1500

1800

# THE DISCOVERY OF THE WORLD

# THE DISCOVERY OF THE WORLD

## ALBERT BETTEX

*269 plates in photogravure*
*36 plates in colour*

THAMES AND HUDSON · LONDON

THIS EDITION © 1960 THAMES & HUDSON
TRANSLATED FROM THE GERMAN BY DAPHNE WOODWARD
PRINTED BY CONZETT & HUBER, ZURICH, SWITZERLAND

# CONTENTS

# INTRODUCTION

The tale of how man set out to discover and explore the earth, and how
after centuries of dogged effort and of hardship endured he finally
triumphed, is one of the finest and most inspiring that history has to offer.
Countless expeditions have made their contributions with accounts of
newly-discovered seas, rivers, islands, mountains, deserts, forests and
frozen continents, and of the strange peoples, animals and plants to be
found there. The records of many of these journeys consisted not only of
entries in logbooks, of diaries, maps and collections, but also of drawings and paintings; the writer, whose name may still be remembered
after centuries, was supported by the illustrator, who was frequently,
though undeservedly, forgotten after a decade or two. It is a breath-
taking experience to open some of these travel books and discover the
fresh, colourful pictures of distant countries and creatures, the beauties
of the world, the vivid episodes from the great drama of exploration,
that they offer in their woodcuts, etchings, lithographs, aquatints and so
forth. These pictures often tell us more than any written description.
Magellan, Cook, Humboldt, Livingstone and innumerable other explorers were passionately absorbed during their journeyings in mental
questing and creative reflection; but all the while their expeditions were
opening up a world that was first and foremost a feast for the eyes. Many

of the pictures express more than this—they reveal the exaltation, the fears or premonitions of man in search of unknown lands. This gives them a vitality which does not fade, a sense of actuality and awe that is imparted in full measure to posterity.

Many of these illustrators were 'on the scene' themselves; others never took part in an expedition. They include the artist who would read a travel description and proceed to illustrate it with his own ideas, concerning himself very little with research for purposes of accuracy. Many of the medieval artists, true to the spirit of their age, indulged their imagination to the full. One of them created the pictures about Marco Polo in the illuminated manuscript known as the *Livre des Merveilles*. More frequently we find the illustrator who did not actually visit any strange lands, but worked from the explorer's sketches or under his supervision, or with the help of specimens such as stuffed animals or pressed plants; he often succeeds in giving an astonishingly close approximation to the real thing. That, for instance, is how most of the illustrations to Alexander von Humboldt's books were made. Those who actually shared the fatigues and dangers of an expedition range from the ship's officer who made sketches and took them home to be worked up by a painter or lithographer, to the skilled landscape painter who was included in every important expedition in the eighteenth and nineteenth centuries. In some very rare instances, the leader of the expedition —Sven Hedin or Julius Payer, for instance—was himself an artist of talent.

The history of exploration leads into far reaches of time and space, and similarly a voyage of discovery through the continent of illustrated travel books, unknown in so many of its aspects, must also cover wide expanses of artistic treasures, originating at very different levels. To make any narrowly-restricted choice from among possibilities so rich and varied is not advisable. Records that are 'true to life' must predominate, of course; but more imaginative works have also their part to play in a presentation of the changing picture of the world, and could not be excluded from a book of this kind. Both are varieties of an art that is trying to express something real; and even where the aim is to render beauty of form for its own sake (as in Caillié's picture of Timbuktu), or where the pleasure of embroidering historical fact with imaginative detail has been allowed free rein (as in Loyset Lyedet's pictures of Alexander's Indian campaign), the claims of reality are never quite forgotten.

And so these artists, delighting in the story they have to tell, not only charm us by the manner of their work, but fascinate us with its matter.

A 'complete' history of exploration, going into all the highways and byways of the subject, would require as many volumes as an encyclopaedia. A single illustrated volume has to pick and choose. It must follow up the trail of the great pioneers, without entirely overlooking lesser figures who, if they did not 'make history', contributed something vital, on the documentary, human and artistic planes. There are good reasons why it should not include photographs; the written word must bridge any considerable gaps left in the story told by the pictures. The further purpose of the text, particularly the notes to the illustrations, is to explain the individual pictures and the connection between them and, in the case of the introductory passages, to describe how the exploration of the principal regions began and what general course it followed.

This is, broadly speaking, a collection of pictures illustrating the achievements of white men and, for the most part, those of Europeans. The non-European regions of the world have undoubtedly carried out a good deal of 'self-exploration' and the illustrations that bear witness to this were often useful to European travellers as well. They range from the lumps of wood in which the Eskimoes, with their primitive tools, scratched the meandering line of some coast, to the ancient Chinese maps on which the world comes to an end at the far side of China. But the history of exploration, in the strict sense of the term, deals with the building-up in men's minds of a complete picture of the world. That picture was created chiefly by Europeans or others actuated by European ideas, and it is worthy to be coupled with the finest flowers of European thought.

In our pageant of the discovery of the world the barrier between past and present disappears; the pictures give us a sense of actual contact with the fullness of life on earth, with the great destinies of its explorers, and with the intrinsic art of the illustrators themselves.

THE CELESTIAL GLOBE OF THE GREEKS AND ROMANS

This shows us the revolving firmament from outside; we have to imagine the earth floating right at its centre. The constellations, circling round the heavens in perpetual motion, are accompanied by their emblems—some of which were set in cosmic space by Babylonian and Egyptian astronomers, others added later by the Greeks and Romans, in a combination of mythological lore and popular superstitions.

Many artists have been inspired by this majestic theme. The engraving reproduced here, which dates from 1571, was probably influenced by the marble globe that rests on the shoulders of the so-called 'Farnese Atlas', a work of the epoch of the early Roman emperors, recalled by the enthroned monarch (unless he is meant to be Zeus in person).

In the Zodiac itself, working upwards along the circumference, we recognize the Bull, with lowered head, the Ram, the Fishes (the left-hand fish has slipped out of the loop of the encircling band), winged Pegasus and the foal, and a fabulous bird with a fish in its beak. In the northern sector of the celestial globe we see, to the right, the Wagonner, a goat on his left shoulder and the guide-rope in his right hand; next comes wing-footed Perseus, holding the Gorgon's head behind him in his left hand; then Ophiuchos, the snake-bearer (the snake has changed into a harmless ribbon) and the Swan with outstretched neck. Passing behind the imperial throne is the woeful figure of Iaside Kepheus, a Phrygian cap on his head, followed by Ketos, the dog-headed water-snake. In the southern section we have a rather plump dolphin (or is it meant to be a whale?), behind which kneels Engonasin, whom many people took for Hercules, battling with stones against the Ligurians.

It was no mere whim that led priests to have the Zodiac painted on the ceilings of so many of their temples, and kings to portray it in their tents; the sight of the star-set heavens prompted them to reflect with awe upon the mighty and eternal order of the universe.

MANKIND AND THE FIRMAMENT

A mood of solemn contemplation has always been induced by gazing at the skies, where the stars follow their timeless courses far above the short-lived generations of mankind. The magnitude and mystery of the creation can be sensed even in this orrery, or model of the heavenly bodies, painted by Joseph Wright (the figure on the extreme right) approximately between 1763 and 1765; it also shows the earth revolving in the orbit of the moon, a philosopher in the middle explaining things, and the circle of thoughtful listeners, lit up magically from below.

## Man sets forth into the Unknown

This woodcut is taken from Thevet's *Cosmographie univer-* ►
*selle* (Paris 1575). The landscape is a fanciful creation, situated nowhere—yet encountered everywhere by men who
have left the firm ground of their native land and launched
out into the unknown, relying solely on their own physical
strength and resourcefulness, a few paltry instruments and
the frail craft they sail in.

The explorers shown here were already better equipped
to sail the oceans than their forerunners in ancient times. The
magnetic compass had been known for four hundred years
past, and with the help of the cruciform 'Jacob's staff' and
the round, flat astrolabe they could read the positions of the
stars and thus calculate that of the ship. But they were still
far from the security of present-day navigation; nearly all
the most prodigious events in the history of exploration took
place in the pre-technical era. The vessels were at the mercy
of wind and weather—lonely specks with no wireless to
keep them in touch with a familiar world, no stores of her-
metically sealed tins to reassure them against the spectres of
hunger and thirst, no modern safety devices to mitigate the
terrors of the vast deep for the explorers of that glorious age.
Yet in 1563 Stephen Borough, who discovered the Kara
Strait and the sea route from England to Archangelsk, spoke
proudly of man's ability, as he sails some remote sea, to
measure with his tiny instruments the whole wide span of
sky above him and, by taking a compass bearing and setting
down a few lines on a sheet of parchment, miraculously to
steer a course to places that lie far out of sight.

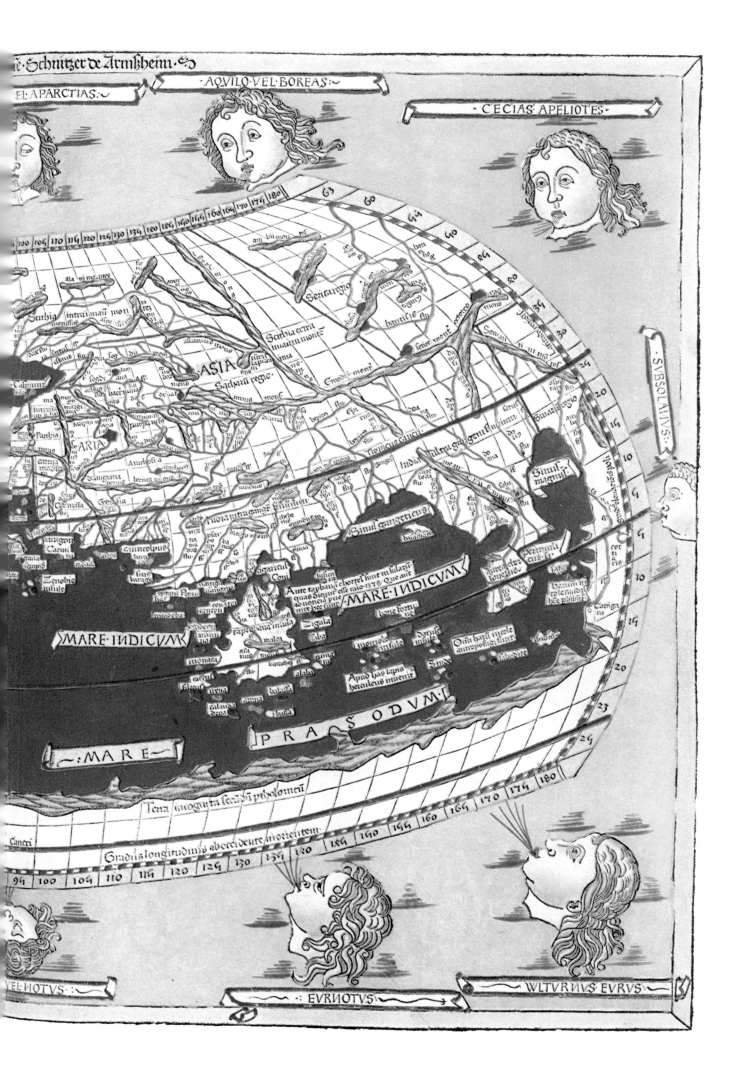

# The World of Antiquity

◄ THE EARTH ACCORDING TO PTOLEMY

The original map said to have been made by the geographer Ptolemy of Alexandria has not survived. It is possible that after his death a map based on his *Guide to Geography* was produced by Agathodamon, an Alexandrian artificer; but that, too, has vanished. In any case it was not until the fifteenth century that copies of Ptolemy's notes and maps found their way back to Europe, brought by scholars in their flight from dying Byzantium. The map of the world shown here is reproduced from the reprint (1486) of the edition of Ptolemy's work published at Ulm in 1482, in the version prepared by Nicolaus Germanus in 1468. The wood-engraver, Johannes von Armssheim, has cut his name on the top edge.

The twelve principal winds are blowing lustily upon the earth out of a clear blue sky. From the north comes cold Boreas, from the south, warm Notus; from the east, dry Apeliotes, and from the west, moist Zephyr; between them genii of other winds. The earth is shown as a globe, imagined to be about one-third of its real size. The picture is dominated by the three interconnected continents known to ancient times; the Atlantic is only a narrow strip of water. America, Australia, the Polar regions and the Pacific are not there at all—for thousands of years they remained concealed from the Old World as though by some magic spell. A significant feature added in the late fifteenth century is the marked projection in the north. Here the editor, Nicolaus Germanus, was following the map of the northern lands recently produced by Claudius Clavus—though not entirely understanding it—on the strength of which he put in a frozen sea (*mare glaciale*) and a handful of Arctic islands. Near the 63rd degree of northern latitude lies a tiny island, 'Tile', floating, as it were, in the northern mists—a hint of the island of Thule, which was so famous in legend.

The Book of Genesis tells how a supreme benediction was vouchsafed Adam and Eve at the Creation, and a world-wide vision revealed to them: 'And God blessed them, and God said unto them: Be fruitful and multiply, and replenish the earth and subdue it.'

'And replenish the earth…' The story of how the human race in fact spread over the uninhabited earth is to a great extent shrouded in the mists of prehistory. Modern archaeologists, studying the skeletons, weapons and tools found in the soil of the different continents, have reached the conclusion that primitive men may have emerged from the mountains of Asia and moved westwards across the Arabian peninsula to Africa and eastwards, over the sea, to Java and other islands in the Pacific; that later they pushed on into Europe; and that much later still, twenty thousand years or more before the Christian era, Asian tribes may have crossed the Bering Strait and spread over the American continent.

In point of fact the explorer very seldom discovers a territory that has never been seen before by human eyes. He is nearly always a re-discoverer: in primeval forest, desolate steppe or craggy mountain pass he is liable to encounter a 'reception committee' composed of distant descendants of the real discoverers—as the American traveller Vilhjalmur Stefansson puts it. But it is this 'second-hand' activity that constitutes true exploration; it reveals things of which mankind has hitherto been unaware, opens a door to the unknown and brings new territories into the general geographical framework.

Every highly cultivated people is eager to chart the face of the earth—to obey, as it were, in the spiritual sense, the command to 'subdue it'. Men have been working for thousands of years to build up a universal cosmography, and various great documents mark the stages of their progress.

Supreme among these is the so-called Ptolemaic map of the world. It summarises the geographical knowledge man possessed in ancient times, and is based on the *Guide to Geography* compiled by Ptolemy, astronomer and geographer, a citizen of Alexandria (*c.* 87–150). This epoch-making work includes a prosaic inventory of every place in the then known world about which its author had managed to gather any information in the course of his wide-ranging enquiries. And the extent of his knowledge was remarkable, for Ptolemy was extremely thorough in scrutinizing and comparing all the geographical traditions to be found in the Greek and Roman records, travel descriptions and directions to navigators, which took in many a fact concerning very far-off lands. Besides, he lived in the wealthiest trading town of his day, where merchants with their caravans, soldiers, experienced travellers and seafarers came flocking from all quarters of the globe: Alexandria was a geographical information-centre of the first importance.

It is true that some of Ptolemy's statements are based on misinformation and hearsay. None-the-less, his work marked a red-letter day for geography. He set about it during the reign of the Emperor Hadrian, when the Roman dominions stretched from the Irish Sea to the Euphrates, from Germany to North Africa; at the same time, in Asia, the Han dynasty was uniting the gigantic empire of China within its isolating circle of ocean, desert and mountains, asserting its authority over the neighbouring regions as far as the Caspian Sea, and, moreover, opening tempting trade routes to the west.

The description of the world that is given in the *Guide to Geography* derives from the clear, logical processes of thought that originated in ancient Greece and introduced a new epoch in the history of science. They enabled the Pythagorean philosophers, five hundred years before Christ, to demonstrate that the earth was a sphere; Hipparchus, in the second century BC, proved that it revolved round the sun. Eratosthenes, working a century earlier with primitive resources, had calculated its circumference with an accuracy that we today have scarcely exceeded. Ptolemy, working with equal clear-sightedness (see map on pages 13 and 14) and guided to some extent by the example of his predecessor, Marinus of Tyre, superposed the earth upon a network of parallels, with an equator and two tropics, dividing it into 180 degrees of longitude (though he spaced them much too widely) from the Canary Islands *(insulae fortunatae)* in the west to the easternmost point of the known world, and into 65 degrees of northern and 25 degrees of southern latitude. There is also an inscription on the left-hand side of the map—a survival from earlier times—which lists the climatic zones of the earth, calculated on the basis of what was then believed to be the longest day.

In ancient times the greatest explorers were the Cretans, Phoenicians and Greeks. Ptolemy was therefore comparatively well informed about the much-travelled coast of the Mediterranean. His surprising knowledge of the remote north-west of Europe—of Albion and Ireland *(ibernia)*—was acquired from the reports of a daring Greek merchant, Pytheas of Massilia (Marseilles), who had penetrated to the fringe of the Arctic. In Scandinavia the outlines break off; but the amber-dealers who roamed the area between the Baltic and the Adriatic supplied our geographer with the names of many races and territories in Eastern Europe. When we realize that Greek products even made their way across the Urals into Western Siberia, we are less puzzled to account for the fact that information reached Alexandria from beyond the River Don (Tanaïs), the boundary dividing Europe from Asia.

Africa, on the other hand—except for its northern coastline—was a world of mystery. Phoenician seamen had sailed as far east as Zanzibar, Greek ships had reached Delgado (Cape Prason). One of the furthest known points to the south-west was the 'Chariot of the Gods' *(the-onochema mons)*—as the Cameroon Mountain was called—near the fifth degree of northern latitude, whose fiery glow, reflected on the clouds at night, had been seen by the Phoenician navigator Hanno in the year 500 B.C. For the geographical outline of North-East Africa Ptolemy could rely on the Egyptians, who had followed it, in their trading activities, from the western desert across Nubia to Palestine and Mesopotamia. His map makes an astonishingly creditable attempt to deal with the Nile, the problem of whose source was not solved until well into the nineteenth century. Arabs, trading in ivory and black slaves, declared that a chain of mountains—the Mountains of the Moon *(mons lunea)*—ran, far upcountry, from east to west; at the foot of this chain lay two great lakes, from each of which a river flowed; these rivers met to form the White Nile, which was joined by what is now known as the Blue Nile, coming from further north.

For Ptolemy nearly all of Northern Asia was wrapped in impenetrable darkness (though he knew parts of the old Silk Route—*Oechardes* signifies the Tarim basin); but great national movements of earlier history provided him with information about India and its approaches. This came, above all, from the campaigns of Alexander the Great and from the extensive trade carried on by the Greeks by land and sea. The *Periplus maris Erythraei,* a book of directions for ships sailing the Indian Ocean which appeared about the year 60 A.D., is surprisingly detailed in its descriptions, even with regard to Ceylon *(taprobana insula),* which Ptolemy shows as enormous. As he moves eastward his account becomes increasingly vague, though he had some acquaintance with the information about Burma, Java *(iabadiu)* and the Gulf of Bengal gathered since the third century B.C. by Mediterranean sailors from the Chinese seamen they had met on their voyages. On Ptolemy's map the Gulf of Bengal borders the *aurea chersonesus,* the Malay Peninsula, east of which lies the *sinus magnus,* the Gulf of Siam. The coast to the east of the Indian Ocean is probably a mixture of Indochinese and Chinese geographical features. Roman coins have been dug up in Indochina! Ptolemy's Chinese contemporaries have left us comparatively accurate descriptions of this region; but he himself shows China as extending far to the south of the equator and joins it by an imaginary coastline to East Africa, so that the Indian Ocean becomes an inland sea. This is the crassest of his errors. For centuries after that many geographers assumed the existence, to the south of the Indian Ocean, of a gigantic continent—*Terra Australis incognita*—straddling the South Pole as a counterbalance to the northern land masses. Not until 1775, when Cook made his daring voyage to the Antarctic, was this misconception finally remedied.

But to this day the mind of the ancients has left its imprint on our geography, and it gleams like a golden thread between the neat plottings on the world-map which Ortelius, Mercator and others have done so much to perfect.

# Alexander the Great in Asia

More or less in the same productive period when Pythias of Massilia was pushing north to the borders of the Arctic, and shortly before Hipparchus, Eratosthenes and others began to measure the earth and provide mankind with a new pattern of the universe, a Macedonian king, in the flower of his youth, set out eastwards at the head of his army, vowing that he would be the first to reach the uttermost ends of the world. This was Alexander, later called the Great (356–323 B.C.). Having conquered the Persians and thus carried out his commission as the military representative of the League of Corinth, he went on towards India on his own initiative, as King of Macedonia, resolved to impose his rule upon half the earth. He led his troops beyond the Indus; but there, wearied even of victory, they refused to go further—though the supposed goal was close at hand. On the way back Alexander ordered Nearchos, his admiral, to chart the entire coastline from the mouth of the Indus to the Euphrates, for he intended to set up a lively trade between Asia, Africa and Europe. His widely ranging mind was already planning the circumnavigation of Arabia and Africa from east to west, his ultimate intention being to control the Mediterranean—subduing Carthage first and then establishing Macedonia's world-wide rule by mastering Rome, whose ambitions were now becoming apparent. But in Babylon he was struck down by fever. As he lay on his deathbed one of his followers asked him at what stage after his decease he should be accorded divine honours. His reply was, 'When you are all happy'—a truly royal farewell which revealed his greatest aim. For Alexander, the pan-Hellenist, had cherished the revolutionary dream of uniting all the peoples of the world, Greeks and 'barbarians', in one community of equal rights and instituting an exchange of merchandise, men and ideas on a world-wide scale never yet known.

Alexander was not only a farsighted general and statesman, he was something of an explorer as well. On his military expeditions his suite included geographers who were expected to gather information about the unknown lands that lay ahead and to survey and map the territory he conquered. Natural scientists were there as well, to follow up the geographers. These companions of Alexander brought back a vivid picture of Asia west of the Indus.

So strong was Alexander's appeal to the imagination that his story has become legend. The most colourful adventures are attributed to the young traveller-king in the eighty versions of the *Alexander Romance* which appeared in twenty-four different languages—depicting him sometimes as a godlike hero and sometimes as a monster of iniquity. Even the sober biographies written by Plutarch, Arrian and Quintus Curtius Rufus give him so noble, passionate and highminded a character as to awaken hero-worship at every period in history when fame and great qualities have been held in honour. So it was at the court of Burgundy in the year 1463, when the gifted illustrator Loyset Lyedet adorned a French translation of the biography by Quintus Curtius Rufus with wonderful pictures of the mighty Alexander as a figure of late medieval chivalry (see pages 20 to 25).

ALEXANDER AT THE WORLDS'S END

Such was the glory of Alexander in the eyes of the ▶ Persians, whose land he conquered, that in their later epics they adopted him and made him into the founder of the Sassanid dynasty. The feats attributed to this Persian 'Iskander' were garnered from Arabian, Greek, Persian and other legends. The poet Firdousi (c. 941 to 1020) raised him to the heights of heroic verse in his *Book of Kings* (Shah-Nama). Our illustration shows the conqueror, after unremitting campaigns, arriving at the world's end. There stands an oracle, a twin-stemmed tree from which men's voices are heard by day and women's by night. Bitter tears fill the young hero's eyes when he hears the prophecy intended for him—the oracle declares that his end is near; invincible though he seems, he will live not an instant longer than is permitted by Death, the ultimate, relentless victor. Conforming to popular legend, the unknown illustrator, who was working for Sultan Ibrahim about the year 1425, depicts the oracular tree not as Firdousi describes it, but with many animals' heads and only one human face.

ALEXANDER SLAYS A PERSIAN LION

In the district of Bazaira, not far from Samarkand, where Persia meets the lands of the northern nomads, the inhabitants used to keep great numbers of wild beasts in woodlands traversed by streams and girdled by walls. There were towers to provide a refuge for hunters. Alexander, at the head of his army, came to one of these parks and gave orders for a hunting expedition. The king was attacked by a lion, an unusually powerful specimen; but he waved aside his friend Lysimachus who sprang to the rescue, and slew the lion unaided, with a single cast of his hunting-spear. At the end of the day Alexander and his army feasted with oriental splendour. The Macedonians are said, however, to have decided that their youthful and impetuous monarch must be protected from himself, and would no longer allow him to go hunting on foot or without a large suite.

ALEXANDER ATTACKS THE CRAG OF AORNOS

On his way to India Alexander had to contend not only with hostile armies but with torrential rivers and precipitous mountains, jungle and desert. On one occasion his forces were brought to a halt at the foot of Aornos, a strongly fortified cliff, full of clefts and gorges, which probably lay north of the River Buner in the Indus valley. The king ordered a near-by wood to be felled; the trees were stripped of their branches to facilitate transport, and the soldiers used them, together with stones and earth, to fill in the chasm at one point. Alexander himself rolled the first tree-trunk over the edge. Catapults were then pushed forward across the artificial dam. The Macedonian archers, spearmen and swordsmen launched an attack, greeted by a hail of stones and spears from above. They suffered heavy losses, and not until the third day did the defenders withdraw. Alexander built

altars to Minerva and Nike on the crest of the cliff in token of his gratitude for this victory.

*Overleaf:*

ALEXANDER BUILDS TOWNS IN ASIA. In the thinly-populated regions between the Tigris and India Alexander founded a score of towns, all of which, like Alexandria in Egypt, were named after him. His architects designed them, his corps of engineers built them, as places where the foreigners from Greece could mingle with the native population and where creative contacts between Persian and Indian culture and the Greek mind could take place. The imagination of our late medieval illustrator (the Flemish artist Loyset Lyedet) has conjured up Burgundian towers and battlements among the hills of 'Asia'.

21

INDIA'S MOST DREADED WEAPON

The Indian King Porus was determined to halt Alexander's advance into the Punjab beyond the River Jhelum. The two armies met on the eastern bank of the stream. At the centre of his battle array Porus had placed two hundred elephants—a fearsome weapon, for the invaders' horses were terrified of them, while those of the Indian cavalry were not; and in the press of battle their huge bodies were a danger to the attacking infantry. By a cunning feint Alexander beguiled the compact mass of the opposing force to break up and drew the enemy cavalry from the flanks, to do battle alone against his horsemen; moreover, Porus's bowmen proved ineffectual, as they could find no firm support on the rain-soaked ground for their bows, which were man-high; whereas Alexander's bowmen, with their smaller weapons, reinforced by intrepid spearmen, managed to master the elephants. Casualties were heavy, all the same. Porus, badly wounded and scarcely able to keep his seat on his elephant, was himself obliged to surrender to Alexander (centre background) who, impressed by his courage, took him as an ally and made him ruler of a great expanse of conquered territory. Near the scene of this battle Alexander founded the cities of Alexandria Nicaea and Alexandria Bucephala (the latter named after his favourite charger, Bucephalus, which had been killed in the battle). Then he resumed his eastward march, across several rivers, towards his ultimate, long-cherished goal—the shore of the eastern ocean, not far beyond the Indus, where, as he and his geographers believed, the world came to an end.

ALEXANDER'S FLEET ENDANGERED BY A TIDAL WAVE

Alexander sailed down the Indus with a fleet that had been built for him in India. Reaching the delta, he gave orders for two arms of the river to be explored, for he planned to bring great merchant navies from Egypt and Babylon into India at this point. While his vessels were sailing down the western channel, they were surprised by a huge tidal wave that rolled up from the near-by sea. The ships were thrown together pell-mell; many of them were holed, others ran aground in the shallows; the sailors, in their excitement, got in one another's way with their poles and oars; and when the flood receded, many ships capsized. After an anxious night the vessels were refloated by the rising tide. When they sailed out into the Indian Ocean, the king sacrificed to Poseidon and threw his golden drinking-cup into the waves.

A Place that no Explorer ever found

The Middle Ages believed that far beyond India there was a range of mountains so high that even the Flood had not reached its crest. Guarded by these mountains and surrounded by a wall lay the inaccessible Garden of Eden, planted by God's own hand. Here, in the Earthly Paradise, our first parents had lived in happy innocence until they disobeyed God and were thrust out to face banishment, pain and death. In the midst of the garden was a spring from which flowed four rivers, known in the outer world as the Indus, Tigris, Euphrates and Nile. The garden could not be entered, however, by travelling up any of these—the seeker would be driven back by rushing waters and contrary winds. Nevertheless, the idea of a voyage of discovery to the Earthly Paradise, as a means of gaining renown, was one that appealed strongly to the medieval imagination. The whole of Europe was familiar with the fabulous travels of Sir John Mandeville, who, one day, as was right and proper, had finally come almost to the threshold of Paradise.

# The World of the Middle Ages
## and the Holy Land

It would be an error to suppose that medieval Europe regarded Ptolemy's *Guide to Geography* as a valuable heritage, to be cherished and amplified. While the might of Rome decayed, and during the centuries of flux and migration that followed, geographical knowledge dwindled; in the early Christian era the teachings of the great pagan scholars were frowned upon. After the fifth century A.D. a timid investigation of ancient lore began; but students of geography confined themselves for centuries to the minor Greek or, more frequently, Roman writers on the subject, delighting particularly in the flowery inventions with which Pliny the Elder, Julius Solinus and Pomponius Mela enlivened their descriptions of strange animals, plants, people and countries. The thirteenth-century philosophers, such as Albertus Magnus and Roger Bacon, who had studied the greatest of the ancient authors, began to introduce more accurate descriptions of the globe, though still accompanied by fantastic reports that had lost none of their popular appeal. A scattered minority even ventured to admit that the earth might be a sphere, not a disk. But geography, like all sciences, was the handmaid of theology, its duty was to bring men nearer to God—in itself a noble incentive which inspired some visions of the universe that were truly imposing, though much impaired by fanciful conceits. Such visions, though fragmentary and dimmed, are reflected in even the most popular of fourteenth-century writings, such as the *Travels of Sir John Mandeville,* presented to an astonished world about the year 1356 by one Jean de Bourgogne, a French doctor.

Practically no impact was made upon medieval cosmography by two events that might well have opened up new regions of the world to Christian exploration. During the ninth and tenth centuries the Vikings sailed from Scandinavia eastwards to the White Sea and westwards, by way of Iceland and Greenland, to the coast of North America; and in the seventh and eighth centuries religious fanaticism, combined with a suddenly kindled flair for world-wide trade, took the followers of the Prophet Mahomet speeding through two separate worlds. First they bestrode almost the whole of the known earth, thrusting out from Arabia to Morocco and across Persia to the borders of China, and thus established one of the greatest commercial empires that history has ever known; and later they mastered the non-Christian traditions that medieval Christendom so signally failed to appreciate. The Moslem geographers, headed by the philosophical Idrisi, unhesitatingly—though critically—took over the antique picture of the earth that they had inherited from Ptolemy, Hipparchus and others, supplemented it with astronomical teachings from Indian sources, and applied to it their own world-wide observations. It was not until the twelfth century that their doctrines began to filter into Europe by way of Toledo and Sicily where translations from Arabic were undertaken.

The most graphic idea of the universe as it appeared to Christian society in the Middle Ages is conveyed by the map of the world that hung for centuries in the Ebstorf Monastery on Lüneburg Heath—the most comprehensive chart to have survived from its period. It was a circular map, over 137 inches in diameter, put together from thirty sheets of vellum and no doubt intended both for instruction and for pious meditation upon the endless miracles wrought by God. It is thought to have been completed about the year 1250; in other words—by no mere coincidence—a few decades after St. Francis of Assisi wrote his hymn to Creation. There is much to suggest a relationship between this map and the cosmographical theories of the learned Gervase of Tilbury, and a similar map is preserved in Hereford Cathedral. The magnificent Ebstorf document—a kind of pictorial encyclopaedia—was destroyed by fire in 1943 during an air-raid on Hanover. A coloured reproduction now hangs in its place in the monastery church.

Comparing this map with Ptolemy's, our first impression is that everything once known about geography had by now been forgotten. The controlling network of parallels has disappeared, outlines and proportions have got completely out of hand, and the earth, a tripartite disk floating in the cosmic ocean, has turned into a burgeoning garden of fantasy. That, at least, is what a first glance suggests. But something quite different has in fact emerged. The earth has come to be regarded in the light of Christian spirituality, so all life is focussed upon the other world; it is the scene of unimaginably rich and rare events, testifying to the dazzling inventiveness of God. The world issues forth from God and returns to Him (as Hermann Hesse puts it) and, however bewildering the throng of scenes and creatures may seem, it is irradiated by the same divine order that governs Thomas Aquinas's *Summa Theologia*. Everything rests in Christ, the Crucified, the Alpha and Omega, who embraces the earth—His head appearing at the top of the map, His hands to right and left of it, and His feet at the bottom of the circle.

Prominently displayed at the very heart of the map, however, is Jerusalem, the place of man's redemption, showing Christ rising from the tomb; and from that point there stretches in an upward direction—that is to say eastwards, towards the rising sun and the Saviour's head—the continent of Asia with all its marvels. Here, inaccessible behind a towering range of mountains, lies the Garden of Eden with the Tree of Life, the four rivers of Paradise, and the Tree of Knowledge. Below this the Ganges, fed by eleven tributaries, flows through a tropical landscape. To the left of Eden, and at a lower level, is the land of the Seres, the Chinese, also hemmed in with mountains—though outside their encircling ring two Chinese are seen gathering silkworms for their most

sought-after article of trade. In the upper Ganges valley India displays one of its innumerable curiosities—a member of the peaceable tribe of Apple Smellers who subsist entirely by inhaling the fragrance of that fruit. To the right, close beside the head of Christ, stand two Trees of Prophecy beneath which Alexander the Great, explorer of India, is consulting the Oracle of the Sun and Moon. Below him is to be seen a member of the Gymnosophists—a sun-gazer, whose eyes are fixed, unblinking, on the radiant orb from which he receives prophetic inspiration. Higher up, to the right, is the land of the Prasii, whose number is as the poppies of the field which serve as their emblem.

An extensive area of northern Asia is cut off by the sweeping curve of the Caucasus. Its principal feature is a territory that projects as a rectangle into the cosmic ocean. This is the home of the dreaded man-eaters Gog and Magog, symbols of all the hordes of oppressors that might at any time overwhelm peaceful humanity. The castellated lines indicate the walls that Alexander the Great was reputed to have built here for extra protection. Even Roger Bacon, progressive thinker though he was, still went in fear of a possible invasion by these demonic powers emerging from their mountainous realm. Slightly lower down and to the west the map-maker has placed the country of the Amazons, guarded by two doughtily armed queens; and still further westwards, under Christ's right hand, stand the flaming altars of Alexander which mark the northern extremity of the world as it was known to the ancients. Looking due south—that is, to the right—from the land of the Amazons, we come first to the city of Colchis on the Black Sea; the golden fleece, which Jason sailed to seek, still hangs from its tower. Above and to the right is Ararat, identified by Noah's stranded ark; and this brings us to the holy regions of the Bible, with which the designer of the map was well acquainted. On the right is the mighty Tower of Babel, in Mesopotamia, and below it, near Jerusalem, are a number of places mentioned in the Scriptures and described by home-coming pilgrims and Crusaders.

Despite St Augustine's mocking assertion that 'men come to Christ by love, not by a sea-voyage', many of the pilgrims who visited the holy places in Palestine in Roman times and through the Middle Ages felt that their sea-crossing and their worship of Christ were in no way incompatible but, on the contrary, in profound harmony. For them, to set foot in the places 'where the feet of the Lord had walked' was an act of devotion that purified and elevated the soul. In early times, at any rate, it was a religious experience paid for with suffering, privation and danger, and therefore justifiably regarded as a sacrifice to One who had offered Himself in sacrifice. During the eleventh century the number of pilgrimages to Palestine increased; it was a period of fervent striving after Christ, a period of penitence and an ardent awareness of salvation. Pope Urban II added coals to this fire when, in 1095, he called for a Crusade to rescue the Holy Places from their Moslem occupiers. Crusades followed one after another from then until 1271, yet the outcome (even apart from the loss of all that had been conquered during that period) was paradoxical. The astonishment engendered by so many unsuspected marvels led to a new delight in the world as such, and among many travellers contempt for Islam gave way to a receptive interest in the intellectual treasures that Islam had to offer—including a fund of geographical lore derived in part from classical antiquity. Beyond the Holy Land the horizon receded further and further into remote oriental regions, whence interesting novelties such as watermelons and the Moorish arch, Persian carpets and Indian myths gradually made their way to Europe. One lasting result of the powerful attraction to the Holy Land was an accurate knowledge of Palestine and Syria which has survived as a permanent feature of Christian culture.

The Ebstorf cartographer had to enlarge Palestine a good deal, so as to fit in all the indispensable features—Bethlehem with the star, the ox and the ass; above that the accursed cities Sodom and Gomorrah, with the waves of the Dead Sea curving over them; higher still, on the Arabian Gulf, Mount Sinai with the phoenix rising from the flames close beside it, to symbolize the resurrection of Christ, whose figure marks the position of Jerusalem in the central rectangle (above and slightly to the right of which is Cana, with the six wine-jars of the marriage feast).

Africa is little more than the segment of a circle, its north and west coasts extending in an almost straight line from the Indian Ocean to the Atlantic, while its south and east coasts describe a shallow curve. Its principal feature is the Nile, bordered by famous ancient cities, strange beasts and even stranger men. The Nile flows out of a lake, in the vicinity of Morocco and near the spot where lies the Garden of the Hesperides—included as a heathen antithesis to the Christian Paradise—within the protecting coils of the feathered serpent, its guardian. Its course runs at first from west to east, through regions inhabited by panthers, ostriches, giant reptiles and so forth—in all, the artist has generously scattered about sixty different animals over his map. Approaching the eastern tip of the continent, the river disappears into the sand; but it emerges to flow in the opposite direction through Egypt, first skirting the region of Meroë (inhabited by dwarfs who ride on crocodiles). At its mouth stands the famous lighthouse of the ancients; and renowned cities such as Berenice, Leptis Magna and Ocea lie here and there along the northern and Atlantic coasts of the continent. Off the west coast the cartographer has placed an empty rectangle to mark the position of the 'lost island' *(insula perdita)* where the seafaring St Brandan discovered Paradise. But rubbing shoulders, as it were, in the southern portion of Africa we find the most weird and wonderful assortment of creatures: the race that does not know the use of fire; the race that has neither nose nor mouth and can converse only by gestures; giants; people with four eyes; people whose upper lips are so huge that they can pull them up over their heads to serve as sunshades; troglodytes riding like the wind on stags (these are level with Christ's hand); Artobatites who constantly fall on their faces as they walk along; four-footed men; snake-charmers on whom poison has no effect; dog-headed men; the centaur Chiron; cave-dwelling giants; and so forth.

In Europe there are none of these mythical and monstrous figures. The countries that border the Mediterranean, with its sprinkling of

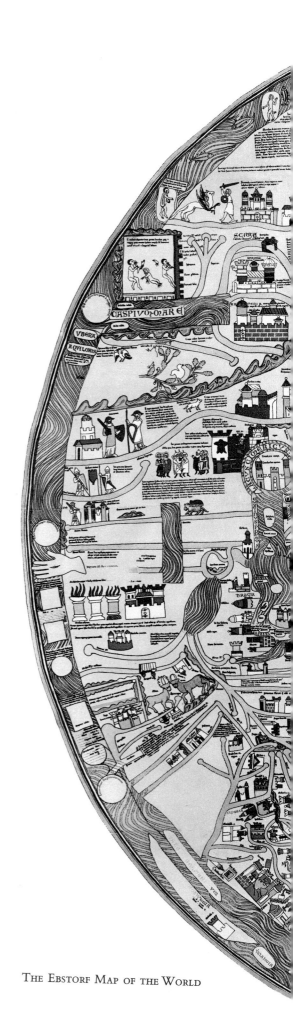

THE EBSTORF MAP OF THE WORLD

31

islands, are easily identifiable. The westernmost is Spain; then come the Pyrenees, turning off at right angles to the Rhone and stretching straight towards the Atlantic. North of these is Gaul, land of many rivers and towns—including 'Parisius'—off whose northern coast lie the islands of Albion and Hibernia-Scotia. In Italy, to north and west of which the Alps curve in a semicircle, we are shown the city of Rome, where seven churches stand within a surrounding wall that has sixteen towers, and Venice, jutting out into the Adriatic. The heart-shaped island lying not far off is Sicily, so the land round which the Mediterranean sweeps northwards must be the Greek peninsula. What is now Switzerland was also known to our author by hearsay; in the northern foothills of the Alps, due north of Rome, he has painted a tower and written 'Curia' against it—this is the town of Chur. Below, on a great bend of the Rhine, are Oberzell, Mittelzell and Niederzell, places on the island of Reichenau. To the north of these the Danube is formed by the confluence of five streams and flows on its way past Urbs Salis (Salzburg), Pattavia (Passau) and Wena (Vienna). One piece of the map is missing, to the left of the Danube, where Lübeck and Hamburg should be. To the north-east, aurochs and elk denote the confines of Russia.

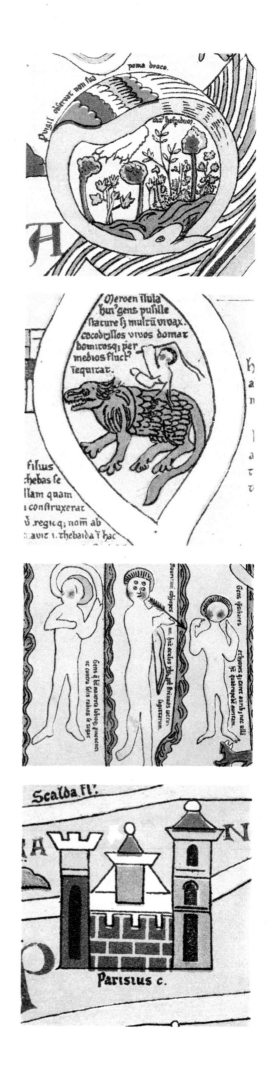

This Ebstorf map is like a geographical romance in pictures; it is comprehensive in design, admirable in execution, and its fundamental concern is to establish a relationship between this world and the hereafter. Its author drew upon classical and Christian traditions and upon contemporary descriptions of fact. Among the ancients he relied more upon popular, highly-coloured source material such as the *Alexander Romance* and the writings of Mela and the elder Pliny than on more dependable authorities such as Herodotus. Also inherited from the ancients were the division of the earth into three parts, and the twelve circles traced in the cosmic ocean—the homes of the twelve winds. Ancient Roman technique has influenced the structure of the map: like the Roman road-plans, it puts things and places in the approximate order in which a traveller would come across them, regardless of exact measurements.

But a certain amount of accurate knowledge is revealed, nevertheless, in Palestine and Europe. Moreover, the medieval imagination occasionally wove its fantasies around facts; for instance, a few of the African natives look like an attempt to interpret pictorially reports of strangely misshapen peoples; and travellers' tales of India, with its areas of dense population and its fakir-like ascetics, may have suggested the pictures of the poppy-field and the sun-gazing Gymnosophist.

The map draws most lavishly of all upon Christian sources—the Scriptures, the Fathers of the Church, the holy legends—and all the other elements of this magnificent synopsis of early medieval cosmography are made to fit into the Christian horizon.

'In no other work of this period, perhaps, either in the graphic arts or in literature, was so comprehensive a picture of the entire medieval world presented, in such a narrow space, as in this map of ours. So it is well worth while studying it closely and repeatedly and trying to discover new items, hitherto unnoticed, among the immense variety of its features,' writes Walter Rosien, the leading authority on it, in his study *Die Ebstorfer Weltkarte* (Hanover, 1952).

Curiously enough, the Ebstorf map serves also as an aid to our understanding of the period of great discoveries which began some two centuries after its completion. For the outlook of the early Portuguese navigators, and that of Columbus too, was conditioned by what they had imbibed of both the ancient and the medieval concepts of the world. Sailing to find the sea route round the Cape of Good Hope, the Portuguese were amazed to discover that the coast of Africa, which looked so short on the map, went on and on without curving eastwards; as late as 1505 the bold seafarer Duarte Pacheco, though a perfectly reliable observer of facts on his own behalf, took for granted the existence of mile-long serpents; and Columbus, coming to the mouth of the Orinoco, thought he had discovered one of the four rivers that watered the Garden of Eden in Asia. The courage with which these explorers sailed into the unknown is all the more admirable because their voyages were fraught, for them, with a vast number of imaginary perils in addition to the considerable dangers they actually entailed.

The impressions of the world recorded by Ptolemy and in the Ebstorf map, both lie—though at different depths—in the twilight zone between experience and dream. Each of them bears noble witness, in its own great cultural epoch, to a great historical process with many ups and downs—to man's growing awareness of the world around him.

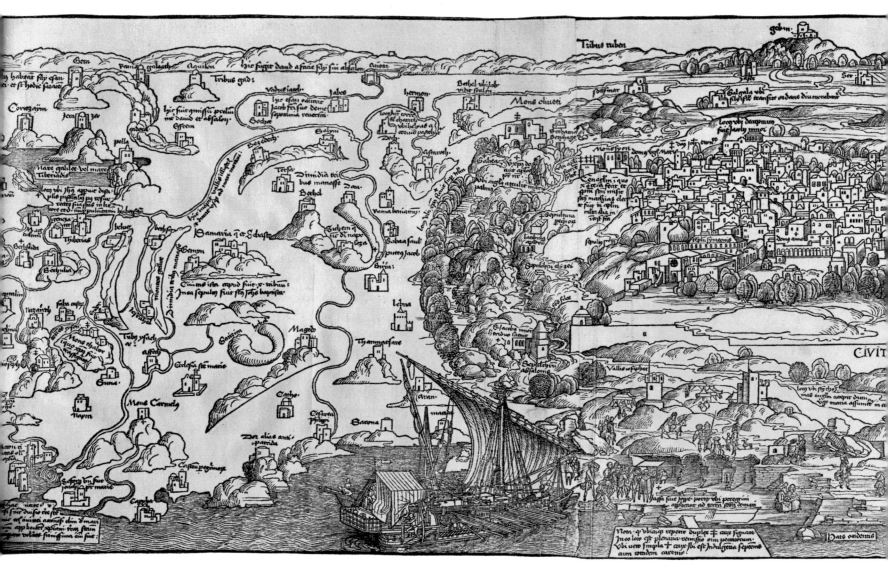

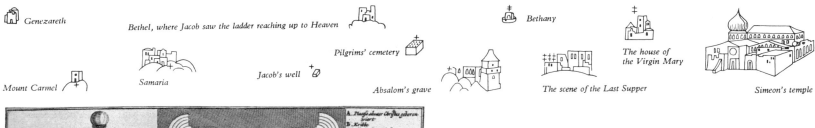

Genezareth

Bethel, where Jacob saw the ladder reaching up to Heaven

Pilgrims' cemetery

Bethany

The house of
the Virgin Mary

Mount Carmel

Samaria

Jacob's well

Absalom's grave

The scene of the Last Supper

Simeon's temple

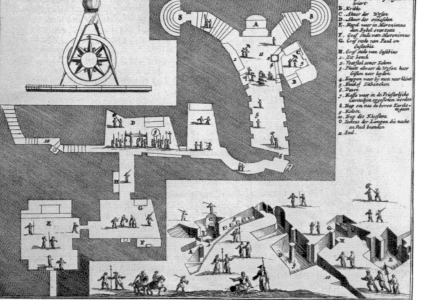

◄ The Underground Chambers of the Church of the Nativity in Bethlehem, which attracts Pilgrims from all over the World. 8, stairway; A, the place where Christ is said to have been born; B, altar where the crib stood, and C, where the Magi worshipped the Child; D, the grotto into which some of Herod's infant victims were cast; E, the spot where St Jerome is said to have translated the Bible into Latin; F, his supposed grave (and H, that of his pupil Eusebius); G, altar for a rich Roman matron of early Christian times named Paula who was buried here. She spent the last years of her life here with her daughter Eustochia in religious meditation.—Dutch print from the Baroque period.

In the view of Jerusalem and its surroundings reproduced above, three double crosses are set above the church of the Nativity in Bethlehem (top right). Those who visited such a place were granted full remission; whereas one such cross implies partial remission.

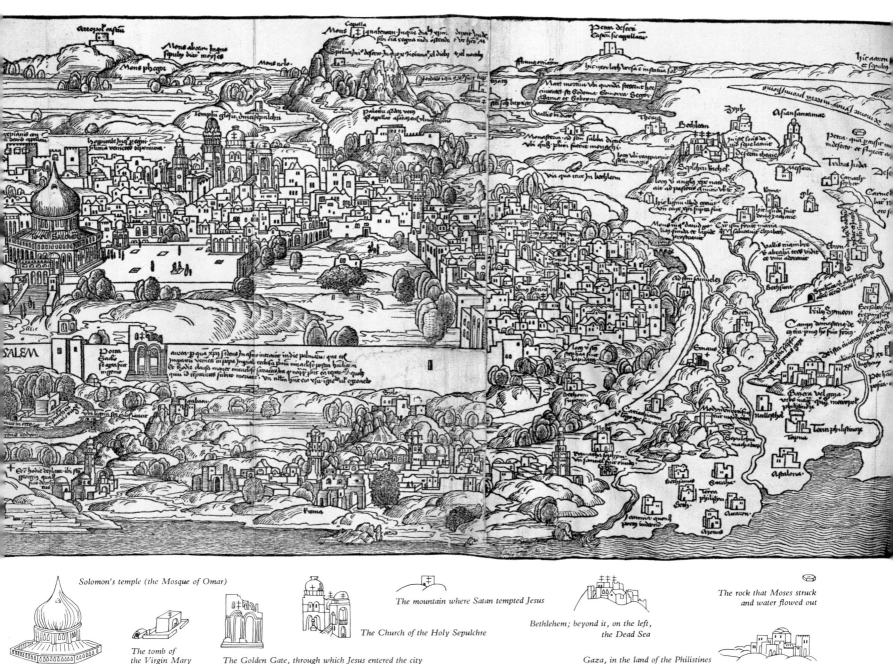

Solomon's temple (the Mosque of Omar)

The tomb of
the Virgin Mary

The Golden Gate, through which Jesus entered the city

The mountain where Satan tempted Jesus

The Church of the Holy Sepulchre

Bethlehem; beyond it, on the left,
the Dead Sea

Gaza, in the land of the Philistines

The rock that Moses struck
and water flowed out

*Above:* VIEW OF JERUSALEM AND THE HOLY LAND. Jerusalem and its neighbourhood—the part of Asia best known to medieval Europe, and the ground most reverenced by Christendom. It was in Palestine that the prophets of the Old Testament and the founder of Christianity had laid down the precepts of the most abundant monotheistic religion that ever influenced mankind, and had borne witness to it with their own exemplary lives. So this scene was often depicted for the outside world. The exceptionally accurate panorama painted by Erhard Rewich, of Utrecht, in 1483 remained unrivalled for a very long time. Rewich accompanied Bernhard von Breydenbach, Prebendary of Mainz Cathedral, on his pilgrimage to the Holy Land, visiting all the places 'where the Holy Bible tells us that some unwontedly great and noteworthy thing took place long since'. His map, part of which is reproduced above, covers the region from Tripoli to Alexandria, and at its centre is an enlarged view of Jerusalem. In the foreground, an Italian pilgrim ship lying off Jaffa.

THE GRANITE MOUNT SINAI in a highly dramatic representation by the Italian engraver Giovanni Battista Fontana (1569). At the foot of the mountain monks belonging to the Convent of St Catherine—which was stoutly fortified against Saracen aggression—are welcoming caravans from Suez or Cairo. Inside the convent wall are many chapels and even, for protection, a mosque; the position of the Church of the Transfiguration is indicated by the halo in front of the cliff. At the top of the mountain stands Moses, at the moment when the Lord 'passed by before him' and consecrated, with His words, the Tables of the Law as the supreme charter of the One God. The herdsman to the left of the convent is also Moses, to whom God spoke out of the burning bush. On the right is St Catherine's Mount, named after the Alexandrian martyr whose body is said to have been buried by angels at its peak. Hermitages, monasteries and cisterns lend life to this wilderness, where the visitor's sense of religious drama and of the drama of the landscape intensify each other.

S.S.

SYNAI

S. Pan-
thaleon

S. chrysostomi

S. maria

S. georgius

Et uitulum
manufactum

Tanduti

S. quadraginta

Antrum

Saxsum aquae

S. Apostoli

S. cosmus
et damianus

Antrum

Bononiae Zalterius Pio lectori

Synai mons est in terra Madian super Arabiam, qui in sacris
etiam literis Coreb, et Ereb est uocatus. Huine utrisq; usus nascitur ut celeriudine dies procedat mons. Hic amigai Deum habitare indicatur, cum igne Moysi in flama ignis de medio rubi apparuisset, incinxissq; ei solutere calciamenta, quia sanctu terra esset

Cuius S. montis perfection cum habuerim certissima linde descriptam a strenuo; gnoq; etiam terram sanctam descriptam fructuosu, typhes ibidi Aere a Jo. Baptista Bontj incidi curaui, incisumq; euulga. Et si tibi meae labores gratae erit cognoscero. Montis Oliueti et Hierusalem descriptionem (ut soleo) accurate iuprimi curauero, impresst. fructes Vale.

THE CEDARS OF LEBANON

All the travellers who crossed the Lebanese mountains in the course of centuries helped to spread the fame of the tall cedar trees that grew there. The psalmist's praise of 'the trees of the Lord, the cedars of Lebanon, which He hath planted' rang in the pilgrim's ear. In the popular imagination these splendid trees are an outstanding feature of the Holy Land. They supplied the Lebanese in ancient times with timber for their ships, and Solomon's architects used cedar-wood for parts of his temple. This picture shows them as they were seen by the French archaeologist Léon de Laborde (1807–69), when they had already been considerably thinned out.

*Right:*

THE VALLEY OF THE RIVER KADISHA (after the French painter L. F. Cassas, 1756–1827). The limestone of these Lebanese mountains has in many places been riven and eroded into strange shapes by wind and water. This wild district, honeycombed with caverns, was for centuries a favourite retreat of pilgrims. The River Jordan, where Christ was baptized by St John the Baptist, flows southwards out of the Anti-Lebanon. Since early times pilgrims had thronged here, wading into the holy stream; many of them wore a linen garment intended to serve later as a shroud.

*Overleaf:*

ON AN ANCIENT ROUTE IN ASIA MINOR between Beirut and Tripoli, near the mouth of the River Lykos, the cliffs come right down to the shore of the Mediterranean. Here, about A.D. 180, the Emperor Marcus Aurelius Commodus Antoninus had a path cut through the rock, to make a better way into what was then the Province of Syria. Egyptian, Babylonian, Persian, Greek, and Roman invaders of Palestine passed this way on their journeys north or south. Weatherbeaten slabs of stone, carved with figures of Assyrian kings (obviously misinterpreted by Cassas) or Egyptian Pharaohs, and Greek and Roman inscriptions, are to be seen in the cliffs as relics of earlier epochs, facing across this magnificent scene towards the sea and into infinite space.

de BERGH CARMELI.

MOUNT CARMEL

On the right, the mountain descends precipitously into the Mediterranean; to the left, beyond the sheltered bay of Haifa (then known as Caiphas), with the town of Acre, in whose harbour St Francis of Assisi landed in 1219 [right, 11], lies the verdant land of Galilee. The caves of Mount Carmel have been used as human habitations ever since prehistoric times. In the ninth century B.C. the prophet Elijah, the most famous of Carmel's anchorites, lived in one of the caves; [8] marks the spot at which he is reputed to have called upon God to send down fire from Heaven. Hermits were living here in the early years of the Christian era; during the period of the Crusades their number increased, and in 1195 they grouped themselves to form the Carmelite Order. [5] is the ancient monastery. In 1240 the Saracens forced the monks to abandon the 'Mountain of God' for a time, and the Carmelite Order spread over the world.

# ASIA

Asia, largest and mightiest of the continents, was long regarded by Europeans both as an inexhaustible treasure-house and as their most dreaded enemy. In almost every field it offered for exploration there was something measureless, something larger than life. Its territory, in the southern belt extending from Asia Minor across India to China, had seen the birth of the five great religions—Christian, Islamic, Hindu, Buddhist and Taoist—the most powerful spiritual forces the world was to know until the victorious spread of emancipated Western civilization. The landscape of Asia—the Taiga, the steppes, the mountains and plains—was on a scale unknown in any other region; the traditional transcontinental journeys, along the ancient Silk Road or the later route across Siberia, were the longest and most toilsome land crossings in the whole history of exploration. 'Travelling in Asia is no bed of roses,' said Sven Hedin—though, like so many others, he had fallen completely under the spell of its stupendous landscape. But with its gems, spices, drugs, furs, precious woods, its rice, cotton, tea, its textiles, carpets, ornaments, inlaid work, pottery and all the other marvels created by its master-craftsmen, Asia was also an incomparable source of wealth.

When its explorers described its natural resources, so far surpassing the common measure of mankind, they never failed to mention the human masses that swarmed in its great cities. 'The throng is greater than at Venice on Ascension Day,' is the wondering comparison made by Odoric de Pordenone, a late-medieval monk. When those masses took arms and invaded Europe they became identified with a terror that the European mind has never quite shaken off. Asia produced world-ravagers such as Genghiz Khan and Tamerlane, and spiritual leaders such as the legendary founders of the great religions, on a scale that the history of no other continent can parallel. Equally unparalleled were the number and diversity of the human races, in their nomads' tents or royal palaces, that European travellers encountered on their oriental journeys. Never in the course of the centuries have the overwhelming physical and spiritual phenomena of Asia ceased to attract, enchant, enrich or—sometimes—ruin those who set out to investigate them.

It was not, however, until Marco Polo reported upon his famous journeys that the extent and wealth of India and her eastern neighbours were brought home to Western minds. True, there had been a long series of earlier contacts, reaching far back into history. Long before Alexander the Great extended Europe's eastern horizon with a vigorous thrust, the European and Asian peoples had been building up a picture of one another, conveyed by merchants along the trade-routes that from time immemorial had linked up Egypt with Mesopotamia, Mesopotamia with India, China with Persia. But no considerable and accurate body of information about the East was assembled until the period of the Moslem Caliphates from the seventh to the eleventh century of our era—when the Arab geographers came to the fore—and the subsequent travels of Marco Polo. For the rest there had only been the reports brought home by Chinese Buddhist pilgrims visiting India in the early Middle Ages.

That extraordinary Arab 'globe-trotter' Ibn Battuta gives us some indication of how far the geographical horizon of Islam—and its trade network—extended in the fourteenth century. A native of Tangier, he left home in 1325 at the age of twenty-one, and travelled for twenty-four years, at the end of which he came back to Fez. His eventful travels had taken him by way of a chain of Islamic outposts, through Mecca, Samarkand, Delhi and Calcutta, to the far-distant court of the Mongol Emperor of China. Never were dramatic adventures described in more sober fashion than in the notes where he set down his experiences—sometimes as the wealthy legal adviser of oriental rulers, sometimes as a destitute victim of shipwreck. Unlike Marco Polo's chronicle these memoirs soon fell into undeserved oblivion.

India's general attitude towards foreign merchants and rulers was one of passive toleration, whereas China's reaction veered, under successive dynasties, from receptiveness and patience to an isolationism that did not shrink from bloodshed, and the extent of information about China in the outside world fluctuated accordingly. Shortly before 1500 Vasco da Gama's voyage from Lisbon to Calicut opened the Portuguese route to India and far-eastern Asia; and this was developed, chiefly by the Dutch, English and French, in a process that continued until the twentieth century.

ORMUZ, WHERE THE THREE POLOS HALTED ON THEIR WAY TO CENTRAL ASIA

Of all the journeys undertaken by Europeans in medieval times, the most astounding was that made by three Venetian merchants—Marco Polo, his father Nicolo and his uncle Matteo. The two older men twice travelled across the boundless stretches of Asia from the Mediterranean to Peking and back—in 1255–69 and in 1271–95. On their second journey they took young Marco with them, and returned by sea from China as far as Ormuz. Their principal base in Asia was Peking. Thanks to Marco Polo's journal, the events of this second residence in Asia, which lasted twenty-four years, have an imperishable place in the history of exploration. It was from his pages that late-medieval Christendom drew its first detailed impressions of India and China.

The three merchants travelled bearing a message from the Pope to the hospitable Kublai Khan, whose rule extended from the Caspian to the China Sea. They made their way across Asia Minor, the deserts of Central Persia, past the once-renowned Bactria, through the icy tempests of the Pamir passes, to the Tarim valley, the oases in the barren tableland of East Turkestan, and finally over the southern reaches of the Gobi desert to Peking—spending three and a half years on their perilous journey.

During a halt at Kirman, a point of intersection on the Persian caravan routes, they braved the scorching heat to visit the Moslem city of Ormuz, on an island near the east coast of the Persian Gulf. Ormuz was an important point of transshipment for the trade between India and West Asia or Europe. The artist who illustrated Marco Polo's narrative in the famous *Livre des Merveilles*, the so-called Master of the Hours of Marshal de Boucicaut, indicates this meeting of the long routes from east and west by showing a typical medieval sailing ship carrying an Indian elephant and a camel from the western desert. Not liking the look of the Indian ships they saw in the harbour at Ormuz, the travellers returned to the mainland and resumed their long journey in the direction of the Pamirs.

MARCO POLO IN PEPPERLAND

India's spices were as keenly coveted as its gems. The names of many spices and products—among them indigo, sugar-candy, copra—found a permanent place in the European vocabulary. Pepper flourishes on the hot, humid mountain slopes inland from the Malabar coast, in South-West India. The medieval illustrator shows Marco Polo, who visited this region on his way home, surrounded by dark-skinned Indians picking black peppercorns.

MARCO POLO IN CHINA. The three Venetian merchants ►
travelled as honoured guests, armed with official golden plaques given them by the Grand Khan which assured them unobstructed passage, free escort and free board and lodging throughout his vast dominions. Young Marco was often entrusted with special missions by the Emperor who was reluctant to let him return home when he finally asked permission. Page 47 shows three of his most lasting impressions.

*Above:* Quinsay, then one of the biggest cities in the world, the present-day Hangchow, capital of the province of Chekiang. It lies not far from the Tsientang river, whose waters fed an enormous network of canals which intersected the town, carrying away all the filth that made so many Chinese cities into hotbeds of disease. In the days of Kublai Khan there were said to be 12,000 bridges crossing these canals to link up the countless streets. Quinsay was a prosperous, well-built commercial city, seething with life, where the produce of the neighbouring provinces—fruit, game and silk—was offered for sale in covered markets or stored in warehouses. There were separate districts for doctors and astrologers. Craftsmanship flourished, the river served as a link with the outside world and with the sea, and entertainments were available in such profusion for its inhabitants that Marco Polo said they might well believe themselves in paradise.

*Centre:* The huge empire was enjoying the tranquillity of the *pax tatarica*. The reins of government were in the firm grasp of the Grand Khan who ruled with a despotism tempered by compassion for the poor and by religious tolerance. He himself attended the great religious festivals—Christian, Moslem, Jewish and Buddhist—partly as a sign of respect and partly to promote the world-wide commercial interests of his empire. If that empire were to be held together, Peking, the capital, must maintain easy and rapid contact with all its provinces. Communications were based on a far-reaching network of roads, their course marked in desert and mountain districts by firmly-planted columns and in other regions by avenues of trees whose maintenance was entrusted to special officials. The European illustrator was evidently quite unfamiliar with such avenues.

*Below:* Paper money was known in China centuries before the Christian era. It served to consolidate the economic and political authority of the Grand Khan, for he had entire control of the Mint, and money could be issued only in Peking. Marco Polo describes the process with astonishment. Mulberry bark was soaked till it became soft, pulped in a mortar and made into paper which was cut into strips of various sizes, representing different values. At a ceremony of Oriental pomp, often attended by the Grand Khan in person, the Master of the Mint and certain other officials impressed their seals on the notes which thus became valid currency.

THE DOG-HEADED ANDAMAN ISLANDERS

The Andaman Islands, in the Indian Ocean, are the peaks of a submerged chain of mountains which in prehistoric times joined Burma to Sumatra. In India Marco Polo was told that the primitive inhabitants of these islands had heads, eyes and teeth 'like those of dogs' and were reputed to be canni-bals. The illustrator of the *Livre des Merveilles* shows them engaged in peaceful trade, thus transforming the cannibal legend into a light-hearted animal story.

A few decades before Marco Polo began his travels, the Church, in an expansionist mood, sent two keen-eyed ob-servers—Giovanni de Piano Carpini, a Franciscan, and Willem de Rubruk, a monk from the Low Countries—on a pioneer journey across Siberia to the court of the ruling Khan; a few decades after Marco's death his report was sup-plemented by two missionaries, Giovanni de Monte Corvino and Odoric de Pordenone. But for a long time Marco was

the man who had seen more of the world than any other European. His eyes—the eyes of a merchant, dispassionately assessing quality and utility—rested on countless Asian pro-ducts; he sometimes writes with the rapt devotion of a lover about choice items such as silk, that 'woven air'; he ob-served unfamiliar men and customs with restrained but un-flagging astonishment, and was cautious about handing on sensational rumours. He never refers to the courage with which he confronted the dangers besetting his way. And, at the end of his report, with a piety and gratitude undimin-ished since childhood, the mature man of the world offers thanks to the benevolent Ruler of the world, of mankind and of the wayfarer in Asia. Of all the travellers of his epoch, Marco Polo undoubtedly brought home the greatest wealth —not merely in gems, precious metals and rich cloths, but in the lasting gold of understanding as well.

# The Portuguese and the Sea Route to India

At the south-western corner of Portugal where Cape St. Vincent juts out into the Atlantic is the sleepy little port of Sagres. Many generations ago a tower stood on a storm-swept cliff beyond the village. Here, in the fifteenth century, the history of exploration entered upon its most glorious era.

This was initiated by Prince Henry of Portugal (1394–1460), later remembered as 'the Navigator'. On this height above Sagres, far from the pleasures of the court, he founded an academy for the training of those who were to sail unknown oceans.

Standing on that promontory one is surrounded on three sides by the sea—the mighty, mysterious adversary against which the Portuguese prince mobilized the cartographers, captains and mathematicians who came to his Academy from many lands. He sent out ship after ship to chart the shores and coastal waters of West Africa, encouraging his mariners by generous rewards. It was many years, however, before any of them ventured further than Cape Bojador. Beyond that headland, according to a theory unquestioned since ancient times, lay the unnavigable tropical zone, with seas that reached boiling-point at the equator. When at last the youthful Gil Eannes sailed round the Cape, a contemporary historian compared his feat to the labours of Hercules. In 1471, when their great patron was already dead, the Portuguese reached the equator. After that they gradually pushed further southwards, establishing trading posts and mission stations at intervals, till they were beyond the mouth of the Congo.

They reached the peak of their achievement towards the end of the fifteenth century. In 1486/87 Bartholomeu Diaz, after discovering that a temperate region lay beyond the reputedly impassable tropical zone, rounded the Cape of Storms, the southernmost point of Africa; his monarch renamed it 'Cape of Good Hope' in joyful anticipation of the future. In 1498 Vasco da Gama, at the end of a nine-month voyage, reached India and landed at Calicut, the capital of the Malabar coast. Thus, nearly forty years after the death of Prince Henry the Navigator, one of the two great dreams that had dominated his life was brought to the verge of fulfilment—Portugal, having found the way round the hostile land barrier of Africa, was about to establish her own trading organization alongside the Afro-Asian mercantile empire of the Moslem peoples. As Grand Master of the Order of Christ and a man in whom the religious mysticism of the Middle Ages still glowed, unsuppressed by his delight in the worldly pleasures of the Renaissance, the Prince had looked upon the discovery of unknown lands and their subjection to the banner of Christ as twin aspects of a single mission. In pursuing this second great dream he again fell foul of Islam.

In Portugal a tiny nation, numbering only about a million souls, had been gripped by a tremendous ambition and was prepared to impose its rule over the entire eastern hemisphere. This was the radiant dawn of the golden age of exploration, when the medieval picture of the world would at last be effaced.

ARABS AND TURKS DO BATTLE WITH THE PORTUGUESE

Trade between Asia, Africa and Europe was controlled in those days by the Moslems, from Timbuktu to India, and their greed raised the price of the goods they handled beyond all reasonable limits. The coastal and caravan routes were blocked by a chain of trading posts. The Portuguese could now avoid these by sailing round them, and they also trespassed on the Arab domains all down the west coast of Africa, wherever ivory, gold or slaves were to be obtained; later they attacked the Arabs in India and Malacca from the east. They had also outflanked the Turkish barrier in Asia Minor. The Italians, who had a monopoly of the carrying trade in the Mediterranean, had been the only Europeans to benefit by the previous situation.

All these trading nations regarded the Portuguese as unwelcome intruders. Counter-measures were numerous. This picture shows one of them. In 1585 the Portuguese Viceroy at Goa decided to send a fleet of galleons and small landing craft on a punitive expedition in the Persian Gulf. Arabs and Turks, reinforced by pirates, met the inefficiently-led Portuguese on the coast, lured them on by retreating inland, and then attacked in crescent formation, cutting off the invaders from their ships and mowing them down.

THE PERILOUS VOYAGE TO INDIA

In August 1585 the Portuguese flagship *San Jago*, bound for India, ran aground on a coral reef between the island of Laurentius (Madagascar) and the mainland of Mozambique, and broke up. By the faint light of a new moon, the negligent helmsman had been steering through the notoriously dangerous passage with all sails set. Five hundred men are said to have crammed themselves aboard the vessel. Only two boats could be launched. While the ship's carpenters laboured to make one of them seaworthy, the twelve occupants of the other were laying about them with hatchets and oars to beat off desperate sailors who tried to clamber into it. Less than sixty survivors reached the mainland, after a twenty-day battle with the sea.

The early sixteenth-century adventurers sailed in tiny cockle-shells; Vasco da Gama's flagship, the *St Gabriel*, was less than 98 feet long! One hundred and seventy men sailed on the first voyage to India; only forty-four reached home again. Hunger, thirst, and the still more dreaded scurvy had taken deadly toll of the crew. The history of exploration is a tale of tremendous sacrifices made for tremendous ends. Not without reason, the spot on the Tagus from which the expeditions set out is known as 'the strand of tears'.

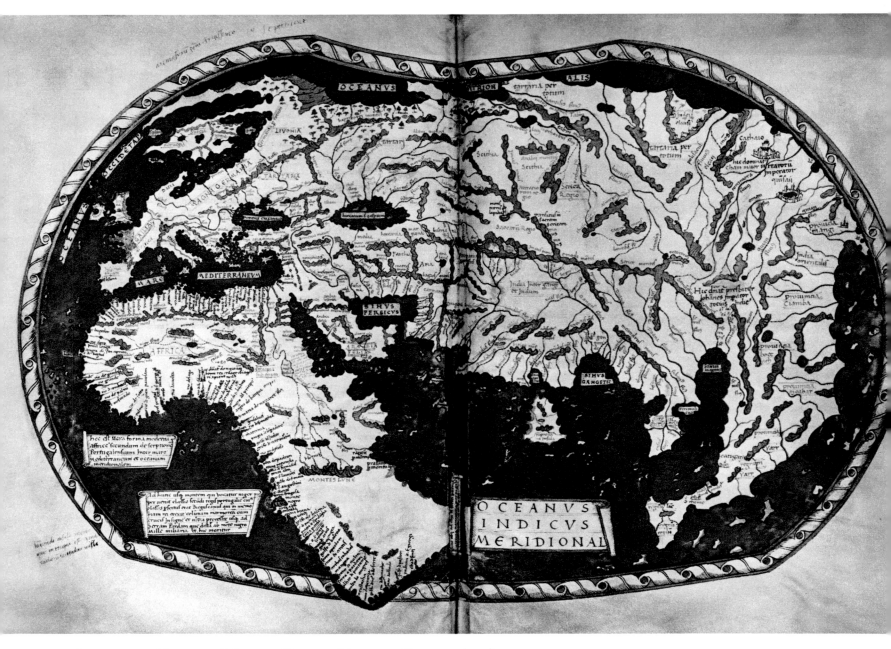

AFRICA ON THE MAP OF THE WORLD BY HENRICUS MARTELLUS GERMANUS (1492)

We can see from this map that the Portuguese had already begun their patient efforts to dispel the obscurity in which the contours of Africa were shrouded for so long. From 1434, when they at last rounded Cape Bojador, they had been making their way southwards, mile by mile, and scattering the coast with a succession of evocative names which have come down to the present day as records of what they saw on their protracted voyages of discovery. A tongue of land projecting from the gleaming white sands of the Sahara they dubbed 'Cabo Branco' (White Cape, 1441); a later explorer applied to the forest-clad shores of his landfall the name 'Cabo Verde'; a third noted the resemblance of palm-stems to masts as he sailed by the 'Cabo dos Mastros', and a fourth gave the name 'Cabo Roxo' to a jutting point of red earth to the south of Gambia.

In the Middle Ages Africa had been assumed to be much 'shorter' (see the Ebstorf map of the world, pages 30–31); the outline of Africa shown on the Laurentinian Portolano map of 1351, on the basis of information gleaned from Arab and Italian merchants who had visited Senegal, was not unduly remote from present-day notions, but it failed to find acceptance. Martellus goes to the other extreme; his immensely elongated coastline hints at the astonishment of seamen at finding that the unknown continent seemed never to come to an end. The information brought home by Bartholomeu Diaz, who in 1487 had reached Great Fish River when his mutinous crew forced him to turn back, is already embodied in this map. Seven years after it appeared—in 1499—Vasco da Gama's achievements clarified the picture of the east coast of Africa as well. Martellus's work came half-way between these two epochmaking voyages, and in the very year when Columbus 'discovered America'. So it is contemporary with some of the notable events in the history of exploration.

THE FOUNDERS OF THE PORTUGUESE-INDIAN TRADE EMPIRE

AFFONSO DE ALBUQUERQUE (1453–1515) was Viceroy of Portuguese India for six years (1509–15), during which he laid the political foundations for the new dominion. He provided flanking defences and an area for manoeuvre by capturing Ormuz to the west and Malacca to the east, and established the whole administrative service at Goa, which he had occupied in 1510. His far sighted policy brought great results. Portugal made no attempt to form a closely-knit empire, but secured naval bases along this stretch of the Indian coast and set up fortified trading posts wherever agreements could be concluded with well-disposed native rulers. Albuquerque encouraged intermarriage between Portuguese and Indians, respected local customs—with the exception of suttee—, and opened schools where Hindu children could learn Portuguese—for he recruited Indians for the Customs, Legal and Financial administration. His example put to shame not only his own king but his successors in Goa, many of whom fell short of his moral stature.

VASCO DA GAMA (1469–1524). His pioneering voyage, which established a link between Portugal and India, lasted for two years and two days (1497–99). Attempting something never achieved before, he sailed with four stout ships far into the unknown Atlantic; and ninety-five days later, after making a wide sweep round the dangerous waters of Guinea, he anchored in St Helen's Bay in South-West Africa. From Mozambique onwards he was in Arab waters, and was exposed to constant danger from the intrigues of native chiefs, captains and pilots. Help came, however, from the ruler of Melinde, who supplied a pilot for the crossing to Calicut, where da Gama found that the local Indian rajah was in league with the anti-Christian Arab spice-merchants. On this first encounter he saw a great deal of fighting; but he brought away, in addition to a precious cargo of spices, a plan for future progress: trading posts were to be established on the territory of rulers hostile to his Arab rivals, and from there he would push further eastwards. . . .

## THE MARVELLOUS FERTILITY OF THE INDIAN SOIL

The reports spread by the Portuguese, and later by the Dutch, about the natural resources of the newly-discovered India are a veritable jungle of words, with their amazing, interminable catalogues of tropical trees and fruits, diamonds and emeralds, birds and fish, cereals and spices, snakes and beasts of prey, precious woods and roots. This illustration is taken from one such report. The trees on the extreme right are coco-nut palms bearing their fruit—the 'Indian nut' (Nuces Indicae). The nut-picker, using the notches in the trunk, is nimbly climbing up to pluck them. The coco-nut palm has something for everybody; its fronds are used to thatch huts, its fibre to make cords and matting, coco-nut milk is a cordial, the flesh tastes like hazel-nuts, and the timber was formerly used even for shipbuilding. Centre, left: A banana tree, bearing its 'Indian figs'. The fruit was declared to be 'as smooth as a mixture of flour and butter . . .; it serves well as rolls or bread, and a man might in sooth make his diet thereof, requiring no other food. . . .' Left: An arequeira, or betel-nut palm (Areca catechu), the fruit of which may grow to the size of an egg. The betel plant, with its peppercorn-like fruit, climbs up the trunk of this tree. Every Indian the early explorers came across was chewing the bitter betel leaf, wrapped round betel-nut pounded up with lime. The mixture fortifies the digestion, sweetens the breath, and induces a mood of serenity.

Looking at such illustrations to the old explorers' reports it is not always easy to decide where fact stops and fiction begins. Some of the pioneers embroidered somewhat on their recollections of luxuriant tropical vegetation, while in many cases the actual illustrators were stay-at-homes, with nothing to guide them except the written tale and perhaps a few rough sketches made by some member of the expedition. Moreover, in the early baroque period the emotions of authors and illustrators alike were apt to range through the whole gamut extending from boundless sensuous delight in a world so packed with marvels, to deep religious awe. Both these feelings were shared by the engraver and publisher Theodor de Bry (1528–98) and his sons, Johann Dietrich and Johann Israel, who collaborated in the most splendid of all the illustrated travel-reports that appeared in the sixteenth century—the multi-volume *Collectiones peregrinationum in Indiam orientalem et occidentalem* from which the illustrations on pages 54 to 59 are taken.

*ficus Judica*

*queira*

*Nuces Judicæ*

MARKET IN GOA

In 1510 Albuquerque captured Goa, a strongly fortified position on the fertile coast north of Calicut, and proceeded to build it up, in the Portuguese style of architecture, as the seat of his government and a principal centre for the trade between Asia and Europe. The market was the great event of each day; it could only be held in the early morning, before the broiling tropical heat reached its climax. Shutters shaded the windows of the low-built houses from the scorching rays of the sun, and the well-to-do on their walks abroad were accompanied by servants holding umbrellas over their heads. Drinking-water was bought from coolies who fetched it

from the only spring outside the town [4]. The women seldom left home; they were carried to church or on visits in litters, with a slit through which they could look out at what was going on [1].

Great numbers of people bought and sold in Goa's crowded market; the national currency of every ship's company was accepted [5], so that at each arrival or departure of a merchant vessel the appropriate exchange-rate would rise or fall; there were dealings in rice and fruit (the women in the background, on the right), fish and horses [2: this particular horse has been decked with little bells, to tempt the bidder], Indian pottery and textiles—and in human beings as well, for we see a slave-girl being auctioned [3]. Generally speaking, the Portuguese were more interested in trade than in cultivating the soil; in that lethal climate, the majority tried to make a fortune with all possible speed. The commercial empire gradually expanded, taking in first Malacca and then Japan; and the flow of people and goods through Goa, its central point, showed a corresponding increase. This view was engraved by the de Bry brothers from a book illustration by the Dutch engraver Joannes van Doetechum in J. H. Linschoten's *Navigatio ac Itinerarium* (1599).

## Ships from the Far East

Here we are shown different types of Far Eastern vessels known to the Portuguese in Malacca, lined up as though for review. In the foreground is a very nimble outrigger craft, steered by an oar; its sail, woven from vegetable fibres, is stretched between bamboo poles. In the background is a vessel used in the coastal freight service; on the right is a two-masted ship with a superstructure, from the South Seas, and beyond that a junk with forecastle and quarter-deck; its sails, which can be rolled up, are made of bast matting reinforced with bamboo stems; it is a foreign visitor from China, a legendary land that now seemed to have drawn much nearer again.

For behind this picture lie vast stretches of space and history. The Portuguese had prevailed over the Arabs and Turks on the western side of the Indian Ocean, and in 1508 Diego Lopes de Sequeira, sailing eastwards, landed at Malacca, to find himself among merchants and seamen—these too of long-renowned skill—from India, Arabia, Burma, Java and China. In 1511 Albuquerque captured the place, which was an important post on the route to China, a collecting-point in the Indonesian and Malayan spice-trade; and in 1514 a Portuguese merchant vessel reached the Middle Kingdom, whose Ming ruler, though he would have no foreign settlers on his territory, was quite prepared to establish trade relations with Europe. As early as 1505 an Italian adventurer, Lodovico de Varthema, had made his way through the Straits of Malacca to Sumatra and the Spice Isles, partly in the tracks of Marco Polo. His reports were useful to the Portuguese who, led by Francisco Serrão, set up a trading post on the island of Ternate, in the Moluccas. In 1529 the Emperor Charles V, pressed for money, sold them the spice-laden Moluccas outright; but before that, in 1523, China had again closed its doors to them, and Japan soon followed suit. For a brief century after this earlier encounter with Far Eastern shipping Portugal's development as a world power continued with meteoric brilliance and rapidity; then the Dutch, English and French began their dangerous inroads upon an empire too far-flung to be effectively protected without assistance.

THE GRAND MOGUL GIVES NEW YEAR AUDIENCE AT AGRA

*Above:* In the Moslem domains of the Grand Mogul, in northern India, the princes used to gather at the New Year, amid oriental magnificence, to offer tributes of gems, golden vessels and precious stuffs to their overlord. Rich tents were set up in front of the palace to lodge the donors.

*Right:* A traditional scene in Asia: somewhere in Bengal, these entertainers are displaying their hazardous art. Two of them are balancing on tall bamboo poles, a third is performing complicated somersaults, while a fourth, fakir-like, bends over backwards, with knives and sabres stuck into his cheeks and held in place by the facial muscles. Wouter Schouten, a Dutchman, drew this scene in India in 1664 and published it in Amsterdam. Dutch books about India appeared in increasing numbers during the seventeenth century, as the Dutch, from their Indonesian bases, began to 'infiltrate' into the Spanish and Portuguese spheres of influence in Asia.

*Overleaf:* COLONNADED HALL BY THE TEMPLE OF MADURA. A seventeenth-century masterpiece of stone-carving in southern India. Bodigais (lotus flowers) hang down from the supports of the flat ceiling; below them are animals—'Diggajas', who bear the universe on their backs. In the middle, slightly to the left, a 'Yali'—a lion with an elephant's trunk—is standing on its hind legs. The pillars are carved with representations of Shiva, prophets, and kings with their consorts—among them, in the right foreground, Tirumala Najak (1623–59), who had this splendid temple built. The English landscape painter Thomas Daniell (1749–1840) spent the years 1784–94 in roaming about India, where his countrymen had already begun to establish a footing. In 1808 he published his splendid colour lithographs in a series entitled *Oriental Scenery*, some of whose plates were a revelation even to geographers.

## The Indian Elephant

The elephant, with his fabulous appearance and huge frame, was a firm favourite with European readers of travel books even before they learnt that in India he was a sacred creature, with magic powers over waters and fields, and that only kings might ride on his broad back. *Below:* Elephants in Ceylon, from André Thevet's *Cosmographie universelle* (Paris 1575).—*Right:* In 1795, when the Englishman Michael Symes led an expedition into Burma—a land hostile to foreigners—the Burmese king showed him this picture of an elephant hunt painted by a Siamese artist on glass. The expedition's artist, a Bengali, copied it and an engraving was later made from the copy, in France, by J. B. Tardieu.

Wild elephants were captured in East Bengal by men mounted on tame, specially trained beasts. The hunter rode cautiously up to the herd and lassoed a selected elephant round the feet. The beast would struggle and rage, but the end of the rope was securely fastened to the tame elephant, and the captor knew how to defend himself. The rest of the herd took to flight while the fettered animal, hemmed in by four trained elephants, was led away to captivity—according to Michael Symes's report.

The Elephant in Ceylon—first bird's-eye view

THE ART OF CAPTURING ELEPHANTS IN THE MOUNTAINS BETWEEN BENGAL AND BURMA

*Overleaf:* THE GIGANTIC OBSERVATORY AT DELHI. Thomas Daniell was the first to present an astonished world with coloured views of the fantastic monstrosities constructed by Maharajah Jai Singh II (1686–1743)—a progressive ruler and an astronomer who made improvements in the calendar—at his residence at Jaipur, with replicas at Benares, Muttra, Ujjain and Delhi. In the middle is the gnomon at Delhi, the Samrat-yantra, erected about 1730; it is over 55 feet high. It served as a giant sundial, with which very small fractions of time could be measured, and also for measuring stars. A right-angled triangle of masonry stands on the longer cathetus, and the hypotenuse, with the steps, lies exactly parallel to the earth's axis. East and west of this and at right angles—parallel to the equator—stretch two quadrants—each with a radius of over 36 feet—on which the hours and minutes are marked. Shadows move over these huge surfaces at a pace that is visible to the eye, so that the time can be calculated by the sun to within a quarter of a minute (note the three observers). In the background is the Misrayantra, a multiple instrument including a sundial, equipment for calculating latitude and other devices the purpose of which is no longer fully understood.

MEMBERS OF THE SCHLAGINTWEIT EXPEDITION (IN DISGUISE) ON THE HIGH PLATEAU OF WESTERN TIBET

Eighty-four volumes of descriptive notes, extensive collections of specimens and 752 drawings and water-colours were assembled by the three brothers Schlagintweit, Adolf, Robert and Hermann, during their travels in the Deccan, Kashmir and the Himalayas in 1855–57. Hermann made this drawing in August 1856, when the expedition was engaged in a weary struggle to investigate the passes leading from India, over the Karakorum range, to Tibet and East Turkestan. Robert and Hermann were hungry and travel-worn, and had already lost seven of their nineteen horses, by the time they and their eight companions reached some meagre grazing-land within sight of the western spur of the Kuenlun range. Piled up in the camp are bales of Tibetan wool-cloth

and Indian cottons which the travellers carried with them partly for barter and partly because they were approaching a region of hostile Moslems, where they must try to pass for Indian merchants. (In this same year, 1856, in spite of this disguise, Adolf—only twenty-eight years old—was stabbed to death by a fanatic at Kashgar.) To the right stretches the broad bastion of the Kuenlun in the dazzling light, its ridge marking the southern boundary of Chotan, in East Turkestan. In front lies the broad plain of rock and alluvial sand through which the river Karakash flows northwards to Turkestan. A sortie across the ridge yielded plenty of fresh geographical and scientific material, together with provisions for the return journey.

# China

'One day when Father Alessandro Valignani, the Jesuit Inspector for India, was gazing from a window of the College at Macao towards the mainland of China, he cried in a loud voice: "O thou rock, thou rock, when wilt thou split open?"' So writes a historian of the mission, and his words reveal one of the two fundamental conditions that governed the history of discovery in China. For that ancient civilization was determined *not* to be explored, let alone converted to Christianity. The resolve to keep out foreigners and all they stood for was a feature of Chinese policy for centuries at a time. But every now and then it would yield to another basic instinct, an eager receptiveness towards things from outside, which originated in the Imperial court and spread from there throughout the country, like a smile on a round Chinese face. At one extreme the enquiring visitor would be received with the utmost friendliness and ceremony; at the other, the Chinese officers of the law would seize him—as happened, for instance, in the eighteenth century, when certain Jesuits were hung head downwards over a trench in the presence of a vast crowd and left there to die.

One period of lively intercourse between China and Europe came at a very early stage—in the time of the Han dynasty (206 B.C. – 220 A.D.) which unified China, organizing it in a way that implied a remarkable knowledge of the internal geography of the country, and extended its sway to the territory west of the Pamirs. During this era silk was brought to Europe by way of Antioch and Aleppo, while at the end of the first century A.D. the Romans sent ships round India into Chinese waters. A second period was that of the *Pax tatarica*: between 1264 and 1368, when envoys travelled to and fro between the Mongol ruler Kublai Khan and the Pope, a flourishing trade was carried on over the longest routes in the world, and the merchant explorer Marco Polo came home to Europe with what long remained the most accurate and detailed report on the wonders of the Middle Kingdom.

After one hundred and fifty years of renewed hostility to foreigners the Portuguese arrived in 1516—the first Europeans to reach China by sea since Roman times. They ushered in a third important period of contacts, though this time, paradoxically, in the face of opposition from the greater part of the country. In 1557, as a reward for the help given by their heavily-armed vessels against Chinese pirates, they were granted a lease of some land on the little peninsula of Macao. Here they set up a trading post and were allowed, under strict supervision, to export cargoes of silk and spices. In the late seventeenth century lacquer, porcelain wares and tea were added to these exports; but by that time the trade was in the hands of the Dutch. During the eighteenth century the English joined in, shipping as many goods from Canton as the Chinese would permit. Frequent reports on China were brought back to Europe by merchants during these centuries.

But it was an event which took place independently of the trade campaigns that proved decisive, when the Jesuits found the key that gave partial access to the interior of the jealously-guarded country. In the seventeenth and eighteenth centuries they became the real explorers of the Chinese mind, and the repercussions of their discoveries were felt far beyond geographical circles. Furthermore, at the very time when the Ming and Manchu rulers were resolutely warding off European intruders, the writings of certain European philosophers, the paintings of Watteau and Cozens, the delicate porcelain figures and lacquer bowls to be seen in private houses, and the pagodas that decorated Chinese-style parks in England testified to the birth of a second China far from China—the European world of the *chinoiserie* (see page 87).

The Chinese proverb first became known in Europe through the publication of a collection in the seventeenth century. Among its gems of wisdom were the following:

'To see through fame and wealth gives a little peace; to see through life and death gives deep peace.'

'He whose vision is narrow cannot be great of heart; he whose spirit is narrow cannot walk far and light-footed.'

'A good student of mankind corrects what he hears by what he sees; a bad one corrupts what he sees by what he hears.'

Examples of Chinese humour also reached Europe for the first time:

'King Huan of Ch'i got drunk one day and lost his hat. He was so ashamed that for three days he shut himself up and would give no audiences. Kwan Chung said to the King: "This is no way for a monarch to behave. Why not do some generous action as a penance?" The King went out and opened his granaries and for three days he distributed food to the poor. The people praised the King's magnanimity and said: "Would that he might lose his hat again and again!"' (Han Fei, died 234 B.C.).

However despite European interest in the Chinese style and wisdom, no really systematic geographical investigation of the enormous Chinese Empire was undertaken until the latter half of the nineteenth century.

THE LAGRÉE EXPEDITION

One of the last great geographical enigmas that remained unsolved in South-East Asia down to the latter part of the nineteenth century related to the upper reaches of the Mekong River in Indo-China, which flows through virgin forest to its wide delta on the coast. How far was it navigable? What were the prospects of trade with the natives who lived on its banks? What was the character of its northern neighbour, the Chinese province of Yunnan? It was the French who put the finishing touches to information handed down by their Chinese, Portuguese, Dutch and English predecessors. In 1859 they chose Saigon as the central point of an extensive tropical territory that remained under their domination until 1885. On 5th June 1866 they sent out their first expedition to explore the region north of Saigon. Its leader was Captain Doudart de Lagrée, the commander of a frigate; its second in command was Francis Garnier, who was subsequently to lead the party down the Yangtse Kiang and back to Saigon by sea—Lagrée having succumbed to a liver complaint when they were already on Chinese soil. Maps and sketches were made by the third in seniority, a young naval lieutenant named Louis Delaporte.

The party got back to Saigon in 1868, having found the difficult southern route into China, discovered that the upper waters of the Mekong were rendered unnavigable by a succession of cataracts, and assembled a wealth of geographical, economic and ethnographical information.

INDO-CHINA: THE LAGRÉE EXPEDITION CAMPS FOR ▶ THE NIGHT. The camping site is near the mighty Khon rapids. In the background the turbulent Mekong rushes past. This is the rainy season and a storm has broken in the early evening. The six boats which, with native crews, have brought the party to this camping-place are moored along the bank of the river, out of sight. The two dozen or so members of the expedition—naval officers from Europe, soldiers, scientists, Annamite interpreters and guards—are at a late supper round the fire. Tall, liana-hung tree-trunks—*dipterocarpus laevis*—rise above them into the darkness.

In the Mountains along the Upper Yangtse Kiang

◄ In June 1867 the expedition left Mekong and proceeded to the village of Muonglim, near the Chinese frontier, there to wait for messengers. The track, which ran through dense forest, had been transformed into a torrent by the heavy rains. Here the party is seen toiling through the jungle. Many of its members were fever-racked; all were tormented by flies and hornets, and leeches fastened on them as they waded across the streams in their path. Before long they were entirely cut off from the outer world.

*Above:*

Having buried their dead leader in his solitary grave near the town of Tungszchewen, the explorers climbed to a height of about 9,800 feet above sea-level and made their way by dizzy cliff paths towards the deep ravine of the Yangtse Kiang, the 'Blue River'. The paths led along precipitous, shaly bluffs, high above tumbling, roaring torrents. On 31st January 1868 the expedition first glimpsed the limpid waters of China's mightiest river, flowing far below. After investigating trading conditions in northern Yunnan, the group travelled downstream to the sea.

*Overleaf:*

North of Luangprabang the Mekong makes a sharp bend at a point where it is 980 feet wide, and rushes along between tall cliffs. In one of these cliffs, at a height of forty-two feet above the river, is a stalagtite cave—a Buddhist shrine for sailors and travellers, crowded with statues, hung with votive offerings (banners, canopies), and tended by priests.

## HUAN-TSANG THE PILGRIM (602–64)

The Tang dynasty (618–907) unified China by force of arms and provided a succession of open-minded rulers. This was a period when religion flourished, when Buddhism and Nestorian Christianity, the creed of 'the second Rome', were free to ramify throughout the land of Confucius. Among those who did most to put fresh vigour into Chinese spiritual life in the seventh century was a monk named Huan-tsang. He was Confucian in his keen, penetrating intellect, his shrewd observation, his moderation, which led him to regard all excess as a sign of stupidity or weakness of character; he was Buddhist in his disinterested striving for that mystic introspection by which man, in the depths of his being, can become inviolable. But the Buddhist traditions in the monasteries of China was clouded, fragmentary, full of inconsistencies. Huan-tsang decided to travel to northern India and there study the most authoritative texts, hold theological discussions, visit the places where the Buddha had dwelt, and seek thus to arrive at the essential truths.

He set out in the year 629 on a pilgrimage that lasted sixteen years. Between him and the Ganges, the sacred river, lay the Gobi and Tarim deserts, the chasms and frozen passes of the Pamirs, and the Indian jungle. He braved the terrors and dangers of the interminably long journey, he withstood hunger and thirst, robbery and destitution. Sometimes he rode, sometimes he walked, sometimes he went by boat. In the Tarim oases he was welcomed enthusiastically by Buddhist princes, who listened, enthralled, to one whose words breathed new life into their faith and revealed unsuspected depths in it. And he reached his goal. In a monastery in Kashmir he found a great teacher of the Mahayana, to which Buddhism owed the force of conviction that made it into a worldwide movement. With the great traditions preserved in Ceylon he had however no acquaintance. He stayed for two years in Kashmir. In Nepal he paid reverent visits to the scenes of the Buddha's birth, enlightenment and death. His was both a spiritual and a geographical odyssey, and sometimes it took on a legendary air—as did pictures, painted in later centuries, which show the traveller heavily laden with Sutras (basic texts, copied out by hand) and reliquaries, and leaning on his pilgrim's staff. He reached home again in 644 and was received with honour. His journey had two results. In the first place it brought about a Buddhist revival in China, chiefly through his many translations from the Sanscrit. In the second place his experience of the world prompted the Emperor to choose him as a counsellor at a time when China, newly unified, was just beginning to reach out towards Central Asia and to conclude pacts with still more distant countries. At the Emperor's bidding he wrote an account of his travels, and thus inadvertently established himself as a classic source of geographical and cultural information. His descriptions of many parts of India and China, with those of certain other Chinese who visited India during the Tang period, for all their omissions and inaccuracies, are among the basic records in which Asians revealed Asia to one another.

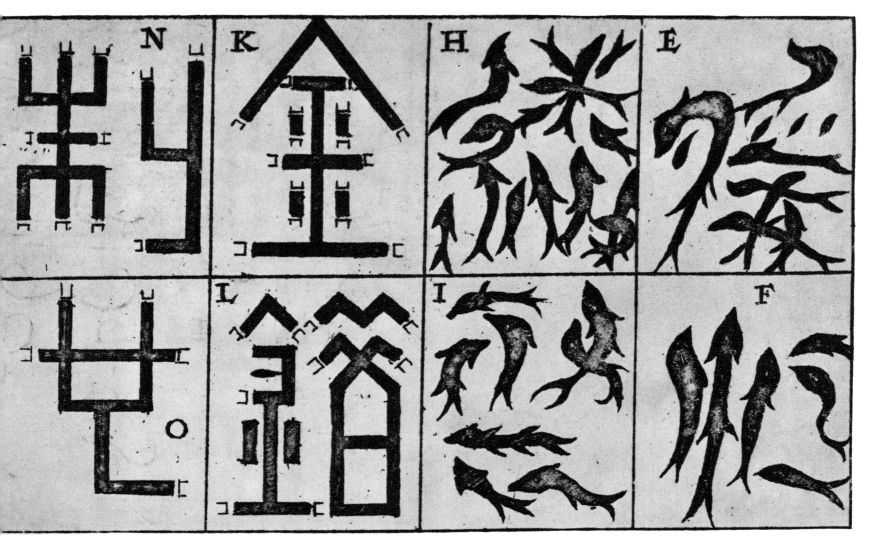

AN ATTEMPT TO REPRODUCE ANCIENT CHINESE CHARACTERS

The Jesuits, whose Order was founded in 1534, occupy a prominent position in the history of discovery. Their most brilliant feats were accomplished in Asia and in North and South America, and they explored not only the length and breadth of each country they visited, but—as their mission demanded of them—the depths of its people's minds and souls. They were also required by their Order to adapt themselves to local conditions. Those who visited the Chinese, an ancient, highly-civilized nation, had first to study in the college at Macao, and thus acquire a respectful familiarity with the language, traditions and customs of China. The leading missionaries had also to have an up-to-date knowledge of the secular sciences of Europe, particularly mathematics, astronomy, geography and medicine. For experience showed that only a 'most learned foreign mandarin' could arouse in the self-assured Chinese a desire to hear about the superiorities of Western erudition and ultimately, in the role of an esteemed adviser, reach a position close to the imperial throne and obtain permission to begin proselytizing—and that in all this he had to proceed with the utmost caution. This was

what made St Francis Xavier regard the mission to Asia as a noble and valiant exercise in the art of human relations. The study of Chinese calligraphy was tirelessly pursued. The Jesuits realized that its characters were ideograms, not phonetic symbols, and the Polish missionary Michael Boym (1612–1659), in his *Delucidatio summaria rerum sinicarum*, distinguished the most ancient of the thousands of symbols from the more recent ones by classifying them in groups according to form—thus following the example of the legendary Emperor Fu-hi. Athanasius Kircher continued the work, including in his book on China (1667), together with other characters, those reproduced above, which had come to notice since Boym's time. Those from E to I are taken, in that order, from the 'fish-shaped' group; those from K to O belong to the 'undecipherable' group. The translations made by the Jesuits had a wide and lasting influence. Leibniz went so far as to declare that Chinese philosophers should be brought to Europe as teachers, and Quesnay quoted Chinese concepts of government to support his theory of enlightened monarchy.

Fig. XVIII

THE MOST ANCIENT VIEW OF THE DALAI LAMA'S PALACE-FORTRESS AT LHASA

The Jesuits were the first to venture upon serious exploration of Tibet. In 1661 two dauntless missionaries, Grüber and d'Orville, even made their way, in disguise, into the Dalai Lama's forbidden city. This was forty years after some Portuguese Jesuits had crossed the Himalayan passes into the strange mountain-land of Tibet, first mentioned over three hundred years earlier by the monk Odoric de Pordenone.— This picture was engraved for Athanasius Kircher's book *China* (1667) from a sketch included in one of Grüber's reports to the General of the Order.

◄ FATHER MATTEO RICCI, S.J., (LEFT) AND A CHINESE CHRISTIAN, LI PAULUS. Ricci was a pioneer who paved the way for the Jesuits in China. He reached Macao in 1582. A year later he was living at Canton, disguised as a Buddhist monk. This was the beginning of a perilous but triumphant progress that ultimately led the shrewd missionary to the Imperial Palace in Peking. Ricci and his successors freely imparted their useful knowledge of medicine, astronomy and even ballistics, as their contribution to this great game of patience. Father Paulus was much respected by Emperor and people alike. Under Ricci's supervision he made Chinese translations of Latin works on astronomy and of other books.

RECEPTION OF PIETER VAN HOORN'S DUTCH TRADE DELEGATION AT THE IMPERIAL COURT OF PEKING (1668)

The semi-official trading companies set up by the Dutch and English competed vigorously for the much-coveted Chinese trading licences, both countries sending delegations to negotiate with Peking, where they appeared with all the necessary ostentation of the day. The mission seen here had come from Batavia—Java being the centre of the Dutch mercantile empire in East Asia. While the Chinese looked on mistrustfully, they brought along their lavish presents on junks and carts, and after these had been carefully inspected by mandarins a high official of the Court took charge of the items desired by the Emperor, which were laid on a table in the courtyard of the building where the audience-hall was situated. The Dutch are sitting on a carpet. In front of them is one of the numerous court officials who had to be bribed with presents by anyone wishing to be admitted to audience and allowed to present a petition. As they went along, the delegations picked up information. . . .

*Overleaf:* THE MODERN EUROPEAN INSTRUMENTS OF PEKING OBSERVATORY. The Court Astronomers of Peking, who were Moslems, had set up their instruments along the south wall of the Imperial Palace at Peking. The Chinese calendar, by which all the year's work and its holidays were regulated, was based on their calculations. The Jesuits managed to prove that this official calendar had got out of hand, and in 1611 they were told, for the first time, to put it in order. Thereafter, as though by magic, eclipses began to occur on the proper dates again; and the Jesuits were allowed to begin missionary work. Despite intermittent persecution they kept their position as Court Astronomers until 1838. They replaced the old-fashioned Moslem instruments in the observatory by new ones—(c) equatorial globe, (d) celestial sphere, (e) zodiac, (f) instrument with compass, (g) quadrant, (h) sextant which they decorated, as a compliment to the Emperor, with dragons and other Chinese motifs.

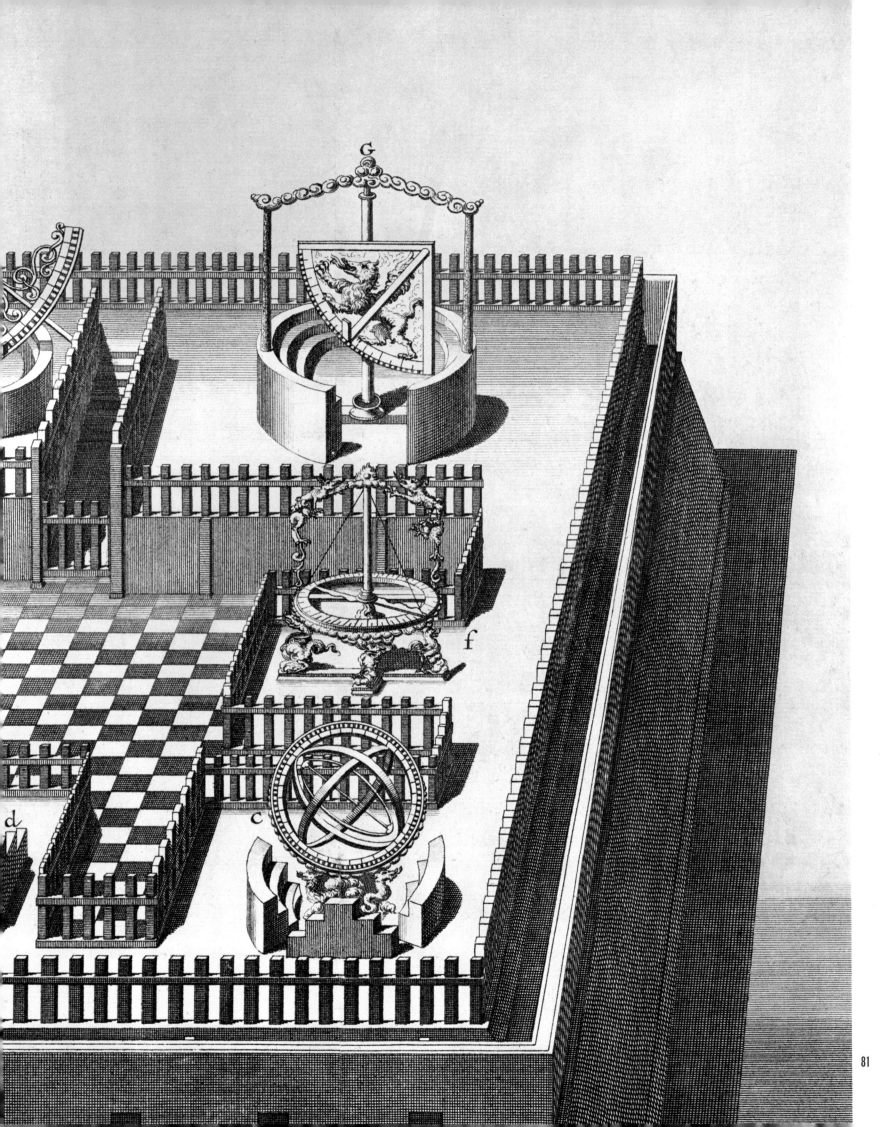

Rottingh

Bamboes

ROTANG AND BAMBOO IN CHINA

On the right is the bamboo, a plant with iron-hard stems, strengthened by knotty joints. On the left is a species of palm, the *calamus rotang,* or Canadian reed. The two pictures are by Jean Nieuhoff (1618–1672), an artist who accompanied a Dutch trading delegation to China.

Suycker Riet. Cannes ou Roseaux.

CHINESE SUGAR-CANE

This plant, the leaves of which have razor-sharp edges, thrives in damp places. When ripe the stems are cut close to the ground and crushed in a mill (seen here in the background). The sweetish sap pressed out of the white pulp is boiled in copper vessels until it becomes thick.

A Pagoda on a Crag in the Province of Fukien

On its way from the seaboard province of Fukien to the city of Peking, Pieter van Hoorn's Dutch trading company (see page 79) sailed through this fairylike landscape along a river they called the Min. 'Towards noon they saw a temple built across a watercourse, like a bridge, so that large ships can sail beneath it at high tide. This pagoda was prettily adorned after the Chinese fashion, with steps going up the side thereof and divers statues standing about,' writes the expedition's log-keeper.

## Chinese Curiosities

FISHING WITH CORMORANTS. The Dutch were astonished
to find that the Chinese could train cormorants—exceptionally greedy birds—to catch fish for them. A bird would dive,
catch a fish and come to the surface with its booty in its beak.
An iron ring round its throat prevented it from swallowing
the fish, which it disgorged when its gullet was suitably
pressed with the fingers. Its work done, the ring was removed and the bird allowed to go on fishing for its own
benefit. The Dutch brought this custom back to Europe in
the seventeenth century, as a sport.

*Centre:* A WAYSIDE PHILOSOPHER. Van Hoorn's people were
struck by the widespread Chinese enthusiasm for soothsay-
ing. They came across many charlatans, self-styled 'magi-
cians', but they were also told of wise old men who lived in
remote hermitages, meditating and preparing for death.
People in need of advice would travel great distances on
foot to consult them, and afterwards spread their fame
abroad.

*Below:* MEALTIME ON A BOAT. Travellers saw many of these
small boats on the rivers of the interior. The broad afterdeck
was divided into two parts, with a place in the middle for
the steersman. A screen of coco-nut leaves kept off the rain.
Here the Chinese company, in the shade of a neatly-woven
awning of reeds, is relishing the pleasures of relaxation, talk
and food—fish and rice eaten with chopsticks out of little
bowls—while the boat glides slowly downstream.

## Ancient Chinese Philosophy of Silence

### From Documents found by Jesuit Priests in China

There are four kinds of silence or reserve of which the ancient rules of wisdom disapprove. To say nothing when one has grave doubts on a subject, or, worse still, to persist in uncouth ignorance instead of seeking enlightenment through enquiry, is stupidity and folly. To keep silence from cowardly complicity, particularly in order to curry favour with the great, is selfishness and sycophancy. To keep silence in order to conceal one's foibles behind a pretence of reserve, is vanity. And lastly, to conceal a heart full of venom and cunning behind a modest silence and an innocent appearance, the better to pursue one's devious, evil purposes, is hypocrisy. None of these is true silence, all are guilty silence. But there is a praiseworthy silence which may be prompted by a variety of pure impulses.

Confucius says that the wise man speaks always bashfully and with simplicity, as though aware of shortcomings in his behaviour and discourse. From the most ancient times, men whose tongues were too glib have been assumed to lack breeding in other respects, and to be unfitted for important tasks. Bashfulness, modesty and restraint are thus in some sort the first initiation to silence, or the art of remaining speechless.

But if virtuous men tend to say little, it is not because they consider taciturnity to be meritorious in itself, or because they are silent for the sake of silence. Their aim is higher: they regard silence as an excellent means of preserving and developing inner strength. Confucius says that to meditate ardently upon a fundamental truth is a means of attaining enlightenment. The least of the advantages acquired is that of escaping the gross errors into which the great majority of mankind is led. To ponder for a long time, quietly, in order to succeed in an undertaking, is rightly believed to denote wisdom and prudence. Above all, self-examination in silent retirement is the most effective means of perceiving our own evil tendencies or the deceits of our self-love. Yen-tse travelled so far along this path that his inner strength won universal respect and confidence, though he spoke with hardly anyone. And the lengths to which this virtue may be carried are shown by the example of Tien. Tien never says a word. And why should he? The four seasons follow one another in obedience to the great Command; everything grows in its due season. Why should Tien speak?...

'Petit discours sur le silence, dont l'auteur est Ouang yong ming', from the *Description... de l'Empire de la Chine et de la Tartarie chinoise*, by Father B. Du Halde S. J., Vol. 2, The Hague, 1736.

---

◄ CHINESE JUNKS AT ANCHOR

On the right is a merchant ship waiting for a cargo; its rudder has been raised out of the water by a cable. The two-masted vessel in the middle bears on its stern its own name and that of the province it comes from; above rises the cabin on the afterdeck, below which is the deep cleft where the rudder moves during the voyage—protected against mounting waves by the high, jutting walls of the afterdeck to either side. The ship on the left is armed; it is one of the escort vessels that used to accompany merchantmen as a protection against pirates. The junk, most picturesque of Asian ships, is square-rigged. Its sails are made of straw matting, with bamboo struts; they catch the wind most effectively, but are not easy to handle.

This lithograph dates from 1827, when China was almost completely closed to foreigners and descriptions became more and more scarce. It was not until after the country had been forcibly reopened by the English, through the Opium War, in 1839–42, and by the French in 1857–60, that scientific geographical exploration began—initiated by an American, Pumpelly, a German, Ferdinand von Richthofen, and by Russians in the north. In the twentieth century events in China took the same turn as in India—the Asians, having learnt from Europeans the scientific principles of surveying, took further detailed geographical research into their own hands.

# The Struggle for an Image of Japan

'The ship's company, about a hundred in number, are of strange aspect. Their speech is incomprehensible, their dwelling place unknown.' That is how the Japanese chroniclers recorded Japan's first encounter with Europeans. Their words reveal the amazement felt by the discovered, which often exceeds that of the discoverers themselves. This was in 1543, when the Portuguese adventurers Fernan Mendez Pinto and Diego Zeimoto had been shipwrecked on the island of Tanegashima during a storm. Their arrival was soon followed by that of merchants and missionaries from India and Malacca, including the greatest of all missionaries to Asia, St. Francis Xavier. However, until the second half of the nineteenth century Japan was to figure in the history of exploration as a larger and sea-girt Lhasa.

Only fifty years had elapsed since St. Francis Xavier's mission, when the military dynasty of the Tokugawa (1603–1868) set itself to impose order upon the feudal nobility with their chaotic rivalries, and make the island realm into a great independent stronghold. The outside influence that had for centuries been exerted over the Japanese mind by Indian Buddhism and Chinese Confucianism remained as strong as ever, but the island was closed to Spanish and Portuguese traders and Christian missionaries. The last Christians were cruelly exterminated in 1638—though this was to some extent the fault of the foreigners themselves, who had become too importunate. An exception was made for the Dutch who were allowed, under rigorous supervision, to use only one trading post, on the tiny island of Deijma in the Bay of Nagasaki. It is by no mere accident that all the information of real interest that filtered out of Japan from the seventeenth century to the nineteenth was conveyed by Dutch employees. They had to smuggle it out after collecting it scrap by scrap, at their peril and by stealth—sometimes with the forbidden complicity of Japanese geographers, who had a fair knowledge of their country and even of the neighbouring territories of Korea and China, with which Japan maintained trade relations. Prominent among the Europeans were two doctors, Engelbert Kämpfer and Philipp Franz von Siebold. It was not until the Americans and English forced their way into certain seaports in 1854, and their example was followed by the Russians in 1855, that the outside world began to form a more detailed picture of Japan, while Western civilization gradually penetrated into that anachronistic setting.

A Deputation from the Dutch East India Company on its Way to the Imperial Court at Jedo (Tokyo) in 1690

The man on horseback marked by the figure 15 was the first European to publish a reasonably comprehensive work on the unknown, mysterious land of Japan. He was a certain Engelbert Kämpfer, born in 1651 at Lemgo, Westphalia—a doctor and student of natural science, deeply learned and much-travelled. He found his real vocation in 1685 while working as ship's doctor for the Dutch East India Company in Persia. He sailed with the Company's fleet to visit all the Dutch bases from the Malabar coast to Batavia, and in May 1690 he went with the annual trading mission to Japan. He remained there for two years—a feat that would have been impossible, in a country so profoundly distrustful of foreigners, but for his usefulness as an exceptionally skilled doctor and to the fact that as a 'Dutchman' he was not unduly suspect. In 1692 he returned from the vast expanses of the Far East to the narrow limits of his native province where, in addition to his exacting work as doctor and as adviser to the local ruler, he wrote a book on Persia. He died in 1716, and eleven years went by before a Swiss scholar, Johann

Kaspar Scheuchzer, of Zurich, rescued his memory from unmerited neglect by publishing an English translation of his important *History of Japan*.

The deputation is seen on its way to the Imperial court, shortly after leaving Nagasaki. 1–2, advance guard, a Dutch and a Japanese cook, with their equipment. 3, two guides. 4, baggage-master. 5, the Dutch envoy's horse. 6, a Chinese soldier. 7, medicine chest. 8, an iron-bound treasure-chest. 9, the envoy in his litter—carried by four men in relays—and three servants. 10, the chief interpreter, in a smaller litter. 11, a second interpreter, with a servant. 12, a legal secretary from Nagasaki. 13–14, two of the delegation's secretaries, each attended by a servant. 15, Dr Kämpfer, medical officer to the delegation. 16, a deputy interpreter. 17, same as 12. 18–19, horse and pike-bearer of the Bugyo, or Japanese supreme commander, who is seen following in a sedan chair (20), attended by servants and porters. 21, friends bidding him farewell. 22, friends of the Dutch party, who have come out from Nagasaki to see them off.

A Portuguese Trading Company arrives at a Jesuit Settlement in Japan

The first European visitor, a Portuguese, landed in Japan in 1543; in 1614 the Portuguese and Spaniards were expelled from the country by decree. This scene relates to the brief intervening period, during which Japanese feudal princes protected the Portuguese, allowing them to bring merchants and missionaries from Europe in their ships. It was probably painted twenty to thirty years later, by which time the foreign religious orders, by squabbling among themselves,

and certain merchants by displays of arrogance, had begun to alienate Japanese sympathies or at least to invite ironical comment (as can be seen from certain touches of caricature).

The gilded cloud-formations that hold the design together are stamped with chrysanthemums and blossoms of the 'imperial tree' (Paulovnia), the armorial bearings of the family then reigning over Central Japan. On the left, a Portuguese ship lies at anchor in the trading port. The Japanese painter,

though very well-meaning, had little technical grasp of the mysteries of a European three-masted vessel. Hence the angular, junk-like shape, the fantastic superstructure, the extraordinary convolutions of the light-coloured anchor cable, and the absence of yards to support the rigging.

On the right is the quaintly caparisoned train of merchants, bringing their tribute of presents (a horse, a dog, a Chinese chair and so forth) for local Japanese rulers.

Two ascetic-looking Jesuits are waiting to receive the party at the foot of the steps that lead to their attractive-looking establishment, on the roof of which a cock or phoenix—a symbol of the resurrection—is perched with outspread wings. Here we have a glimpse into the life of a Jesuit mission—which in this case obviously serves as a 'base' for merchants—with its austere Fathers, young seminarists and Japanese neophytes of the Christian Church.

THE 'KAMI' COURTYARD OF THE GIWON (SACRED GROVE) AT KYOTO NOW KNOWN AS THE YASAKA-JINJA

*Above:* Shinto temple area, after Siebold. Shintoism, the leading Japanese religion, has an immense number of great and lesser kamis—divine spirits that dwell in cosmic space, in the underworld, and also, though invisibly, on earth. Its wooden temples are cheerful places, built in delightful surroundings to ensure that intercourse between gods and men shall be pleasurable to both. In the middle is the main building, the Honden (1), where people come to pray or lay votive offerings before the Moon Goddess. No. 3 is a subsidiary temple. Each of the small shrines (14–36) contains the emblem of the particular Shinto divinity for whose worship it is reserved. Below, on the right, is the entrance—a ceremonial arch (Torii) with two stone lanterns beyond it. No. 38 marks wash-houses (ritual ablutions form part of the prescribed ceremonies). The unrelated pagoda-shaped building on the right (5), behind the trellis for a honeysuckle plant, is a Buddhist shrine; for Shintoism may embrace Buddhism.

JAPANESE MILITARY EXERCISES, as Siebold saw them, had been used from the most remote times to foster skill and courage. Originally reserved for the Samurai, they were later introduced even into Japanese schools. Even the matchlock, first brought to Japan by the Portuguese, was still in use in the nineteenth century as a kind of sports equipment (1–2). The end of the fuse is held in a groove in the cock, the remainder of its length being wound in loose coils round the marksman's left arm. 3–6: postures of the Kendô: fencing with swords and sticks. The sword has been replaced by a bamboo cane. In ancient times the fencers were unprotected, but now their faces, necks, breasts and arms are shielded. Victory goes to the one who lands the greatest number of blows on these portions of his opponent's body. —Below is the Sôjutsu, or lance-fighting, another very ancient practice. The lances, ten feet long, are made of oak and tipped with leather pads to avoid injuries.

THE ATAGO-SAN NEAR KYOTO

This mountain, 3,038 feet in height, is a place of pilgrimage with a shrine dedicated to Atago, the fire-god. Atago was greatly to be propitiated, for the Japanese wooden houses were easy and frequent victims of fire.

It must be remembered that Japanese officialdom regarded these pictures, together with all Siebold's notes, as contraband goods, and that getting them together was a secret and perilous enterprise. This, although Siebold himself was treated with comparative favour. Like a few privileged Por-tuguese and Dutch travellers before him, he was an instructor of highly-placed doctors at Tokyo (European medical textbooks were not allowed into Japan till 1720, and then only those printed in Dutch!) and thus enjoyed a certain freedom of movement. Even so, misfortune lay in store for him. In January 1830, when he had been in the country for seven years, it was discovered that he had persuaded the Court Astronomer to give him a copy of a map of Japan. He was expelled, and the guilty astronomer died in prison.

ONTAKE, THE SACRED MOUNTAIN

Ontake (10,049 feet), which stands in what is now the district of Nagano, is, with the exception of Fujiyama the most sacred mountain in Japan. The Shinto shrine that crowns it is still visited each year by many pilgrims. It is situated in the 'Japanese Alps'; at its base a hot spring bubbles forth.—Siebold commissioned this and other pictures, ostensibly for a work on Japan by native artists—in this case the painter Tojoske. This lessened the danger of his being imprisoned as a spy, and also gave the book a strong aesthetic interest.

THE GREAT TOKAIDO HIGHWAY, ALONG WHICH SIEBOLD TRAVELLED

The Tokaido highway ran from Kyoto through the provinces bordering the Pacific to Jedo (Tokyo). It was used by merchants, pilgrims and porters, and by the local princes with their great retinues, on their way to the statutory audiences with the Emperor at Jedo. Siebold, too, in the suite of the Dutch envoy, came by way of this rest-house, these stone signposts and milestones. Porters and litter-bearers were encountered more often than horses or pack oxen. Goods were carried, for preference, in long wooden panniers swinging at either end of a pole balanced on the shoulder.

Travellers sat on their heels in wooden litters or in sedan chairs made of wickerwork or light wood and slung from a pole carried on the shoulders of two bearers. Experienced bearers would move so smoothly that the passenger could read or write in comfort; the unskilful would transform the journey into a torture. Siebold praises the hardihood and adroitness of the people. The road, which in many places ran on an embankment, was shaded by pines, cedars, cypresses and other trees. In the evening, master and servants would take a welcome bath at their inn.

# Exploring the Himalayas

The history of exploration includes several 'late-comers', regions so inaccessible that their soil remained untrodden for thousands of years, though the surrounding territories were criss-crossed in all directions by traces of man's passage and sojourn. Among these regions are the North and South Poles, a number of virgin forests and deserts, and above all the world's loftiest range of mountains, the 1,500 mile-long chain of the Himalayas. Not that the whole length of the range was unfrequented; at a remote period traders were already travelling to and fro between northern India and the interior of Asia by way of a few perilous, snow-swept passes at a height of about 14,000 feet. These were routes that served practical requirements; salt, woollen cloth and musk were carried southwards along them, grain and sugar were brought northwards; they were seldom used for military purposes, but from early times priests and pilgrims passed by this way while on their spiritual errands, for that incomparable mountain-chain has been revered by millions as holy ground. It is the dwelling place of the mightiest Hindu divinities and the inaccessibility of its white peaks gives it a religious significance. The *Skanda Pwana* promises the faithful who brave the toils and dangers of the mountain journey that 'even as the dew is dried up by the morning sun, so are the sins of mankind redeemed by the sight of the Himalayas'. About the year 1815 the Scottish traveller J.B.Fraser, overwhelmed by the majesty of the holy mountains, wrote that 'Mahadeo could not be more divinely enthroned than in the recesses of the Himala Mountains.'

This comment was made at a time when the geographical study of the region was just beginning to penetrate beyond the narrow strip to either side of the tracks followed by merchants and pilgrims. The distant snow-peaks are mentioned in the reports of earlier travellers such as Grüber, and were described by Huan-tsang; but they were not systematically explored until the nineteenth and early twentieth centuries, chiefly by Englishmen, from the south. The British wanted to gain control of the mountain peoples; they wanted to screen India from the risk of attack by the Chinese to the north-east and the Russians to the north-west; and last but not least they were eager to solve, from the purely scientific standpoint, the mysteries of the gigantic range—to investigate its geological structure and the laws governing human, animal and plant life at those great heights. The forerunners included the painter Samuel Turner, who reconnoitred the State of Bhutan in 1783, painting watercolours as he went. The versatile J. B. Fraser performed some astonishing feats of travel in Gharwal and Nepal in 1814–15. In 1808 Webb discovered the source of the Ganges; in 1820 Moorcroft explored Kashmir and Ladakh; in 1848–51 the botanist J. D. Hooker made his way as far as Sikkim in the teeth of fierce opposition; in 1855–56 the three Schlaintweit brothers from Munich reached various points of the range, including Kamet, where they attained a height of 21,998 feet—an amazing feat in those early days. On their expeditions to the borders of Tibet the English took with them Indian scholars, known as Pundits; and about the turn of the century Sven Hedin made his admirable maps of the northern side of the range, the Trans-Himalaya, supplementing the records compiled by the English in the south. After efforts that had taken scores of years to complete, the contours of the world's highest mountains were more or less established. But it was not until 1903 that Gaurisankar (23,435 feet) was distinguished from Everest (29,141 feet), which had been named after the Englishman who directed the survey of India from Calcutta to the Himalayas in 1823–43.

This loftiest peak defeated all attempts to scale it until twentieth-century technical resources were brought into play (the New Zealander Hillary and the Nepalese Sherpa Tensing were the first to reach the summit, on 24th May 1953). Those who did not look upon such climbs as merely a sporting venture, felt impelled to achieve the utmost of which the human body and spirit were capable and thus bring out what was best and greatest in man. Thus it was that Everest came to be known as 'the third pole'. And so the Himalayas became sacred ground for their explorers, as they had been from time immemorial for the Hindu pilgrims, though in another sense. And that great mountain climber, expedition organizer and leader of men, C. G. Bruce, when asked by the Superior of the Rongbuk Monastery in Tibet why the Europeans were so eager to reach the top of Everest, could reply in all sincerity that some of them came in order to purify their souls on the highest mountain in the world.

JAMES BAILLIE FRASER NEAR THE SOURCES OF THE GANGES

In 1814 the English declared war on the fiercely independent Gurkhas whose sporadic incursions into northern India from their home territory of Nepal were causing insecurity in that part of the British dominions. After a mountain campaign, with heavy losses, Nepal was more or less annexed. A peaceable Scottish painter, J. B. Fraser (1783–1856), came up with the reserve troops from the scorching northern plains into the region of Gharwal, with its precipitous crags, where the English found allies among the petty rulers who were also oppressed by the wild Gurkhas. Fraser left the troops and, with a few companions, made his way onward and upward, sometimes following the course of the Sutlej, towards Nepal and the snow summits—probably the first explorer to see them at such close quarters. In June 1815 he was in Rampur; from there he crossed the territory of the Rajah of Seran and reached the spot where he was to receive his most intense impression of the power the Himalayas exert over the human spirit. This was the Temple of Gangotri, a Hindu shrine which stood near the source of the Bhagirati Ganges. On his return he published a folio volume containing twenty colour-plates of boldly-depicted landscapes, many of which had never before been seen by any European. The plates were executed in aquatint by R. Howell from Fraser's water-colours. The same year, 1820, saw the publication of Fraser's *Journal of a Tour through part of the Snowy Range of the Himālā Mountains...* a mixture of geographical description and military reporting, in which the daring artist foretold that the future would witness the opening up of great Himalayan passes through which a steady flow of traffic would link India with China and Central Asia.

*Overleaf:*

THE HINDU SANCTUARY OF GANGOTRI on the upper reaches of the Bhagirati Ganges. Shiva sits enthroned, unapproachable, amid the eternal ice of the eastward peaks; the most holy of the Ganges tributaries rushes down through inaccessible mountain gorges to the valleys far below. Here, at man's furthest outpost on the way to the dwelling of the gods, stands a place of worship, the little pilgrim temple of Gangotri. The neighbourhood is full of memories of saints and recluses who withdrew to these wastes and dedicated their lives to Shiva. The long, perilous, purging road followed by the pilgrims ends beneath the projecting stone eaves of the temple, on the left, with its convex upper storey and reddish cornice. On the far left is a shelter for pilgrims. The tumbling, ice-cold mountain waters cleanse the believer of his sins, while the Brahmin priests pronounce blessings upon him. Nor did they withhold their benison from James Baillie Fraser, the first European to visit this mountain land. Moreover, its bestowal was followed by rare and auspicious omens—the sky cleared and the level of the stream rose. In memory of all this, the artist shows a glow of transfiguring radiance from above—like that which falls from the wide-opening heavens in so many pictures of the Baroque period—bathing the place where 'all is mythological if not holy ground'.

THE WORLD OF PEAKS TO THE WEST OF NEPAL (detail from the picture by J. B. Fraser reproduced below)

◄ The Rajah of Seran lived from time to time in a kind of residential fortress on the near side of a gorge through which the Sutlej flowed. Beyond it, the distant Himalayan peaks look down over forests where deer, pheasants and monkeys live in undisturbed tranquillity. The buildings form a rectangle surrounding a courtyard. The two towers belong to temples; the Rajah's daughter and the young heir to his throne have smaller buildings to themselves. Centre right, a Gurkha fort —a reminder of times when the Rajah, as yet unallied to the English, was at the mercy of his warlike neighbours.

99

THE LITTLE SELIPUK MONASTERY IN SOUTHERN TIBET

◄ A TIBETAN MENDICANT LAMA SKETCHED BY SVEN HEDIN. Tibet and the neighbouring territories—Chinese Turkestan, the Tarim basin, the trans-Himalaya and the Karakorum— together with the Gobi desert, were the principal fields of activity of the remarkable Swedish explorer Sven Hedin (1865–1952), who was driven by an insatiable thirst for information about unknown regions. He was a gifted draughtsman and continued to work as artist on his own expeditions, even after he took to including cameras among his equipment. His second great expedition (1899–1901) took him— coming from the north—up on to the Tibetan plateau. It was in the spring of 1901 that he made this sketch of a mendicant lama whom he met near Manasarovar, a lake held sacred by the Hindus. Slung over the man's right shoulder is a pair of fur-covered wooden soles, worn on the hands for protection as the pilgrim proceeds round the Tashi-Lumpo monastery, prostrating himself in obeisance at every step. He carries a prayer-wheel and round his neck hang a rosary, a necklace of shells and a 'sao', or reliquary, containing a picture of one of the gods, a present from the august Tashi Lama. Pilgrims looked upon such holy mendicants as mediators between gods and men, and were generous in filling their begging-bowls.

*Above:* On 27th June 1908 Hedin pitched his tent outside the Selipuk lamasery, situated 15,696 feet above sea-level. He was coming to the end of his third great expedition (1905 to 1909), in the course of which he had made eight journeys through the vast trans-Himalaya range—which he himself had discovered—mapping his routes as he went. On 8th July

he and his party crossed the Dingla Pass (19,308 feet) and went down into India, where the British Viceroy received the distinguished explorer with great honours. In the large section of a water-colour by Hedin, which is reproduced above, Selipuk looks like a ship decorated with festive pennants. Its white walls with their broad red horizontal stripes overlook one of those remote, desolate mountain plateaux whose borders have always been favourite sites for Buddhist monasteries. The roof is topped by a chorten, an imitation of the Indian stupa, erected in honour of some particularly enlightened Buddha. The shapes at the corners, which look like closed umbrellas, are emblems of lordship over the world. The banners and the innumerable pennons are inscribed with prayers, especially the magical formula of propitiation, 'Om mani padme hum'. Every gust of wind scatters their silent intercessions to all quarters of the globe; the Tibetans believe there is virtue and salvation even in the mechanical multiplication of prayers by means of flags and prayer-wheels. A grim office was frequently entrusted, in these Tibetan monasteries, to watchdogs like the one seen here in the foreground. In a region where the ground was frozen as hard as iron for six months in the year they were expected to help the vultures in devouring the bodies of the dead, which were deposited in the open, at some distance from the monastery. 'As soon as the religious ceremonies are over and the dead man has been carried out of his dwelling or his monastery cell, he is held to have departed this life, and the perishable husk in which the liberated soul was formerly housed is delivered over to the great solitude and the temple dogs.' So writes Hedin in his book *My Dogs in Asia*.

AN ENGLISHMAN REACHES UNPRECEDENTED HEIGHTS—SIR JOSEPH DALTON HOOKER ON THE CHUNJERMA PASS IN 1848

Between 1847 and 1851 the botanist J. D. Hooker (1817–1911) was exploring the unknown eastern regions of the Indian mountains. The Rajah of Sikkim having at first refused him permission to enter the country, Hooker had to begin by withdrawing into the mountains of north-west Nepal. The route from here to Sikkim crosses the Chunjerma Pass. Hooker climbed it, with one native companion and a few porters, and lingered for an hour in the ice-cold, rarefied atmosphere at the top. His barometer recorded 15,260 feet above sea-level. Hooker was a meticulous and tireless observer, with notebook constantly at hand, and his porters were laden with telescope and sextant, collecting-boxes for insects, presses for plants, and so on. The party included a taxidermist. The hour that Hooker spent on the pass was the last before sunset. To the south, far below him, India lay, shrouded in thick mist; to the north the peak of Jannu, near the main range of the Kangchenjunga, rose like some white Himalayan Matterhorn to a height (according to Hooker's calculation) of 25,312 feet. In his *Himalayan Journals* (1855), one of the classical works on the subject, he declared that never had he witnessed any nobler spectacle than met his eyes on that unforgettable day—5th December 1848.

# The Opening-up of Siberia

In the seventeenth century, when the Dutch were already encroaching on the Portuguese trade empire in tropical India and the intellectual world of China, like some new continent, was gradually yielding up its secrets to the Jesuits, Russian-sponsored expeditions began to explore Siberia, the mysterious, inhospitable region that made up the northern third of continental Asia. In ancient times, and well into the Middle Ages, little was known of Siberia except through rumours brought back by traders who had ventured beyond the Urals. The first systematic attempts to penetrate its measureless wastes began after 1582, when Cossacks in the pay of the Strogonovs—a family of merchants—led by one Yermak broke through the Tartar lines along the banks of the Irtish. From then on, for over a century, they were the only pioneers in this territory—actuated partly by obedience to the Tsars who sent them to collect tribute from the unknown tribes to the east, partly by genuine lust for adventure and partly by eagerness to exploit the possibilities of a land that swarmed with fur-bearing animals.

The early history of the exploration of Siberia is a savage, primitive chronicle of spine-chilling events, marked by that harsh delight in the sheer vastness of nature which is shared by so many of those who travel in Asia. To venture into Siberia was to plunge back into primeval ages of physical and cultural life. The wild, boundless territory lured its explorers into marshes and forests as large as many a European country, into a region of wolf and bear, where dark dwellings in the ground were the only shelter the few inhabitants could find from the ice and snow of the interminable Arctic winters. They were uncouth people, these Tungus, Yakuts, Bureti and Chukchi—hunters, fishermen and peasants working with Stone-Age tools and practising a shamanistic religion. Primitive, too, were the Cossacks who came to their country as fur-traders or representatives of the Tsar; most of them were barbarous extortioners; few died a natural death. But the Tsarist regime was equally primitive in its administrative machinery on the further side of the Urals. The occasional reports sent in by Cossack leaders were apt to vanish without trace into some government office—as probably happened to that of Deshnev, the Cossack who arrived on the Bering Strait in 1648, the first explorer to reach the easternmost tip of Asia. Even when Vitus Bering, the greatest of Siberian explorers, sent back his reports to St. Petersburg, not half of what he said was believed in that city where calumny found ever-open ears. Forty years later, however, Cook paid respectful tribute to Bering and declared, in vindication of his memory, that his map was an excellent one.

The Cossacks gradually pushed further, advancing up the great rivers and lesser streams of Siberia. Yakutsk, on the Lena, was founded in 1632; in 1697–99 Atlasov subdued Kamchatka; and in Semen Remesov's *Siberian Sketchbook*, published about 1700, the territory is roughly but recognizably mapped.

It was Peter the Great (1672–1725) who prompted the first really scientific exploration of Siberia. With the headstrong ruthlessness of a despot and the zeal of a reformer he set himself to raise the cultural and economic level of his vast empire and open it to world trade on all its frontiers. As an essential preliminary to this he needed a comprehensive geographical survey of his Asian dominions. The Cossacks' pioneering must be followed up, answers must be found to a number of fundamental questions. How did Siberia's northern and eastern coasts run? Did North-East Siberia join up with North-West America, or was there a sea dividing them? What was the interior of the country like, in its geological, zoological, botanical and ethnographical aspects? What did the neighbouring coast of America look like? What was the best sea route to Japan and China? It was to answer these questions that two expeditions were sent out under Bering's leadership—the first in 1725 and the second, which produced decisive results, in 1733 (see the description, right).

These heralded a third epoch in the history of Russian exploration, when the Cossacks' early feats and Bering's great, many-sided scientific expeditions were followed by the investigation of regions far beyond the frontiers of Russia itself. In the first half of the nineteenth century several Russians were sent out to sail round the world (among whom were Krusenstern, von Kotzebue and Bellingshausen), chiefly with a view to the consolidation of Russia's political and economic position in the Pacific; and they made various new discoveries in the South Pacific and the Antarctic (see page 342). In the latter half of the century we find Russian explorers headed by Przewalski as rivals of the Chinese in Manchuria and Mongolia and of the British in the Tarim valley and the region of Tien-shan.

## THE 'GREAT EXPEDITION'

In 1733 Vitus Bering, a Danish sea-captain in the service of the Tsar, set out for Siberia on the greatest of all the expeditions undertaken by Russia. In 1749 the last stragglers from that enterprise got back to Russia, eight years after the tragic death of their leader, whose 'Great Expedition' had solved some of the most important geographical problems relating to Siberia. At one time he had been in charge of a cumbersome organization comprising not far short of six hundred craftsmen, seamen, scientists and soldiers. Huge quantities of stores and all the rigging, canvas, anchors and other iron pieces had been hauled across the continent before the two largest of the expedition's ships, built from timber felled in Kamchatka, could be fitted out in the harbour of St. Peter and St. Paul, which Bering had constructed in Avacha Bay. Among the scientists, Georg Wilhelm Steller was the outstanding figure. For three years of unspeakable hardship the expedition's headquarters were at Yakutsk, which resembled a military camp; for another three years it was based in Okhotsk. During this period almost the entire Arctic coastline of Siberia was explored by five subsidiary expeditions, many of whose members failed to return. The Kurile Islands, too, were explored. Bering carried a crushing burden—anxiety over the subsidiary expeditions which often ran into danger; exasperation at the schemes hatched against him at court; despair due to the inefficiency of those around him, the Siberian winters that brought everything to a standstill, and his own personal tragedy—that of a man prematurely aged and worn out by years of humiliating delays, to whom a tremendous task had now been entrusted, too late. In the eighth year of the expedition, he and his second ship managed to sail close up to the Alaskan coast, near Mount St. Elias, and Steller was allowed a mere ten hours on the little outlying island of Kayak on 20th July 1741. 'The preparations took ten years, and only ten hours was allowed for the task itself,' he commented wrathfully. After that, the approach of winter and the shortage of supplies obliged the party to turn back. For forty days Bering's ship was delayed off the Aleutians—beating up against winds that blew with hurricane force along that short stretch of coast. She was not far from Kamchatka, and safety, when the storm flung her on the shore of the island now named after Bering, where he and some of his companions in misfortune died wretchedly of scurvy. Despite appearances, however, he died a victor, for he had discovered, once and for all, the nature of the territory between North-East Asia and North-West America. Of the seventy-seven men in his company, thirty-one were dead by 8th January 1742; the others, in a boat they themselves had built, got safely back to harbour at St. Peter and St. Paul, as did the remaining ship.

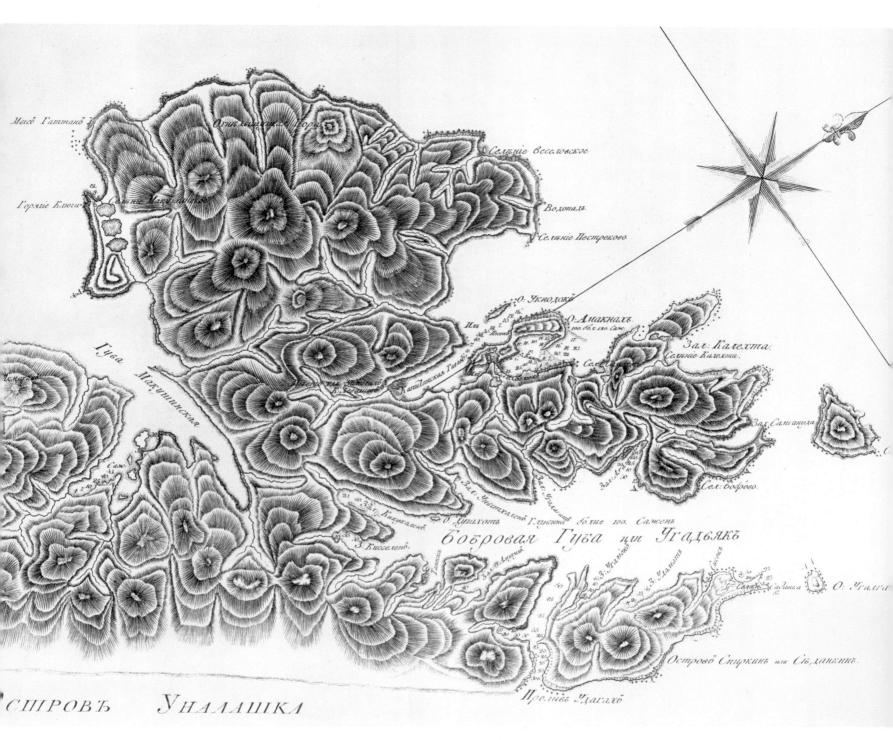

Со ПРОВЪ   УНАЛАШКА

SECTION OF AN EARLY RUSSIAN MAP OF THE ISLAND OF UNALASKA IN THE ALEUTIANS (1790)

For all his conscientious striving for scrupulous accuracy the cartographer, whose technique is a combination of stratified contours and shading, has been unable to cope successfully with the rugged volcanic landscape of this island, the second largest in the Aleutians. On the left the Bay of Makitinski cuts in obliquely from above; on the right, horizontally, lies Beaver (or Ugadja) Bay. The map was made by Gavrila Saritchev, a member of the Russian expedition led by Captain Joseph Billings, which spent the years 1785–94 in attempting to follow up Bering's traces and establish more accurately the situation of the islands in the Bering Sea. Its leadership was bungling and irresolute, so that the hardships entailed in crossing Siberia—which were tremendous at the best of times—took on atrocious proportions. The work done in the Aleutians did not add very much to the maps which had been made by Cook. But at a time when Spanish, Swedish and British rivals were already appearing in this area, the economic and ethnographical observations brought home by the party were of considerable importance. The latter were illustrated with great skill, as will be seen from the following illustrations by the expedition's artist, Lukas Varonin. Martin Sauer, its chronicler, declared bitterly that the inhabitants of Unalaska, with their Stone Age culture, were far superior to the toadies who made up the Court circles at St Petersburg and who had no culture at all. An echo of Rousseau in the Arctic!

## An Impression of the Life of the Tungus

In the neighbourhood of the seaport of Okhotsk, in eastern Siberia, Captain Billings's expedition met with wandering hunters, fishers and reindeer breeders belonging to the Tungus, a Mongol tribe. Their weapons were the bow and arrow. They vaulted on to the backs of their reindeer without the help of stirrups and rode with their legs hanging over the front edge of the flat saddle. They took their children on their journeys, carried in baskets. They caught fish in the rivers, and foxes, wolves and hares in the mountain forests; their clothing and shoes were made of sheepskin and reindeer hide. 'Their tents' (from which the smoke of the hearth escapes through a hole in the top) 'are covered with the inner bark of the birch-tree, which they render as supple as leather by exposing it for a time to the steam from boiling water, and to the action of smoke,' wrote Martin Sauer, secretary to the expedition.

*Overleaf:*

The Island of Unalaska in the Aleutians showing Captain Billings's ship, *Slava Rossiji*, and her small escorting craft (June 1790). Bering discovered the island in 1741, and Russian fur traders, seal fishers and sea-otter hunters soon began to arrive there. The natives were declared to be Russian subjects, and tribute, in kind, was extorted from them with the utmost brutality—'Heaven is high and the Tsar is distant.' James Cook landed on this island in 1778. Gavrila Saritchev spent his time from 3rd to 13th June 1790 in drawing the map reproduced on page 107. The island he was surveying lay beneath a cloudy sky at a point where the cold Siberian winds and the icy currents of the Arctic seas encountered warmer air and water from the South Pacific, so that storms, fog, rain and snow were frequent. The scenery was volcanic—a rugged, treeless, stony world rising from a sea thickly strewn with rocks. Yet these wastes were inhabited—by a race akin to the Eskimoes, who lived in huts covered with turf or soil, propped up inside by baulks of driftwood and whalebones, and often dug out of the ground like cellars. These were entered from the top by climbing down a notched beam (clearly seen in the picture). The interior was lit and heated by fish-oil. All dwellings stood near the shore, for the people depended on the sea for their livelihood; the most they could hope to find on land was a starvation diet of berries and roots to help them through an emergency. The men were adept at fishing and at capturing seals and whales, with the help of arrows whose sharp points were dipped in poison made from the root of the aconite plant. But their greatest skill was in handling their kayaks; on the right of the illustration we see one of these craft, raised on supports; it can take several men, and is covered with the hide of seal or sea-lion. The native women wore the 'barkas', a kind of shift made from the skins of sea birds or the pelts of seals. In 1867 the Aleutians were sold to the United States.

SHAMANISTIC RITES AT THE BEDSIDE OF A SICK YAKUT

The Shamans—omniscient priests with magic powers—lived in the Yakut community as a kind of religious order to which women also were admitted. They interceded between mankind and the realm of the good and evil spirits. They established contact with these spirits by working themselves into frenzied trances, and it was thus that they learnt to know forces of destruction or of healing. In the ceremony depicted above the frenzy is being intensified by a flood of sound that rises progressively to a crescendo. (Its effect can be seen in the child and the dog.) The noise is produced by a flat drum—a skin stretched over a hoop—and by pieces of metal fastened to long strips of leather which are whirled round. The magic is strengthened by hanging miniature horses on a cord. At the climax of his frenzy the Shaman announces the cause of the sickness and the method of curing it.

Chappe d'Auteroche, the French astronomer (1728–69), ▶ travelling by sledge from Petersburg to Tobolsk, to observe the passage of Venus (1761), made a halt at a peasant's cottage at Melechina, a hamlet in Siberia. The illustrations for his account of his Siberian impressions were engraved by J.B.Le Prince who knew Russia at first hand.—The traveller was admitted to the cottage by a bearded peasant carrying a pinewood torch. The first thing he noticed inside was a hanging cradle, behind which an old woman had fallen asleep at her flax-spinning. The young mother was just getting up, still half asleep. The other members of the family lay, snoring or gossiping, on top of the stove or in a kind of loft. The whole scene is reminiscent of a story by Tolstoi. After a few hours' rest the stranger went out again from the warm, stuffy room into the frozen Siberian night.

THE VOLCANO KLUCHEVSKAYA SOPKA (16,120 feet) ON THE KAMCHATKA PENINSULA, FROM A DRAWING MADE IN AUGUST 1828

A picture dating from a period when specialised research was already going on in Siberia, and when, on the other hand, the Russians had sailed round the world a number of times and thus overstepped the boundaries of their own sphere of influence. Among the members of their fourth round-the-world expedition (in 1826–29, led by Lütke) was Friedrich Heinrich Freiherr von Kittlitz, the ornithologist, born in Breslau in 1799. He climbed the church tower in the village of Kluchev to draw this view, from which a lithograph was made later and used by another circumnavigator, the physicist Georg Adolf Erman, of Berlin (1806–77), as one of the illustrations to the atlas accompanying his *Reise um die Erde durch Nord-Asien und die beiden Oceane*. Erman, an intrepid and enthusiastic observer, made his way in September 1829 to within about 1000 feet of the crater of this most

magnificent of all East-Siberian volcanoes, which towers up higher than Europe's Mont-Blanc. In the foreground, beyond the Tundra-like expanse, we see the undulating tops of a belt of trees—alders and birches—favoured by hunters pursuing bear and reindeer. To the left is a small, lava-covered hummock of volcanic origin, thrown up by a secondary eruption. Then, after a stretch overgrown with stunted willows, the ground rises steeply to the crater, the rim of which consists of lava, ashes and an infinite number of minute glacious particles. The ribs of the volcano stand out like buttresses, coated towards the top with snow and ice interspersed with patches of lava. Von Kittlitz believed it to be extinct, but only a year after his visit Erman found that smoke and ashes from the crater were again being wafted far over the surrounding country.

# Unveiling Ancient Civilizations of the Near East

'Assyria, Babylonia and Chaldea are still shrouded in darkness,' observed Austen Henry Layard, a young Englishman travelling in the East in 1840. This was the great void that baffled all who tried to form even an approximate idea of the ancient kingdoms between the Euphrates and the Tigris, about which they had read in Herodotus or Strabo or in the Old Testament. The ancient writers gave little or no reliable information on the subject, and the strange, long mounds that here and there rose abruptly to a height of sixty-five feet above the scorching sands of Mesopotamia had not yet surrendered their secret. True, the site of ancient Babylon was known, and the spot on the Tigris, opposite Mosul, where the remains of Nineveh lay in heaps of rubble had been correctly located by some of the few travellers to pass through this region. It was legend among the nomads that curious images hewn out of black stone lay buried in the mounds. The local people sometimes fetched stones from the rubble-heaps to build their huts, as the ruins of Babel were plundered to build the town of Hillah, but their attitude towards their country's past glories can be summed up in the fatalistic words of the Moslem who wrote to one of Layard's friends: 'Praise God, I do not seek for things of which I have no need.'

Yet less than ten years after Layard had commented on the darkness that covered this region, an impressive sequence of illuminating works on the subject began to appear in Europe. Layard's own *Nineveh and its Remains* was published in 1848–49, Emile Botta's *Monument de Ninive* in 1849–50; in 1850 H.C.Rawlinson produced a key to Babylonian and Assyrian cuneiform inscriptions; and so it went on. The Louvre and the British Museum held their first exhibitions of newly-discovered reliefs, statues and other objects, which filled room after room. Since then, and especially since Robert Koldewey's excavation of ancient Babylon around 1900, the picture of oriental life in ancient times has grown rich and colourful. Two or three thousand years after the collapse of those mighty empires they began to find their rightful place in the awareness of educated Europeans.

The great archaeologists of the eighteen-forties were spurred on by the magnificent harvest of pictures brought back to Paris in 1841 by the painter Eugène Flandin and the architect Pascal Coste from a two-year sojourn among the antiquities of Persia (see pages 120 and 121), and still more by the discoveries of the youthful Claudius James Rich, the first to establish beyond doubt that the mound opposite Mosul was the site of ancient Nineveh.

There was keen competition among archaeologists during that glorious period. The enthusiasm of Julius Mohl, the German orientalist, fired the French naturalist Emile Botta who after long, fruitless digging in the mound at Khorsabad (1843–46) suddenly came upon the fortress of Sargon, King of Assyria. In 1842 Botta had shown young Layard round the excavation site facing Mosul, thus spurring him on to greater effort. In October 1849 Layard, in his turn, led his compatriot H. C. Rawlinson through the murky passages into the mound of Nimrod, where he had found the walls of the palace of Kalah, the ancient Assyrian capital. Rawlinson, studying on his own, had recently worked out the key to the cuneiform script; and in 1852 he took over from Layard. With his brilliant pupil George Smith, he became the great interpreter of the clay tablets in the library of King Assurbanipal—already discovered by Layard—which yielded up so many secrets of the past.

All these pioneering, competing seekers and finders were passionately excited by a number of questions, the answers to which had to be wrested from dumb objects that had lain buried in the earth for thousands of years. Where should they begin digging? In what direction? Which was the outer and which the inner side of a new-found stretch of wall? What was the meaning of the marks on those clay tablets? And of the scenes on these alabaster reliefs? How did such and such fragments fit together? To what period did they belong? What was missing? Fever and thirst, the scorching desert sun, dilatory workmen, prowling marauders, the wiles of hostile Turkish governors—none of this daunted the men with the spades. Their triumph was to come with the first great resurgence of a mighty epoch from its ruins. They were the re-discoverers of what is historically one of the most 'numinous' regions of the world. And so their place is here, at the end of our review of Asian exploration, as the equals of those by whom Asia's mountains, deserts and forests, living nations and civilizations, were revealed to Western eyes.

AUSTEN HENRY LAYARD (1817–94) AT NINEVEH

Layard, brave to the point of recklessness, was one of those men who are irked by a sheltered middle-class life and gladly abandon its comforts to seek a full, creative, individual existence in the outside world. He began his career as a London barrister, but he was an avid reader of J. B. Fraser's Persian tales, Rich's reports, and the *Arabian Nights*. The East, with its imaginative people and primitive patriarchal communities, was the goal of his aspirations; above all, he felt the lure of the mighty Tigris, with the ancient, mysterious city of Nineveh still lying buried on its banks. At the age of twenty-five he went out to Constantinople to work under the English envoy, Sir Stratford Canning, and three years later Canning generously provided him with funds to try his luck at excavating in the traces of Rich and the Frenchman Emile Botta (1845–47). Layard proved to be fortune's great favourite among archaeologists. Within twenty-four hours of his arrival the hit on he definitive entrance into Nimrod's mound; and by the end of his second expedition (1849–51) he could see in his mind's eye a group of monumental Assyrian buildings standing in much the same arrangement as shown on the two following pages. Going out as the representative of the British Museum, he surpassed even his own record by discovering King Assurbanipal's library of over 24,000 clay tablets, under the mound of rubble at Kujunjik.

This was Layard's last visit to the scene of his archaeological triumphs. Returning to England he entered politics and carried the dauntless courage he had displayed as investigator and lone wolf into the House of Commons where he launched many attacks on corrupt protectionist practices and smug routine.

A FLEET IN THE TIME OF KING SENNACHERIB OF ► ASSYRIA (704–681 B.C.)—A BAS-RELIEF FOUND BY LAYARD IN THE MOUND AT KUJUNJIK

Sennacherib, who subdued Babylon and besieged Jerusalem, is believed to have employed Phoenician crews and vessels for his voyages and naval campaigns. The sea is indicated here by starfish, crabs, tortoises, fish and wavy lines. The bigger ships have masts and sails, and are fitted just below the water-line with a metal-shod beak for ramming enemy craft. They resemble the mastless galleys in having two decks, with two banks of oars on the port and starboard sides (the lower rank cannot be seen). The spearmen's bucklers surround the upper deck like a fence.

RECONSTRUCTION OF A ROW OF MONUMENTAL ASSYRIAN FAÇADES ALONG THE TIGRIS

Layard took these great buildings for part of ancient Nineveh. Nowadays we know that in that case the city must have been the size of twentieth-century London with all its suburbs. In reality this was part of the earlier Assyrian capital, Kelach or Kalchu, some 18 miles to the south of Nineveh; its ruins were later given the name of Nimrod. Nineveh, first chosen as the capital during the reign of Sennacherib, was buried under two mounds—Kujunjik and Nebi Junus, both 65 feet high—exactly opposite Mosul.

The remains of the buildings shown here were found by Layard on the eastern bank of the Tigris. They are, from left to right: a tower, rising in diminishing storeys, in which was an empty vault assumed by Layard to be the tomb of King Sardanapalus; in its shadow, two temples which may have been built by Assurnasirpal III; then the wide front of the 'North-West Palace', begun by the same monarch and restored by Sargon (its shattered halls and galleries, with their bas-reliefs, were among Layard's most magnificent finds). In the middle of the picture is the 'Central Palace', built by Tiglathpileser III; and last of all comes the latest and proudest building, the 'South-West Palace', dating from the reign of Assarhaddon, who died in 668 BC.

All these buildings stand on a platform high above the river. Great steps, cut like gullies in its sides, lead down to the water. Layard assumed that the walls of the towers and palaces, with their colourful facing of terracotta tiles deco-

rated with great figures and mythological symbols, must have formed a glittering spectacle that could be seen from far and wide. The mural reliefs and clay tablets found inside gave a wealth of information about life in ancient Assyria; the national archives had been stored in these palaces and temples. Light probably entered the buildings through openings in their flat wooden roofs.

The broad façade of the South-West Palace was adorned with winged bulls—the tutelary genius—and with a gigantic frieze, 16 feet high, depicting battle scenes, triumphal processions, the offering of tribute and the performance of religious rites; events in the life of a race of despotic rulers, who at one time controlled the vast territory extending from Babylon to Israel and Egypt, from the Euphrates to the Nile. Hardly sixty-five years after their power had reached its apex, Assyria met its doom. The Medes, from Persia, allied themselves with Nabopolassar, ruler of the new kingdom of Babylonia, and in the year 606 a devastating onslaught was made on the Assyrian cities. Such buildings as escaped the flames crumbled into dust or were gradually buried under heaps of earth and rubble, lost in a night that lasted for two thousand years—until the excavators' spades restored the remains of the cities, their reliefs and plaques, the magnificent dying lioness and the clay tablets relating the epic of Gilgamesh, to the light of day and granted them the triumphant immortality of all great things.

48 Cannelures.

BASE ET CHAPITEAU DES COLONNES DE L'OUEST.

3 mètres

THE RUINS OF PERSEPOLIS, RECORDED BY E.-N. FLANDIN

Buttressed to the north by a semicircle of cliffs, a terrace, partly of artificial construction, extends southwards for nearly 1,540 feet, forming a majestic plinth from which the residences of the Persian monarchs Xerxes, Artaxerxes III and Darius looked down upon the city and the open country to the south—until, in 330 B.C., Alexander the Great came that way and, in a wanton mood, had the whole place destroyed by fire. *Above:* These pillars, with fifty-nine others, adorned an audience chamber and an atrium. On the extreme left is the entrance to one of the residential palaces. *Left:* The main portions of a fluted column—one of twelve which stood in the lateral portico of a neighbouring building. Carved on its capital, and supporting the beams of the architrave, are two kneeling bulls, firmly reined in, as symbols of controlled strength. The nobility and precision of this drawing are typical of the work of Eugène-Napoléon Flandin

(1809–76), the classical artist among Far Eastern archaeologists, who won fame in Europe in the eighteen-forties.

*Overleaf:*

The excavators of Nineveh, Babylon and Persepolis occasionally varied their explorations by jaunts into the little-known regions that lay around the ancient sites. Layard collected information about Kurdistan, and Flandin followed up his archaeological work on Persia with a volume on *La Perse moderne.* Among its illustrations is this view of Yezd-I-Khast, a little town with mosque and minaret standing on a cliff not far from Persepolis, beside the road from Shiraz to Isfahan. Its lower windows look straight out over the cliff —a sheer drop of at least 130 feet. The sheltered cluster of houses is inaccessible except at one of its narrower ends. A few ruins of ancient buildings can be seen.

121

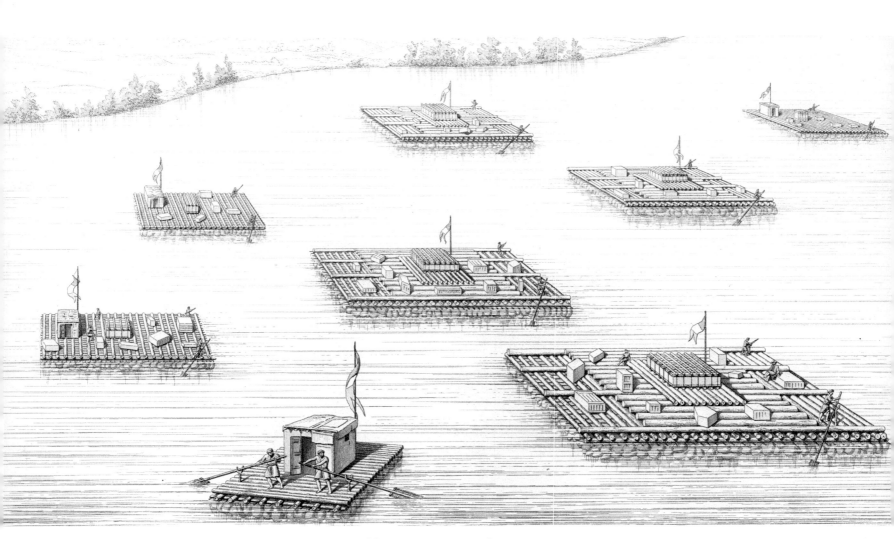

How the Finds were brought from the Mounds in Mesopotamia to the Ships

Once the reliefs, statues and tablets with their cuneiform inscriptions were safe on board ship at Basra, the meeting-point of the Tigris and Euphrates, the archaeologist breathed a sigh of relief. The river between Nineveh (Mosul) and Basra had many dangerous shallows and rapids, and its banks were infested with parties of would-be robbers. The Frenchman Victor Place lost a precious cargo which sank to the bottom without trace. The rafts did not always float downstream so smoothly as in this picture.

The packing-cases containing the booty, padded with matting and felt, were arranged on the raft with their weight evenly distributed. Goatskin or sheepskin bags were fastened underneath the logs to give extra buoyancy, and were pumped up afresh every now and then. The convoy was manned by experienced raftsmen, sometimes protected by firearms. Victor Place, who found some important sculptures at Khorsabad where he worked as Botta's successor in 1852–55—shortly after Layard's return to England—sent them in this consignment to the Louvre. There and in the British Museum eager crowds gathered to form a picture of an aspect of Asia now newly revealed to a world that would never again be entirely unaware of it.

# AMERICA

## Columbus

'Westward, ever westward! There the land must lie!' That is how Schiller's poem sums up the epoch-making notion that fired the spirit of Christopher Columbus, the explorer who left his home—the little house of a poor Genoese weaver—and knew no rest until he reached Central America and planted there the first European flag ever seen on its soil. Already in his early youth, as a seaman sailing the length and breadth of the Mediterranean, he had felt a deep longing 'to penetrate the mysteries of the universe'. His vision took clearer shape when he read Marco Polo's description of the golden realms of China and Japan; it was confirmed when his clandestine search of the Royal Archives of Portugal brought to light a map made in 1474 by a Florentine astronomer, Toscanelli, on which the alluring eastern coast of Asia seemed to be no more than a few weeks' sail from Western Europe. And his dream became an unshakable conviction when he read in certain holy books that a predestined spirit—surely himself—would one day 'bring together the ends of the earth—linking Europe and Asia across the Atlantic—and unite all peoples and tongues under the banner of Salvation'.

Obsessed by his great plan, he fought for it desperately from 1478 to 1492. It was rejected by his native city, by the Portuguese court, by Henry VII of England and by a junta of learned Spaniards. 'I am a Genoese seaman, reduced to beggary because the kings will not accept the realms I offer them'—so he declared when finally obliged to seek admission to the monastery of La Rabida, near Palos. At last, after the fall of Granada (1492), when Spain, unified since 1479, was beginning to nurse ambitions, its rulers granted him three small caravels with which to try his fortune—they had a great deal to gain and little to lose. And on 12th October 1492, after a voyage lasting seventy-one days, his belief was triumphantly confirmed—the dream-coast lay clear before his eyes. All that he discovered on his four voyages—Cuba, Haiti, Jamaica, Trinidad, the coast of Venezuela, Honduras and Veragua—he firmly believed to form part of Asia. His mistake is perpetuated to this day by terms such as 'Red Indians' and 'West Indies'.

This in no way detracts from his fame as an explorer and, through all the intervening centuries, he has stood as the very archetype of the man devoted heart and soul to a single idea, who triumphs with it against a host of gainsayers and obstructionists. It is true that this single-mindedness went hand in hand with an insatiable craving for wealth and power and an imagination that led him into some most disconcerting pseudo-logistical trickery. Whenever anything happened to disturb his vision of himself as the greatest explorer of all time, he promptly and effectually disposed of the evidence. For example, he concealed his knowledge of the Toscanelli records; he suppressed the bonus to which the sailor was entitled who, aloft in the crow's-nest, first sighted the island of Guanahani, where his great idea was verified; and he blamed others for his inefficient administration of the lands he discovered.

Five hundred years before his time the Vikings had already 'discovered' America, to the north. Seven years after his death (1506) Balboa crossed the Isthmus of Panama and proved that the places where Columbus had landed were not in Asia; in 1520 Magellan's ship *Victoria* really brought the ends of the earth together for the first time. The new continent was not named after the great Genoese explorer but after his compatriot Amerigo Vespucci who had explored the Brazilian coast in Portuguese ships during the first decades of the sixteenth century. But Columbus's feat had the effect of turning the energies of the Spanish, French and English explorers of the sixteenth and seventeenth centuries in a new direction—westward, where little by little they discovered an entire hemisphere about which (to quote Alexander von Humboldt) Europe had till then known even less than about the dark side of the moon. Moreover, Columbus did more than almost anyone else to stimulate the urge for discovery which rose to a frenzy during the Renaissance. Its chief spokesman was Petrus Martyr (1455 to 1526); over a period of several decades his letters and the notes he published *(De orbe novo)* formed the first important records of this supreme era in the history of exploration. A Lombard by birth, he rose to high religious office and was entrusted with the education of the young Spanish grandees. He thus had ready access to all reports of fresh marvels and could question the explorers themselves when they came to court to relate their adventures. 'Things not known since the world began are now beginning to manifest themselves,' he declared, and longed for the eloquence of Cicero that he might do justice to an age which, as a subsequent commentator put it, had doubled the works of the creation.

TORDESILLAS

It looked at one time as though the entire world lay either in the grasp of Spain, with its rapidly-growing colonial empire in America, or in that of Portugal, with its trade empire in Asia and the Pacific. Clashes with young, ambitious nations such as England, France and Holland, seemed inevitable; as early as 1530 Francis I protested, 'Where do we find written, that the earth is already divided up?' It seemed equally inevitable that there would be quarrels between the two powers themselves, now that the heroism of their explorers had given Europe unmistakable precedence in the world. Spain appealed to the Vicar of Christ on earth,— the medieval view being that all newly-discovered land belonged to him—to bestow it as a fief upon the kings, who would convert its inhabitants to Christianity. After violent argument, Pope Alexander VI laid down, in the Treaty of Tordesillas, the most extraordinary political frontier-line ever decreed in history. This was only two years after Columbus's first voyage. The boundary ran approximately along the 49th meridian, and divided the earth into two halves, like an apple. Africa and Asia (with the exception of eastern Siberia) lay within the Portuguese sphere of influence, while Spain received the Americas (except for eastern Brazil) and a handsome share of the Pacific. All this did not prevent other nations from undertaking further exploration, to an ever greater extent, as the sixteenth century drew to its close.

COLUMBUS'S EGG

In actual fact it was not Columbus but the great architect Brunelleschi who had the brilliant idea of routing his opponents (they declared that the dome he had designed for the cathedral at Florence was a structural impossibility) by standing an egg on end, after they had all tried and failed to do so. But posterity has stubbornly attributed the famous experiment to a much more sensational figure, the heroic navigator and discoverer. Mankind will never forget the legend, in any case, for it illustrates with overwhelming simplicity the fact that ability to achieve the impossible is confined to those pre-

destined to true greatness. In this instance the non predestined are the Spanish grandees, sitting at dinner with Columbus, the foreigner they secretly despise, and flattering themselves that plenty of other men could have brought off the discovery of the New World. Whereupon the seafarer put the most popular of all the questions attributed to him: who could make an egg stand on end? Nobody had the right idea, until a light touch from the hand which had planted the Spanish flag in the New World set the egg, with its tip slightly flattened, upright before the abashed company.

COLUMBUS TAKES POSSESSION OF THE ISLAND OF HISPANIOLA (HAITI)

This scene, a tribute to Columbus engraved by Theodor de Bry, the etcher, in 1594, combines two separate incidents. On the left it shows the explorer, in admiral's uniform, landing on the island of Guanahani. Relieved of the tremendous inner tension of his voyage, he dedicated the island to the Saviour, calling it San Salvador. Here the Cross is erected, and Columbus carries the royal spear ashore—two symbolic acts which show that his aim was not solely to achieve a personal triumph but to spread the Christian religion and the rule of Spain. On the right we see him meeting the people of Haiti, on 6th December 1492. At first they fled before the new arrivals, but later, on the orders of their Cacique (Prince), they came back, bringing presents—objects made of gold, the avidly-sought metal which was also used for their earrings and the bracelets they wore on their arms and round their ankles. Gold was poured out like water here, reported the explorer, who had only knives, mirrors and coloured cloth to offer in exchange. The arrival of Columbus's three caravels at Guanahani wrenched the whole American territory, from south to north, out of its protecting circle of oceans, and for centuries after that it remained under European influence.

PORTRAIT OF COLUMBUS, attributed to Ridolfo Ghirlandaio. ►
It illustrates the legend that his hair turned prematurely white during his years of bitter struggle.

129

### THE PEARL-FISHER'S PARADISE OFF THE COAST OF VENEZUELA

On this third voyage (1498–1500) Columbus left San Domingo and sailed due south towards Haiti, still hoping to light upon a way into the Indian Ocean round the tip of some cape. Landing on the island of Cubagua in the Bay of Paria, his sailors noticed that the native women wore exceptionally beautiful pearls and would exchange them without hesitation for the most worthless trash. Off-shore, Indians were diving from their canoes for shells, from which they extracted pearls to sell in heaps to the Spaniards. Columbus had found a store of the treasure which, in those early days, came second only to gold in the navigators' esteem. But it was raided in the next few years by favourites of the Spanish Court—Alonso de Ojeda, Peralonso Niño (who had formerly sailed with Columbus) and Rodrigo de Bastidas—whose company included an aristocratic but as yet obscure youth named Balboa. These men used the maps drawn by Columbus and brought home a rich booty, while the real discoverer was in Spain, fighting unsuccessfully for his disputed rights as governor and privileged exploiter of the 'Indies'.

COLUMBUS ARRESTED

Columbus's third voyage, just referred to, ended in the deepest humiliation. The Spanish courtiers, with their love of intrigue, soon found out that the great explorer was making a poor show as Governor of the New World. He could control neither his own ambition nor the greed of the Spanish noblemen who would suffer no constraint in their efforts to win boundless wealth in the new lands; and the Indians were the scapegoats in the whole affair. But the Spanish royal house was obliged, for reasons of state, to ensure that the determination to incorporate the new colonies into a single empire, under one leadership and with one religion, should prevail over all private interests, however powerful. So the honourable Francisco de Bobadilla, Commander of

an Order, was despatched to Hispaniola in 1499 as plenipotentiary, to restore order. He was received with great respect (the illustration shows him landing from the ship on the left); but Columbus, returning from a journey to the interior, contested his authority. Thereupon the royal envoy gave orders for Columbus to be put in irons and sent back to Spain with his two incompetent brothers, there to give an account of himself (right). The prisoner drew advantage even from this defeat, by refusing to disembark except in fetters. Ferdinand and Isabella, thus put to shame, received him with honours, and in 1502 he was allowed to return overseas, though his original privileges were never restored. In 1506 he died, by no means impoverished, but a broken man.

# The Spanish Conquistadors

Columbus was the pioneer who discovered many of the islands and coasts of Central and South America, but it was the intrepid Conquistadors—adventurers and conquerors, most of them drawn from the less wealthy families of the Spanish nobility—who opened up the interior. In a brief half-century they cut a network of tracks over the whole vast region between the Missouri and the River Plate, where no white man had ever set foot before.

In 1513 Balboa landed in the Gulf of Darien and made his way through trackless mountains to the shore of the Pacific. In 1519–21 the Aztecs with their advanced civilization were subdued by Cortes. In 1528 Pamfilo de Narvaes set out from Florida with four hundred men to explore the northern shores of the Gulf of Mexico; eight years later a party of Spanish horsemen riding down the east coast of the Gulf of California met with four tattered scarecrows who proved to be their fellow-countrymen, the last survivors of that expedition. In 1541 Coronado, coming from the direction of the Grand Canyon, first glimpsed the great herds of bison in the American prairie.

Towards the middle of the century the explorers lost interest in the regions north of Mexico. Meanwhile the outside world had been thrilled by reports that a new and even richer Mexico had been discovered in Peru; the kingdom of the Incas had fallen a prey to the brutal Pizarro. Then, in 1536, another Conquistador, Quesada, came upon the highly-civilized Chibchas, who lived on the mountain plateau of Bogotá and Tunja. But the Spaniards' great urge was to press southwards. As early as 1535–37 Almagro, a companion-in-arms of Pizarro, made his way far down towards Chile; in the summer of 1542 about fifty Spaniards, led by Orellana, sailed in a roughly-made boat down the 'green hell' of the Amazon and reached its mouth. In 1516 de Solis had reached the mouth of the River Plate; four years later Magellan, seeking a way into the Pacific, had explored all the inlets from there to the Straits named after him; and in 1535 de Mendoza had founded Buenos Aires as a base from which to penetrate into the interior.

The opening-up of Central and South America by the Spanish Conquistadors was the greatest tour-de-force in the entire history of exploration. It demanded unparalleled physical endurance, self-sacrifice and far-sighted confidence. But in no other period of exploration was so much superhuman valour accompanied by such ruthless destruction and oppression of ancient peoples and civilizations.

Even while this atrocious cruelty was still rife in Central and South America the benefits of expanding communications were gradually becoming apparent to the Old and the New World alike. The gifts of nature—maize, potatoes, tobacco, silver and precious woods—found their way in increasing quantities to Europe and beyond, while the Old World began to supply Spanish America with iron, sugar-cane, cattle, rice, wheat and many varieties of fruit. The picture of a new continent took shape and on the ancient soil of that continent there began a dramatic succession of interpenetrations and clashes between civilizations which has continued down to our own time.

EARLY SPANISH CONQUISTADORS ON THE ISTHMUS OF PANAMA

The Venezuelan coast and the Atlantic shore of the Isthmus of Panama were the goals to which the Conquistadors first aspired—attracted in the one case by the pearls and in the other by the gold which Columbus had described so vividly. At the end of 1509, spurred on by the newly-founded Colonial Office—which, under the direction of Bishop Juan Rodriguez de Fonseca, was ruthlessly pursuing the interests of the Empire—King Ferdinand allotted two great stretches of land to two individuals—pitiless Conquistadors—to be held in fief and explored by them. Alonso de Ojeda received a strip running from the Gulf of Maracaibo in Venezuela to the middle of the Gulf of Urabá; Diego de Nicuesa's territory continued this in a westerly direction and extended along the north coast of the Isthmus of Panama to the mouth of the Veragua.

Here we see some episodes from Nicuesa's tragic expedition. One stormy night during the search for the mouth of the Veragua, the flagship lost touch with the other caravels. Assuming that the Captain had been drowned, a certain Lopez de Olando took over the leadership; it was agreed that the party should go ashore for a time. Olando, taking a long view and wishing to ensure against desertion, deliberately allowed the ships that had so narrowly survived to be dashed to pieces by the surf. He soon regretted his over-hasty decision, however, and ordered his carpenters to build a sturdy vessel from such driftwood as they could recover (bottom, right), eked out with native timber (top, centre). This was probably the first ship ever built by Europeans on American soil. Olando had Spanish-style wooden houses put up alongside the Indian huts, and the surrounding land was sown as a precaution against starvation—an ally relied upon by the Indians who had taken to flight.

Four months had gone by, and in this tropical climate the first harvest was already close at hand, when a boat suddenly arrived, bringing three of Nicuesa's men who said they had left their Captain and a large party, in a half-starved condition, at a point further west. The starving companions were all brought over, but Nicuesa had Olando put in irons immediately, charging him with abuse of authority. Although harvest-time was so near, he harshly ordered them to sail away southeastwards, to Darien on the Gulf of Urabá, on whose western shore Balboa had meanwhile established the flourishing settlement of La Antigua. Ojeda, however, had decamped—after needlessly sacrificing 250 of his 300 men—and the colonists, forewarned of Nicuesa's reputation as a slave-driver, would not let him land. They forced him back to the open sea, where he vanished. The survivors of the two ill-fated expeditions were taken in hand by Balboa—a born leader—and developed into a small colonial élite.

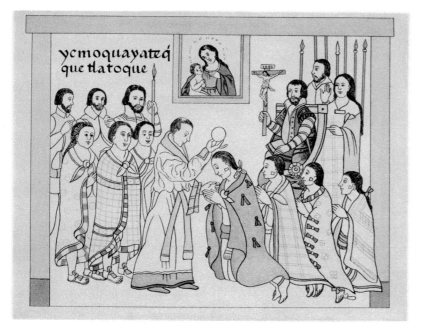

### THE BATTLE FOR MEXICO

Cortes opened his Mexican campaign by scuttling all but one of his ships off Vera Cruz. Having thus put his faithful followers into a mood of grim determination, he led them up to the plateau where the city of Mexico, at that time called Tenochtitlan, stood in its lagoon. In 1519 to 20 five hundred men with muskets, swords and armour, with fifteen horses and six cannon, fought their way through unknown country, amid a hail of arrows and stones from hostile Indians. They found allies, however,—tribes in rebellion against the dictatorship of Montezuma whose rule extended from Mexico over the whole country. Many of their chiefs were baptized and given first communion by the priest, Juan Diaz. Here we see them kneeling, distinguished by the golden pegs in the lobes of their ears—the newest vassals of Christ and His Spanish Majesty. Cortes holds the crucifix; by his side—she never left it—is Marina, the daughter of a Mexican chief, who was Cortes's interpreter, adviser and mistress. Spanish and Aztec nobles are looking on.

*Centre:* The Spaniards and their allies from Tlaxcala, in a very tight place. They had marched unopposed along one of the dykes that crossed the lagoon and into the highly-civilized city of Mexico. Montezuma, torn between the instinct of self-defence and the superstitious idea that these foreigners were white gods returning to the country who should be given a hospitable welcome, had admitted them and lodged them in the Axayacatl Palace. Before long the guests seized their host to serve as a hostage, while resentment, aroused by the brutal conduct of the Spaniards, ran high outside the palace. It exploded in June 1520. Burning arrows set fire to parts of the palace, including the chapel with its holy pictures. The occupants tried to put out the flames with pitchers of water (bottom, centre). The Spaniards defended themselves with cannon-shot and sorties. Montezuma was compelled to appear on the tower of the palace and address his people, calling for peace (above, left); he was hit by a stone and died a few days later. Cortes had underestimated the fighting spirit of the Aztecs. He was obliged to withdraw from the city in the dead of night, a very perilous operation.

*Below:* The Conquistador's army, reduced to a quarter of its original strength, assembled at Tlaxcala. Reinforcements were brought in, and the leader's fierce determination rallied his men to the attack again. Here we see a clash, on one of the dykes in the lagoon, between the Spaniards and a valiant party of Aztecs. In the middle, on a sort of scaffold, is the head of a slaughtered prisoner. To the left, a group of the Spaniards' allies has just gone past Marina, who is cheering the soldiers on; their leader is distinguished by the device on his back—a heron. His opponent has clad himself in a jaguar skin, to inspire terror. Both men are fighting with the 'obsidian sword'—a kind of wooden club with a groove along its narrower edge, in which sharp splinters of vitreous lava are stuck. Two Spaniards are hastening up from the right, one of them in protective armour. Aztec boats are attacking on one side of the embankment, and on the other side is one of the large, rapid Spanish craft—a new weapon which played a decisive part in the fall of the city.

ycpolinhq mexica

CORTES ACCEPTING THE SURRENDER OF QUAUHTEMOC, LAST KING OF THE AZTECS

On 13th August 1521, in his badly battered capital, the new, youthful ruler of Mexico, accompanied by his nobles, surrendered to the foreign conquerors. Unarmed except for a shield, he is escorted by a chief who has a pinion-shaped badge made of quetzal feathers. (Above him, at the top of the picture, is the Queen.) In contrast to this simplicity the three Tlaxcalteks who are advancing proudly in the foreground behind the Spaniard display the full splendour of the ancient Aztec ceremonial dress, dictated by the highly-developed sense of social and military hierarchy that prevailed in a community where the different classes rose one above another in a structure as rigid as the steps of their temples. In their midst is a warrior carrying a staff round which twines a kind of serpent made of yellow parrot-

feathers; it is tipped with a tuft of the red feathers of the ara bird. The man behind him carries a V-shaped war emblem, a very costly affair, made of small gold or silver discs and tipped with bunches of feathers.

During the next few years Cortes, as Spanish Governor, made strenuous efforts to explore the great territory, pacify it, extend its frontiers and open it to world trade; but before long, orders from Spain relegated him to a huge estate near Oaxaca, and another Viceroy was appointed in his place.

The dramatic chronicle of the conquest of Mexico was illustrated by, among others, a Spanish-trained artist from Tlaxcala, whose work in the *Lienzo de Tlaxcala* combined the traditional Indian style with that of Europe. We show four of his pictures here.

THE CONQUISTADORS INTRODUCING NEGRO SLAVES INTO HAITI

At the very beginning the Spaniards in America took Indians as their slaves. Great stretches of land reverted to desert because this method of work was repugnant to the Indian character, and the lash of the whip even more so. Only a small minority of the new rulers was prepared to take a personal hand in the labour. This led to a suggestion that introduced a completely new human element into American history: the proposal to import African Negroes, who were tougher and more willing. They were first set to work on plantations and in the gold and silver mines of Hispaniola, as shown in the picture.

Twenty years earlier a monk, Bartolomé de las Casas (1474–1566), had landed in San Domingo, to spend fifty years as a missionary among the Indians and as a champion of their despised rights—in defence of which he was tireless, carrying his impassioned pleading to the very steps of the Habsburg throne. 'The Christian faith deprives no man of his liberty, it robs no man of his birthright on the ground that nature has destined him to slavery; and it would well beseem Your Majesty to root out so monstrous an oppression at the first beginning of Your reign . . .' he wrote to the Emperor Charles V. Tragically enough, it was Las Casas himself who recommended the introduction of Negro slaves for the heavier work—though he later retracted this advice. The Leyes Nuevas promulgated under his influence by Charles V in 1542 at last gave some degree of protection to the Indians.

ATAHUALPA THE INCA KING EXECUTED BY THE CONQUISTADORS

Peru lay in the path of the group of Conquistadors who pushed southwards into unknown territory from the town of Panama, founded in 1519. The driving force in this case was the iron-willed Francisco Pizarro. He was already more than fifty years old when he and his comrade-in-arms Almagro began the gruelling expeditions that were to enable them, after a period of years, to build up a picture of the north-western portion of South America. The Spanish royal family had to send him fresh funds before he could set out on his decisive journey. Armed and equipped in the same fashion as Cortes, and travelling along the amazing roads built by the Incas, he carried war into the heart of their country. The autocratic Inca state, which organized the lives of its peasants and artificers down to the minutest detail, was torn by the rivalry of two Regents, and this explains its collapse, in 1532, before a force of scarcely two hundred invaders. Pizarro seized Atahualpa, who was ruling at Cuzco. The royal prisoner offered gold in profusion to pay his ransom. Pizarro accepted it, but just after the negotiations (seen in progress) he shamelessly broke his word by bringing his victim before a so-called court of justice, which sentenced him, on a charge of 'conspiracy', to a horrible death by strangling. Negro slaves of the Spaniards acted as executioners. Through the windows we see some fanciful representations of Inca buildings; the Spaniards were astounded by the immense scale of Peruvian architecture.

HUMAN SACRIFICES ON THE 'TEOCALLI' OF MEXICO. The temple-pyramids in Mexico were bloodstained places. To keep up the Sun-God's strength and ensure that the sun would pursue its course (see page 147), the Aztec priests offered up human sacrifices on the platforms of the teocalli (pyramids), outside the chambers where the idols stood. Prisoners-of-war were the customary victims. The Spaniards themselves were obliged to look on, in the city of Mexico, while some of their captured comrades-in-arms were flung upon the sacrificial block for the officiating priest, with his obsidian knife, to cut the hearts out of their bodies—which were afterwards thrown sideways down the temple steps. Cortes completely stamped out this cruel religious custom which contrasted strangely with the gentleness of the race in other respects. The Mexicans were not long in extending their devotion to the Virgin Mary and the Christian Saints, who henceforth occupied a place in their worship equal to that of the gods of the Sun, Rain and Wind.

*Centre:*

BALBOA THE GOVERNOR OF DARIEN and his followers were the first Europeans to gaze down from an eminence in the New World upon the boundless expanse of the Pacific Ocean. This was in September 1513. They and their Indian porters had crossed the Isthmus of Panama at its narrowest point, cutting their way through jungle and marshland, lured on by rumours of a mighty sea to the south-west, fringed with lands rich in gold. A few days later Balboa strode into the water, carrying his sword and shield, and called to his companions, who stood with their bloodhounds on the shore, to bear witness that this sea, with its islands and coasts and the lands bordering upon it, were henceforth Spanish possessions, 'so long as the world shall endure, and until the last day of Judgement'. Not many years went by before the new Governor of Darien, egged on by Balboa's enemies, had the heroic pioneer beheaded.

*Below:*

A SPANISH SHIP IS WRECKED AT THE MOUTH OF THE RIVER PLATE. Buenos Aires, the fortified settlement founded in 1535 by Pedro de Mendoza on the edge of the pampas, was dogged by ill-fortune. The Indians attacked it persistently, and hunger and sickness ran rife inside its walls. Mendoza sent two ships to St Catherine's Island to meet a relief vessel which was expected, under the command of Alonso Cabrera, and to take off immediately as much food as they could obtain for his starving settlers. During the return voyage one of these ships, with its irreplaceable cargo, was driven ashore by a storm in the night, and broke to pieces. Only a few of the crew were able to save themselves, clinging to masts and pieces of wreckage. They reached dry land and made their way for fifty miles, feeding sparsely on berries and roots, to the harbour of St Gabriel on the River Plate, where they found one of the other ships safe and sound. Buenos Aires was abandoned in 1537 and not rebuilt until 1580.

THE CONQUISTADORS—'EVERY MAN FOR HIMSELF'

Almagro, Pizarro's companion-in-arms, pushed further southwards in 1535–37, at the head of several thousand natives, and reached a point halfway down the coast of Chile—blind to the beauty and fertility of the region, for it had no gold to offer. A Conquistador's hand was always on his dagger; violent altercations among the Spaniards themselves and between them and the natives (the last Inca King did not lose his life until 1571) or the emissaries of the Spanish court, were the order of the day. Almagro quarrelled with Pizarro about the ownership of Lima; Pizarro's brother, Hernando, sentenced him to death by strangling (right), and his body was publicly beheaded (note the spectators). Vengeance came three years later, however. Pizarro was struck down in Lima, his new capital, by Almagro's partisans.

*Overleaf:* A STRIKING VIEW OF THE PYRAMID OF EL TAJIN near Papantla in the administrative district of Vera Cruz. In the eighteenth century the world began to turn its attention to the mysteries of the ancient, gigantic buildings of Central America, which had lain forgotten for so long. C. Nebel, an architect, spent five years in Mexico and published in Paris, in 1836, the first accurate views of the structures. The jungle growth was just cleared away, when he came across the building shown here, believed to have been dedicated to Tlaloc, the Rain God. Its distinguishing features are its 366 large and its twelve small niches, presumably intended for idols. The Mexican pyramids, unlike the Egyptian, do not contain tombs; their interior is simply a mound of earth on which the shrine is raised high above the countryside.

NORTH-WEST CORNER OF THE RUINED PYRAMID OF XOCHIALCO WHICH LIES SOUTH-EAST OF CUERNAVACA

From the fortified top of this hill a stepped pyramid with elaborate carvings once reared, its peak visible from far and wide. All that now remains of it is a portion below the first terrace, with the oblique buttress wall, the frieze (45½ inches in height) and the forward-leaning cornice. It ends, on the right, with one side of the vanished double staircase. Eduard Seler, the archaeologist, declares this to be a temple of Xochiquetzal, the Earth Goddess, for her attributes include the serpent and the coyote, and the latter figures repeatedly among its carvings. What looks like the head of the plumed serpent, with the tip of the tail curling towards it, can be seen on the buttress. The figures sitting cross-legged on the frieze may be priests; each holds in his left hand a bag containing incense-burning equipment.

*Right:* These two figures, in this same attitude, are repeated fifteen times on the cylinder-shaped 'Tizoc stone' in Mexico city (it is 33 ½ inches high). On the left, in his fluttering raiment of feathers, is the Aztec ruler Tizoc (1482–86); in front of him, in each case, a defeated warrior—identified, by hieroglyphics which differ in each instance, as the representative of a conquered territory—meekly bending his head. In his left hand this figure holds a bundle of javelins, in his right hand the javelin sling. The monarch appears in the awe-inspiring guise of Tezcatlipoca, Lord of Night and Warfare, recognized by the smoking mirror near his right temple and by his left foot, which looks like a trail of smoke. The stars gaze down upon the roughly-stylized scene, which rests on the back of the Earth Monster.

## Cortes at the Great Temple in Mexico

'One hundred and fourteen steps led up to the temple. At the foot thereof we found six priests and two high officers of State, sent by Montezuma to meet us and to assist our leader during the climb. He, however, refused their aid.

'Reaching the top, we saw before us a platform which served for the slaughter of the wretched victims. It was all smirched with blood and many sacrificial stones lay about, before a great idol shaped like a dragon and other hideous images. Montezuma, with two priests, came forward to greet us, out of a chapel where the idols of the temple were arrayed. He showed us great friendship, saying "Thou art doubtless weary, Malinche, from so lofty a climb", to which Cortes answered that weariness was a thing unknown either to himself or to us. Then the King took our Captain by the hand and led him forward, saying "Look down upon my great city and the many townships beside the lake; from here thou mayst behold all, even as far as Tlatelulco."

'And in sooth that accursed temple overlooked the whole land. We could see the three roads that ran along dykes into Mexico—the road from Iztapalapan, by which we ourselves had entered the mighty city four days earlier; the road from Tlacupa and the road from Tepeaquilla; we saw clearly the bridges that carried these roads over the gaps in the dykes where the lake water flowed in and out, and the great aqueduct that brought sweet water from Chapultepec to all parts of Mexico. In that city, and in the townships beside the lake, one could go from house to house only by way of drawbridges, or by boat. The lake was strewn with vessels that made their way in all directions, and in the townships the white sacrificial temples rose high above the terraces of the dwelling-houses, with little towers and chapels—a sight, in truth, of wondrous beauty. We gazed and gazed with ever-renewed delight, until at length our eyes fell on the great market and the press of folk buying and selling there, bringing merchandise or bearing it off. With all this was a buzzing and an uproar that could be heard an hour's march away. Certain of our comrades-in-arms, who had been in many cities, vowed that nowhere before, even in Rome or Constantinople, had they beheld a market so thronged with people, yet withal so orderly, as in this place.

'And with the city and the land lying so before us, Cortes turned to Father Bartholomew of Olmedo and said "What think you, should we not one day ask Montezuma's consent to build a Christian church in this place?"

'"That would in truth be a goodly deed", replied Father Bartholomew, "but the time is not yet ripe, and Montezuma would deny us."

'Meanwhile Cortes had bidden Marina speak thus for him to the King: "Your Majesty is indeed a mighty monarch; may your power ever increase. We look with delight upon all this mighty city. But we desire greatly to behold as well the images of your gods."

'Upon this Montezuma took counsel of his priests, and they led us into a little turret. Within was a chamber with two lofty eminences, as it were altars, whereon stood two massy figures, as tall as giants.

---

◄ THE 'AZTEC CALENDAR'

This famous stone, a symbol of the solar disk, on which the Aztec chronology and cosmology are set forth, measures 12 feet from rim to rim, and, like the Tizoc Stone, was discovered late in 1790 among the ruins of the great temple-pyramid of Mexico. C. Nebel made most careful drawings of both these 'documents'. In the centre of the calendar is the Sun-God, to whom everything shown on it bears a definite relationship. The signs in the four rectangular spaces surrounding the God represent the four previous Suns, i.e., the epochs in the history of the Earth which were respectively governed by them. At the end of each of these epochs the sun was destroyed—by a flood (the epoch of the Water Sun, bottom right); by the collapse of the sky, caused by a jaguar that devoured the sun (the Jaguar Sun, top right); by fire from heaven and volcanic eruptions (the Fire and Rain Sun, bottom left); and by whirlwinds (the Wind Sun, top left). The present (fifth) Sun was born in the year whose hieroglyph, '13 cane', is seen above, between the serpents' tails. Earthquakes will one day bring its epoch to an end. To avert the evil portents of this fatalistically catastrophic calendar, the sun had to be strengthened by annual potations of human blood. This accounts for the Aztecs' custom of human sacrifice and for many of their military campaigns—the purpose of which was to bring home prisoners to be sacrificed. It also explains the two serpents that twine round the calendar stone; they represent the Fire-God and the God of War, for in this gloomy religion sunshine and war were closely linked.

The Aztecs divided the year into eighteen months of twenty days, adding an extra five days to the year to keep it in step with the sun. The symbols of the twenty days form a ring from which four V-shaped symbolic rays emanate. These symbols run from right to left and include Lizard, Viper, Skull, Stag, Water, Dog, Ape, Tiger, Eagle, Rain, and Flower.

'The figure on the right was Huitzilopochtli, the God of War. He had a broad face with great goggling eyes and he was all set about with gold and pearls and precious stones. Round the body of this monster were entwined great serpents made of gold and gems, and he bore in one hand a bow, in the other an arrow. Beside him stood his page, a small idol, bearing his lance and his shield, which was all of gold and jewelled. Huitzilopochtli had a necklace of human faces and hearts of gold and silver, set with blue stones. Before him stood sundry basins wherein, amid clouds of incense, there burnt the hearts of three Indians who had been sacrificed on that day.

'The image on the left was of the same stature as the War God, and studded with as many gems. This was Tetzcatlipuca, the God of Hell, who had power over the souls of the dead. His visage had much the aspect of a bear's snout, his flashing eyes were made of the mirrors of that country, which are called Tetzcat. A line of little devils with serpents' tails wound about his body, and human hearts were laid before him. But the floor and walls of the chapel were black with blood, and the stench was fouler than in any slaughterhouse in Spain...

'On the platform of the temple was a great drum, whose note was so dismal that it might well be called the drum of hell. They told us it could be heard at more than two hours' march; it was made from the skin of a monstrous serpent. We saw on the platform divers other devilish instruments and objects, trumpets and slaughtering knives, all bloody, foul and damnable. Therefore our Captain turned to Montezuma with a smiling mien and said: "In truth, I wonder that so great and wise a ruler has not understood long ere this, that these idols are not gods, but evil demons. Would that you would allow me a chamber in this temple, wherein to set up a crucifix and a picture of the Mother of God; then should you and your priests behold the terror of your idols, by whom you are thrust into eternal perdition."

'Then the priests glared in anger and Montezuma's brow darkened as he answered: "Had I looked for such insults from thee, Malinche, I had never shown thee my gods. We deem them to be just gods, answering our prayers with life and health, food and drink and victory in battle. Presume no more to speak such blasphemies."

'Seeing men's minds so heated, Cortes let the matter rest, saying in friendly fashion: "The time has come, perchance, that we should both go hence."' [1]

[1] From the report of the discovery and conquest of Mexico by Bernal Diaz del Castillo.

MARE del NORT.

rra
di
ARIA.

A Flood at the Mouth of the Orinoco observed by Sir Walter Raleigh

As the adventurous century of the Conquistadors was drawing to its close, the passion for conquest flared up anew, fed by reports that in the primeval forest along the lower reaches of the Orinoco there was a city called Manoa, whose streets were paved with gold. The dying Quesada, conqueror of the Chibchas, left his fortune to Antonio de Berrio, the husband of his niece, charging him to seek for Manoa. Berrio made three unsuccessful attempts between 1584 and 1591. He then found himself confronted with an unexpected rival in the person of Walter Raleigh (1552–1618), an English conquistador, poet, soldier, statesman and explorer, filled with ambition for his country, a favourite of Queen Elizabeth I, eager to capture some earthly paradise in America. Raleigh had heard of Manoa. The efforts he had made during the 1580's to found an English colony in what is now

Carolina had failed, but they had shown England the way to her future North American settlements. Since then Raleigh had fallen into disgrace; but the legendary golden city of Manoa enabled him to regain favour on two occasions. The first time was in 1595 when he equipped four ships; the second was towards the end of his life when, after James I had kept him prisoner in the Tower for many years, he secured his release by promising to find and capture gold-mines on the Caroni river. The expedition came home discomfitted, and Raleigh was beheaded on 29th October 1618.

*Above:* Raleigh's report mentions the floods at the mouth of the Orinoco during the rainy season. The natives (who, to judge from the figures in the right foreground, had cannibalistic tendencies) are seen here taking refuge on the highest islets and in the tallest trees.

MARIA SIBYLLA MERIAN VISITS SURINAM

In August 1699 a fifty-two-year-old woman, weary of European life, landed at Paramaribo. She was Maria Sibylla Merian, daughter of the engraver Matthias Merian the Elder, a native of Basle. Well known as a flower and insect painter, her entomological studies were her chief source of pleasure in what was a hard life; and she was a fervent Christian who looked upon nature as a pageant of divine miracles and the successive metamorphoses of insects as the symbol of man's resurrection.

A community of her fellow Labadists had settled in Dutch Guiana (Surinam), and this gave her an opportunity to visit the tropical world whose natural beauties she was eager to immortalize in pictures. She and her daughter travelled forty miles up the Surinam river to a plantation known as 'Pro-

videntia'. The engraving on the title-page of the French edition of her *Metamorphosis Insectorum Surinamensium* (1705), with its sixty folio plates, gives an imaginative view of herself at work, and a glimpse of a Guiana plantation. Ill-health obliged her to return to Amsterdam after barely eighteen months. Her book, its plates sometimes coloured by her own hand, is one of the most perfect artistic records of tropical nature in its lesser manifestations.

*Right:* Sibylla Merian was not always able to put a scientific name to her insects and herbs. In such cases she had to be satisfied—as we see in this coloured engraving—with placing an accurate record on paper, in her mature style, and leaving it nameless. This is a plant from her garden in Surinam.

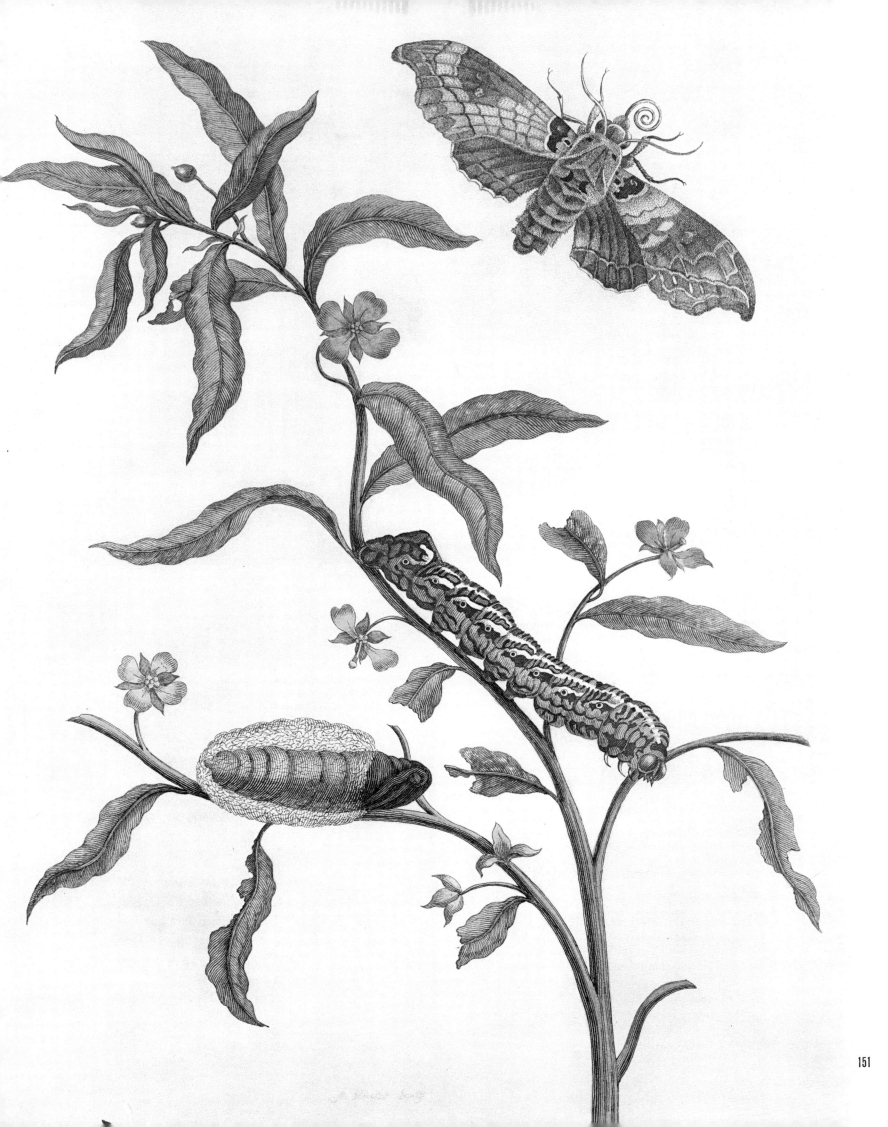

THE LEGENDARY GOLDEN CITY OF MANOA

Spaniards, Englishmen and Germans vied with one another in the sixteenth century in seeking for the golden city of Manoa. The town and its district on the Orinoco where it was thought to lie were also known as Eldorado. This was an erroneous transposition of the name given to a Chibcha Cacique who, at an annual ceremony on Lake Guatavita (see page 158), used to be coated in gold-dust and then bathe in the lake. Since then the word Eldorado has been the synonym for a land of heart's desire. Walter Raleigh's report sug-

gests that Manoa, which he never saw with his own eyes, was the capital of Spanish Guiana (which now lies in southern Venezuela), a land flowing with gold, gems, spices and other eagerly-sought products. It stood on the large lake of Parima, and was linked to the surrounding regions by much coming and going of canoes. The inhabitants of the Essekebe river-basin used to travel upstream for twenty days till they came within a day's journey of the lake; they then carried their boats, goods and provisions overland to the lakeside.

# Alexander von Humboldt

The Spaniards allowed no foreigners to set foot in Central and South America, thus won for them by the Conquistadors. Geographical research was left to a small number of scholars, mostly Spanish Jesuits. But a second great era of discovery—which was to continue until after Latin America had broken away from Spain and Portugal—opened with La Condamine's expedition. This began in 1736, its first exploit being carried out on the crest of the Andes, at the equator, where the distance between two degrees of longitude was measured with an accuracy never achieved before. It concluded in 1743–44 with an eight-month voyage of discovery down the Amazon. In 1799 the history of exploration entered upon its most happy phase, heralded by the arrival in South America of Alexander von Humboldt, most brilliant of natural scientists, and his faithful companion, the French botanist and zoologist Aimé Bonpland.

Humboldt, who came of an aristocratic Prussian family, was then thirty years old, and this journey was the decisive episode in a course of development that established him as the most versatile and reverent of all nineteenth-century adepts of the natural sciences. He learnt to discipline his seething mind and make it the servant of an ambitious programme of research. He had an endless curiosity about individual natural phenomena, coupled with an equally vivid interest in the vaster implications of his subject; he flung himself body and soul into all his undertakings; to the end of his life he eagerly pursued his discussions with the intellectual élite of his day, his study of the master-minds of earlier centuries, whilst his enthusiasm for the terrestrial globe as an inexhaustible source of factual information never flagged. His interest embraced the entire cosmos, from the planets to the humblest forms of human activity, and extended to every aspect of nature.

The years 1799 to 1804 found Humboldt travelling through the Venezuelan jungle, up the Orinoco—whose connection with the Rio Negro and the Amazon basin he established once and for all—and far beyond. Always accompanied by Bonpland, he studied the people and the economic system of wealthy Cuba; climbed by perilous tracks up the Colombian Andes, examining the rock formations as he went; risked his life in Ecuador on his famous attempt to scale Chimborazo; visited the ruins in Peru and made deductions from them about the Inca civilization; and finally reached Mexico where his investigations resulted in an impressive general picture of the geography, economy, social structure and cultural history of the ancient Aztec kingdom and the new colonial territory.

The journey was incredibly productive. This is evident from the thirty-volume account of it which appeared in Paris (1805–1832). Humboldt had financed the expedition itself, and this publication swallowed up what remained of his fortune. He and Bonpland had identified 3,500 new species of plants and made a fundamental contribution to plant geography. Humboldt described many hitherto unknown animals. He investigated the structure of volcanos and studied their action on the earth's crust. He published a host of cartographical notes, magnetic measurements and meteorological, astronomical and oceanographic observations. With masterly skill he described the people of the regions he visited in relation to their surroundings; and his comments on the political and economic institutions of South America reveal a liberal and statesmanlike mind.

The great stream of his knowledge sometimes bursts its banks, but is promptly brought under the control of a will bent upon fitting all the riches of nature into place in the general scheme of things. His descriptions all culminate in recognition of a cosmic law; and the acknowledgement of that law leads him, in turn, to apprehend the existence of a primal cause which bears some resemblance to the universal mind sensed by the thinkers of the romantic movement. 'Whether in the Amazonian forests or on the ridge of the high Andes, I was ever aware that *one* breath, from pole to pole, breathes *one* single life into stones, plants and animals and into the swelling breast of man.' (Letter to Caroline von Wolzogen, 14th May 1806)

To look upon the earth in such a way is to transform geography into a truly majestic science. In his writings Humboldt strove ardently to rouse the innermost consciousness of mankind to awareness of the visible universe. To this end he commissioned talented artists to work on his sketches, displaying the beauty of the world to the eyes of his readers. His *Ansichten der Natur* (1808) and his *Kosmos* (1845–62) pursued the same educational purpose.

In the course of history the explorer appears in a variety of guises, several of which are often combined in one individual. He may be a merchant, setting up trading posts—a conqueror, oppressing the lands he has discovered—a missionary, bringing a new creed and striving to read men's souls—a colonist, settling down to sow and reap. Humboldt was the supreme example of the explorer bent upon research, wholly disinterested, seeking knowledge for its own sake alone. The two extremes of the explorer's nature are exemplified by Humboldt, the scholar who felt the soul of the universe breathing on the Andean heights, and by Pizarro, the illiterate adventurer who in those same Andes crushed a great civilization. These two attitudes, appearing in the same region during the discovery of Central and South America, produced the special human atmosphere of its exploration, from the Conquistadors to the expeditions of Humboldt, Martius and Darwin.

ALEXANDER VON HUMBOLDT SEEN IN 1856 IN HIS LIBRARY IN ORANIENBURGERSTRASSE, BERLIN

Paris, in those days the intellectual capital of Europe, was Humboldt's elected home. He was there in 1804 when he saw his magnificent *Voyage aux régions équinoxiales du Nouveau Continent* through the press. But by 1827 his money had given out and he was compelled to return to Berlin. He lived there as the courageous liberal adviser of an extremely conservative king (he was known as the 'Court democrat') and the revered patriarch of natural science. In 1829, commissioned by the Tsar, he made a journey to the Russian territories in Central Asia. People travelled great distances to visit him; a tremendously active correspondence kept him in touch with the scientific world of his day; books, maps, geological specimens and so forth poured in to add to his own collections; and thus the world continued, as it were, of its own accord to visit the great explorer now that he had ceased to visit it. The American writer Bayard Taylor gives the following description of Humboldt's surroundings: 'He ushered me into a room, filled with stuffed birds and other objects of natural history; then into a large library which apparently contained the gifts of authors, artists and men of science. I walked between two large tables heaped with sumptuous folios, to the further door, which opened into the study.'

Humboldt's life of exemplary creative activity came peacefully to an end in Berlin on 6th May 1859. He was mourned by the whole civilized world.

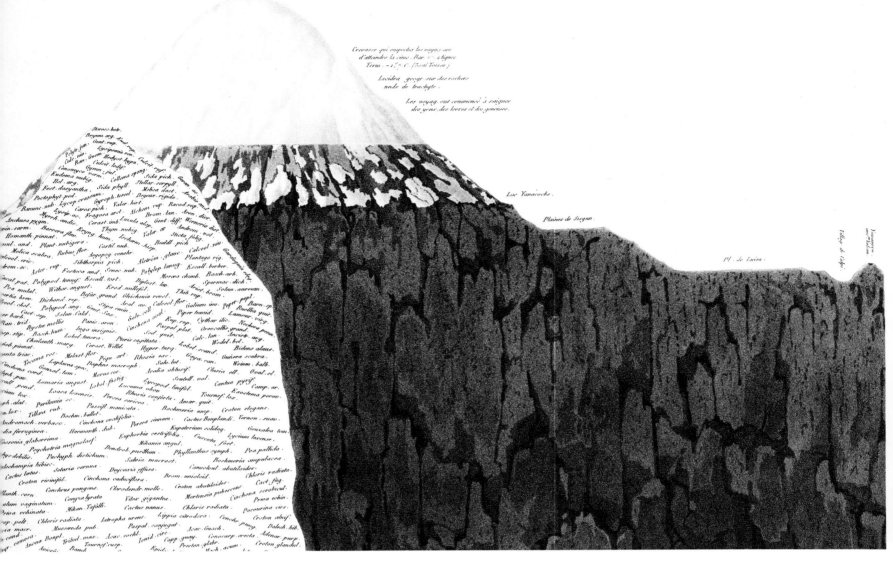

PROFILE OF THE VOLCANO CHIMBORAZO (20,702 FEET) SHOWING WHERE VARIOUS PLANTS WERE FOUND

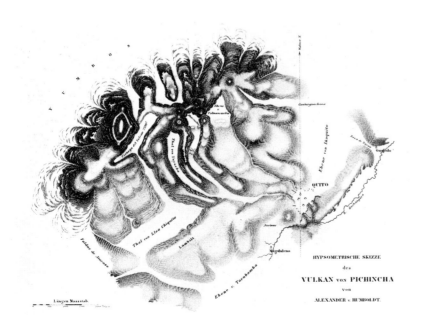

HYPSOMETRISCHE SKIZZE
des
VULKAN von PICHINCHA
von
ALEXANDER v HUMBOLDT.

THE VOLCANO PICHINCHA, in the Western Cordillera of Ecuador, shown with the help of an improved style of shading devised by Humboldt who, as a cartographer, was stimulated by the difficulty of accurately depicting the volcano's numerous peaks, with their complex structure. The result is a little work of art.

To discover the secrets of volcanic activities was one of the great aims of Humboldt's work.

Pichincha, which is not far from Quito, rises from flat ground to a height of 15,672 feet. Humboldt, the most reverent of explorers, held it particularly sacred in memory of a great event: on one of its perilous summits there stood a cross, erected by La Condamine sixty years previously, for the purpose of the accurate measurement of a degree of longitude which he was trying to make from the Andes. (See page 163.)

THE PEAK OF ORIZABA IN MEXICO SEEN FROM THE FOREST OF XALAPA

*Page 156, top:* Chimborazo, from a working sketch by Humboldt who has written the names of a vast number of plants at the levels at which they grew, ascertained by means of the barometer. Certain notes recall particularly unpleasant episodes in the daring attempt to scale this mountain made in 1802 by Humboldt, Bonpland and a local *mestizo* called Montufar. They struggled up into the eternal snows, blinded by clouds of mist and whirling snowflakes, fighting against mountain-sickness, with bleeding lips and gums, till they were brought to a halt by an impassable crevasse. Their last scientific observation was made at a height of 16,920 feet where they found a tiny cryptogamic lichen, *lecidea atrovirens.*

Humboldt and his companions climbed to a height of 19,290 feet above sea-level before turning to make their way down again over precipitous rock-faces.

*Above:* The volcano Orizaba was as familiar to sailors as Mount St. Elias, Table Mountain or the peak of Tenerife; for it was a landmark that guided them, from a great distance, towards Vera Cruz. In making this picture of it, Humboldt was actuated by a motive different from that which prompted his profile of Chimborazo. Orizaba towers above the amber-trees and arbutus of the surrounding forest with the 'silent grandeur and nobility characteristic of nature in the tropics'. Wherever the majesty of nature thus transcended man's descriptive powers, Humboldt relied upon 'the scientist's ancient alliance with poetry and artistic sensibility' to give expression to it, enlisting the help of painters and engravers in Paris, or in the German artists' colony in Rome. In this particular case he chose Eduard Hildebrandt, who executed this aquatint in 1805, under Humboldt's supervision and from a painting by Baron A. J. Gros.

Lake Guatavita to the North of Santa Fé de Bogotá

At the time of the Spanish invasion led by Quesada, this mountain plateau in what is now Colombia was inhabited by the Chibchas, a highly-civilized nation. They held an annual ceremony during which the Cacique of Guatavita, after being anointed with oil and sprinkled with gold-dust, was rowed out over the lake into which he dropped gold and jewels and in which he then bathed, as a tribute to Bachue, the mythical Mother of the Universe. Meanwhile priests and people, gathered on the steps leading down to the lake, performed the appropriate rites to the accompaniment of chants. The Spaniards referred to the Cacique as 'El Dorado' (the Gilded One)—a name later transferred, by error, to a gold-seekers' region in South America (see page 152).

A Suspension Bridge over the River Chambo near Penipé (Peru)

The agave grows everywhere in Central and South America. Its roots are used for medicinal purposes, the highly intoxicating *pulque* is brewed from its sap, its thorns serve as needles and nails, its leaves make good thatch, and the ropes spun from its fibres are so strong that they can even be used to make suspension bridges, such as the one shown here. Bamboo staves are laid across the floor of the wobbly structure. Some specimens of the marvellous plant can be seen growing, in the right foreground and on the slope.—Humboldt drew both scenes in his sketchbook when he was on the spot, and Pierre-Antoine Marchais, the French painter, used the sketches later for two of his brilliant and enduring illustrations to Humboldt's account of his travels.

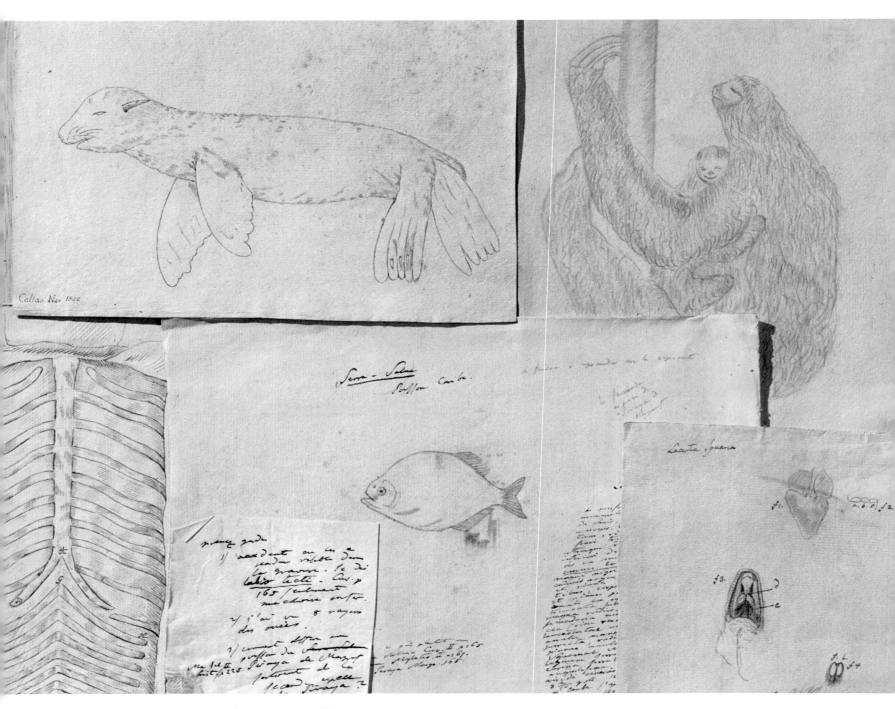

DRAWINGS OF ANIMALS BY ALEXANDER VON HUMBOLDT

During his great voyage of scientific exploration Humboldt made thousands of sketches—scraps from which to build up the great general view of nature which was his ultimate purpose. Top, left in this picture is a variety of seal; right, a female three-toed sloth—a climbing tree-dweller. Below on the left is a study of the remarkable rib-structure of the crocodile; on the right, portions of the body of the iguana—a species of lizard; and in the centre (with notes jotted down by Humboldt for his Swiss friend Johann Jakob von Tschudi) the piranha, a dangerous predatory fish that will attack even men in the water. The whole page gives a selection of South American fauna extending from Cãllao, on the Pacific, to the Orinoco on the Atlantic.

*Right:* The Mexican *Acacia acapulcensis*, one of the innumer- ▶ able species of plants discovered and described by Bonpland and Humboldt. They found this acacia growing in sandy soil on the Pacific coast, near Acapulco (hence its name). Its leaf and flower are fragile miracles. The leaves react with the greatest sensitivity to changes of light and temperature—as Martius put it, they lead the 'mysterious life of automata'. The flowers (1) grow in close-set spikes; twenty-six or twenty-seven very long stamens project (2) from the short-petalled corolla, which is held in a five-pointed calyx. The pollen is arranged in tiny lentiform patches, with four grains in the middle and eight round the edge. The picture was made from a water-colour by P.J.F.Turpin.

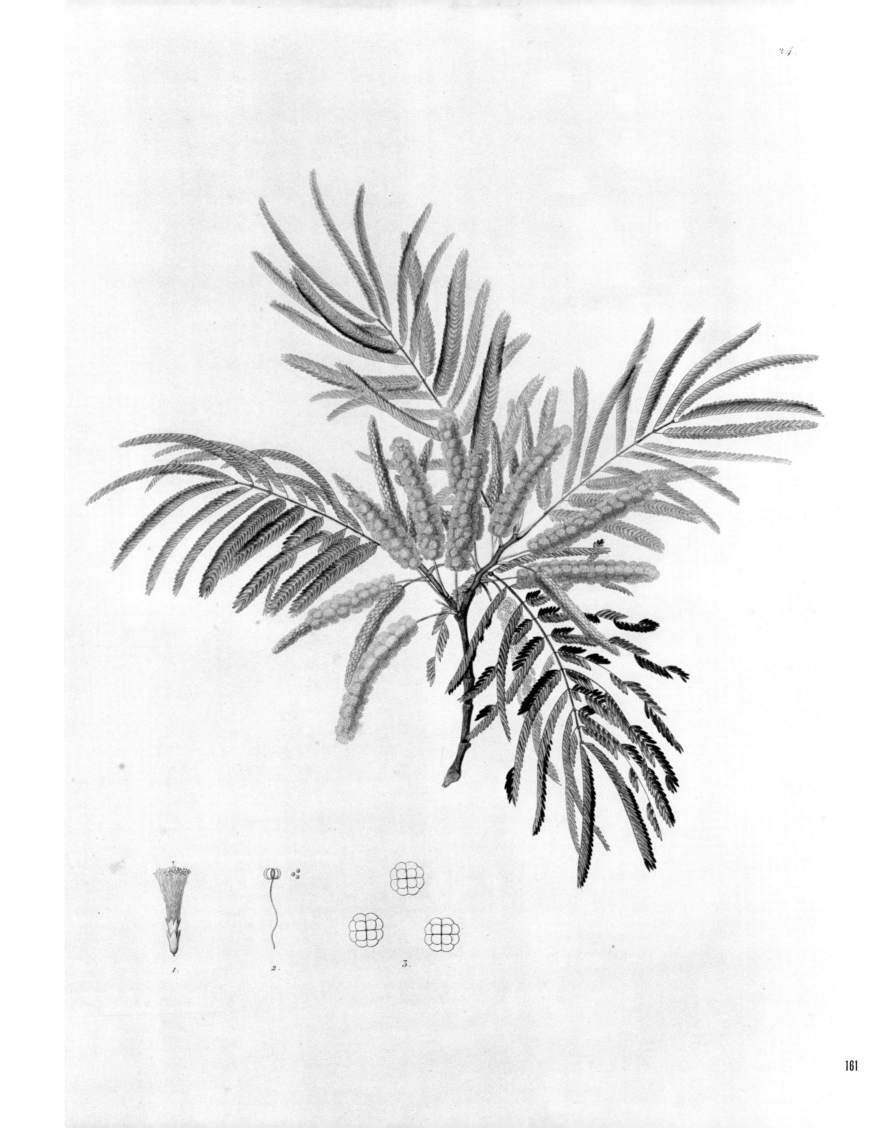

AN INDIAN SHOWS AN EXPLORER THE RUINS OF PACHACAMAC

Five hundred years before the Conquistadors destroyed the Aztec, Maya, Chibcha and Inca civilizations, the oases that fringed the scorching Peruvian coast were the sites of towns doomed to be ultimately swallowed up by the sand. Pachacamac, the most brilliant of these cities before its capture by the Incas, was once the Rome of the Andes, the chief place of pilgrimage for worshippers of *Pachacamac*, the animating spirit of the universe, and of the sun, the moon, the sea and the stellar divinities.

The Swiss naturalist Johann Jakob Tschudi (1818–89) visited the dead city in 1842, on his way down from the high Andes. In 1851, in collaboration with M.E. de Rivero, the Peruvian geologist, he published the first really scientific work on the civilization of the Andean races before the arrival of the Spaniards. It includes a description of *Pachacamac*.

The temple (A) once towered over several rings of fortifications rising one above the other. The remains of the pilgrims' quarter can be seen at the foot of the slope (d); the townspeople's homes were on the far side of the hill. Below on the hill that rises to the left are the ruins of the great cloisters reserved for the virgins in the temple service (D). On the expanse of ground between the spectators and the hills and the fresh-water lagoon on the right we see the signs of the victory of the Incas, who subdued the whole region from the mountains to the coast: on the left, the Temple of the Sun, which they built; and in the middle, slightly to the right, the foundations of the Inca palace (C).

*Overleaf:*

MEMBERS OF LA CONDAMINE'S EXPEDITION IN DEADLY PERIL
IN THE TOWN OF CUENCA. In 1793 the French Académie des
Sciences assembled an impressive group of mathematicians,
astronomers and biologists who betook themselves to the
Andes, near the equator, set up an extensive surveying net-
work, and measured three degrees of a meridian.

Having completed their work, they were all in the town
of Cuenca when, on 29th August 1739, the hatred of foreigners that was always latent among the South American
Spaniards broke out in full force.

There was to be a bull-fight in a public square. The atmosphere was tense, for in one of the boxes sat young Diego de
Leon (D) with his father-in-law the Alcalde (judge) Serrano
and their declared patron, the Apostolic Vicar to the Arch-
bishop of Quito—a notorious intriguer (E); while diagonally
opposite (a) sat their deadly enemies, Manuela Quesada
(recently and shamefully deserted by the faithless de Leon
for the sake of the influential Alcalde's daughter), her father,
and their guest, Seniergues, surgeon to the French expedition. Seniergues had attempted to obtain for Manuela the
sum de Leon had promised to pay as compensation for his
desertion. Leon's partisans were up in arms because of this,
and his friend Neyra (C) sparked off the quarrel. He found
some pretext for beginning a heated argument with the
detested foreigner who was sitting in Manuela's box; the
crowd joined in, the Alcalde Serrano hurried down from his
box to take a hand (B). The Frenchman sprang into the ring
and prepared, in his turn, to face the yelling mob with dagger and pistol (A), while de la Calle, the Mayor, strove in
vain to drive back the crowd at the point of his rapier (G).
While several priests and a group belonging to the expedition (right foreground) were still uncertain as to what was
happening, Seniergues had to give way before a shower of
stones. 'Kill him!' screamed the Alcalde, beside himself with
rage; and indeed the unfortunate Frenchman, fatally in-
jured, collapsed in front of his countrymen's box, near the
entrance to the ring (7). The case was brought to trial, but
no one dreamt of carrying out the sentence pronounced on
the murderers. (Drawing by La Condamine.)

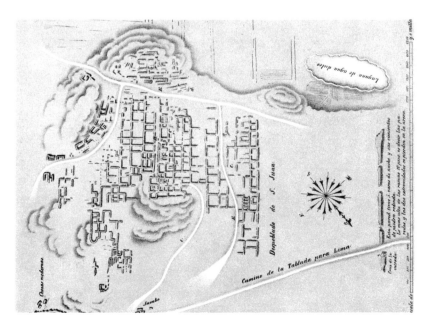

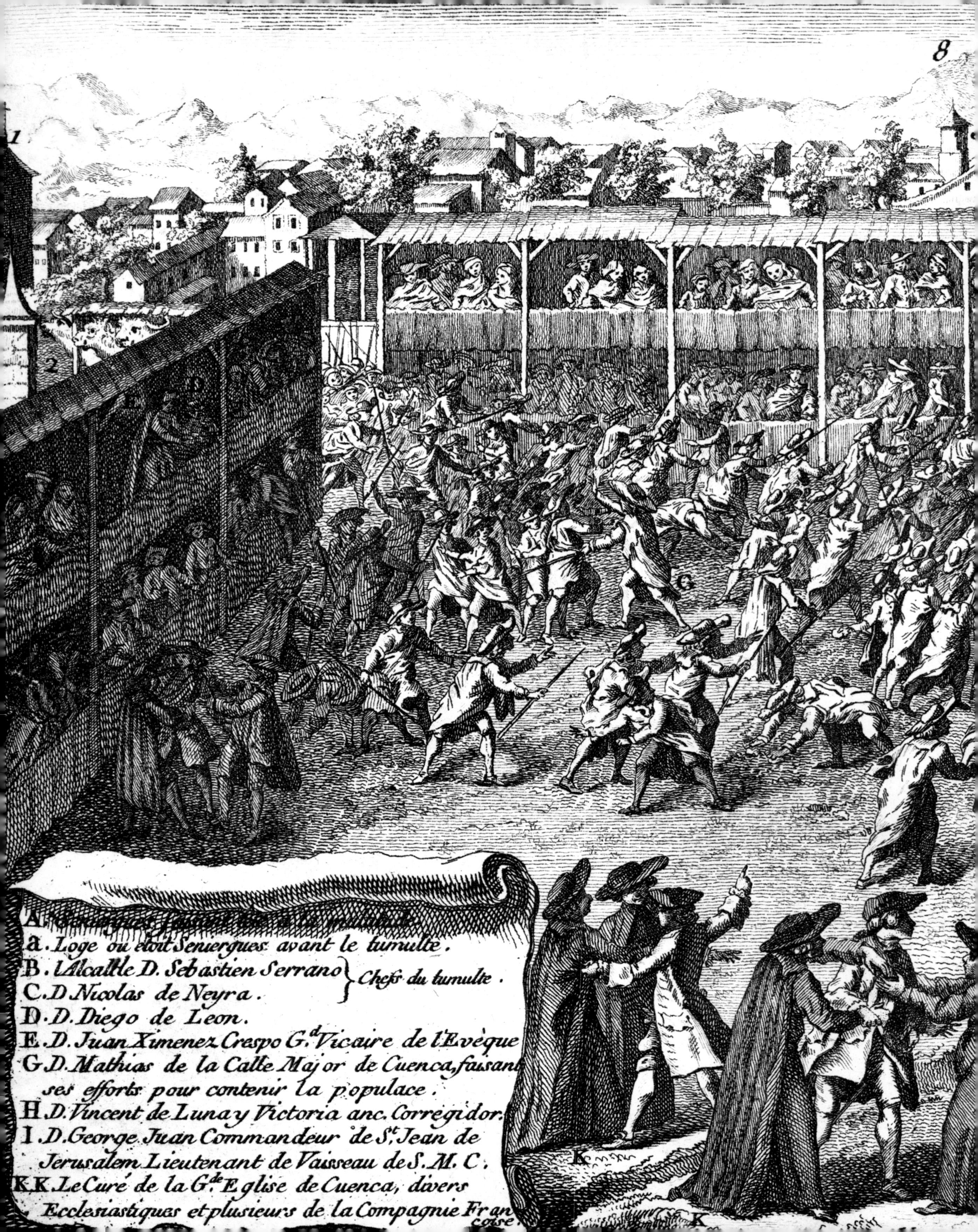

8
1
2
G
A. Seniergues faisant
a. Loge où étoit Seniergues avant le tumulte.
B. l'Alcalde D. Sebastien Serrano } Chefs du tumulte.
C. D Nicolas de Neyra.
D. D. Diego de Leon.
E. D. Juan Ximenez Crespo Gd. Vicaire de l'Evêque
G D. Mathias de la Calle Major de Cuenca, faisant ses efforts pour contenir la populace.
H. D. Vincent de Luna y Victoria anc. Corregidor.
I. D. George Juan Commandeur de St. Jean de Jerusalem Lieutenant de Vaisseau de S. M. C.
K.K. Le Curé de la Gde. Eglise de Cuenca, divers Ecclesiastiques et plusieurs de la Compagnie Françoise
K
K

1. l'Eglise de St Sebastien de Cuenca.
2. Cimetiere de l'Eglise et Parc des Taureaux destinés pour la fête.
3. Eglise principale sur la G.de place de Cuenca.
4. Eglise des Jesuites.
5. Eglise des Dominicains.
6. Eglise des Relig.res de la Conception.
7. Balcon d'une partie des Academiciens François, et de leur Compagnie.
8. Montagnes de Vavalchuma et autres qui bornent l'horizon de Cuenca.

MANNING A PUMP ON BOARD THE FRIGATE 'AUSTRIA' DURING A VOYAGE TO BRAZIL (1817)

The frigate *Austria*, in gala trim, sailed from Trieste in April 1817, carrying the Archduchess Leopoldina of Austria, daughter of the Emperor Francis I, with a large suite, to join her future husband, Dom Pedro, Crown Prince of Brazil, at Rio. The joyful event was also to be marked by the despatch of a scientific expedition to explore some little-known regions in Brazil, so the passengers included, among other distinguished scientists, three Austrian professors, Schott, Natterer and Pohl. When these returned to Vienna they brought with them considerable zoological and botanical spoils gathered in the territory between Bahia and São Paulo, together with hundreds of drawings and water-colours made by the painter Thomas Ender (1793–1875), who accompanied the expedition. As can be seen from these two water-colour sketches, Ender found an inexhaustible source of inspiration for his lively, impromptu style of work before he even left the ship and its company. *Above:* deck-hands on board the *Austria* manning a pump; *right:* one of the many deck concerts that helped to pass the time for the passengers during the eighty-two days of their voyage.

*Overleaf:*

Two Bavarian passengers—the zoologist Johann Baptist von Spix (1781–1826) and the botanist Carl Friedrich Philipp von Martius (1794–1868)—who were travelling on their King's orders, took leave of the Austrians at Rio. Now that the bar-riers erected against foreign explorers in South America were beginning to yield, they were bent on making up for centuries of neglect in this particular sector of their respective sciences. They stayed in Brazil from July 1817 to June 1820 and brought back not only a wealth of geological and ethnographical notes, but collections of specimens intended for the museum at Munich—among them 3,300 animals and 6,500 plants—which were so vast that it took more than a generation to catalogue and arrange them.

Passing through lush green woodland along the Rio Francisco on their way to the Amazon, the chief scene of their investigations, they paused to watch the myriads of birds that peopled some large pools. 'Hundreds of pink spoonbills (*Platalea Agaja, L.*) were standing in long rows on the banks, like troops on parade, or wading slowly forward and hunting diligently with their beaks in the marsh. Great storks—Jaburús and Tujujús (*Ciconia Mycteria Temm.* and *Tantalus Loculator, L.*)—were pacing solemnly by themselves through the deeper water. Flocks of ducks and waterhens were gathered on a little island in the middle of the pool, and innumerable plovers were darting round the fringe of the wood, hunting for insects. All these different species of birds kept up a perpetual cackling, screeching and twittering, and the longer we watched the strange spectacle, the more reluctant we became to disturb the tranquillity of their natural habits by firing a shot among them.'

169

SPIX AND MARTIUS IN THE DEPTHS OF THE AMAZONIAN PRIMEVAL FOREST

◄ A WATERFALL IN THE TROPICAL FOREST. This magnificent scene made an unforgettable impression on the members of the company that sailed round the world with Baron H. Y. P. Florentin de Bougainville in 1824–26. On the southern side of the Corcovado, near Rio de Janeiro, the River Tejuca spills over a cliff and plunges in several falls down a rock-strewn slope walled-in on either side by the green jungle, hurtling against gigantic blocks of stone wrested from the banks by its own tremendous force, to vanish at last into unknown depths. This picture was made by Sabatier from a sketch by E. B. de la Touanne.

*Above:* On 4th October 1819 the two explorers, accompanied by nine Indians, set out from Villa Nova de Rainha, a village of palm-thatched huts below the point where the Rio Mauhé flows into the Amazon. They entered the crepuscular world of the primeval forest where the tree-trunks reminded them of the stone pillars in some vast cathedral; only far above, so high up as to be almost indistinguishable, did boughs and foliage grow out of those huge columns. It seemed as though time had stood still here for thousands of years. Martius reckoned that these Amazonian trees must have been saplings during Christ's lifetime on earth. 'There is more to be found in forests than in books'—the awe-struck explorers soon came to realize the truth of this phrase coined by a Brazilian expert of forest lore. What had once been roots now rose like a kind of buttress to merge with the trunk at the height of a house. The nine Indians, standing with linked hands at the foot of one of these trees, came nowhere near to girdling its 82 feet circumference. On the thickest trunk grew a *Eugenia muricata* with its evergreen leaves; plants of the spadiciflores species were found here and there, together with a *Clusia alba* with its aerial roots, and various other jungle plants. The silence was broken only by the peculiar whirring, gnawing and sawing noises produced by an army of beetles, ceaselessly pursuing their work of destruction.

EXPLORERS LANDING NEAR A VILLAGE OF CARIPUNA INDIANS ON THE RIVER MADEIRA

◄ GEONOMA MULTIFLORA. 'So long as palm-trees are named and known, the name of Martius will be famous', declared Alexander von Humboldt—thinking of the *Historia naturalis palmarum*, published between 1823 and 1850, in which Martius deals with the life of the palm in all parts of the world, but with special reference to South America. It is from that work that we take the illustration on the left, which shows a stemless variety of Geonoma and another with a slender, ringed trunk.

Spix succumbed to the after-effects of tropical fevers only six years after his return to Europe and so published little about the great numbers of animals he had found in South America. But Martius lived to a ripe old age and was able, with the help of a series of collaborators, to garner the full harvest of his travels. These are immortalized in part by the dozens of folio pages of plates and descriptive notes that make up his *Flora Brasiliensis* in which he tried to give a systematic account of Brazilian plant-life in all its aspects. It is a work almost without parallel in botanical literature. Some idea of the quality of its illustrations can be gained from the reproduction given on page 171. Many of them were taken from drawings made by Martius himself.

*Above:* This boat, with its palm-thatched roof, arrived in 1867 bringing Franz Keller-Leuzinger (1835–90), a German engineer and painter, who had been commissioned by the Brazilian Government to discover the exact course followed by the River Madeira and to decide whether a railway line should be built there.

The rowers, with their broad-brimmed straw hats, are Moxos Indians. The forest comes right down to the river bank; orchids grow in clumps on the huge branches, which are hung with curtains of Louisiana Moss *(tillandsia);* palm-trees stand in the shadows, among them the fan-shaped *strelitzia*. Behind the boat are two Indian canoes, each made from a single piece of bark turned up at both ends and laced like a shoe. A jungle path leads down to the brink of the sluggish river; women, children and warriors of the Caripuna tribe stand there waiting for the boat to tie up. This was a period when the Indians were being gradually driven back into the forest, and mistrust was rife. The balance of forces was different now from what it had been in the far-distant days around 1549, when gunner Hans Staden was captured by Indians in Brazil and reluctantly became their first ethnographer (see page 174).

## Gunner Hans Staden among the Brazilian Indians

Little is known of Staden's life before or after his two voyages to Brazil, except that he came of a middle-class family in Hesse. But his experiences among the primitive people of the tropics, in 1547–48 and 1549–54, set him apart.

Gunner Hans Staden related his experiences in his *True Description of a Landscape of the Wild, Naked, Ferocious, Man-eating People, situated in the New World of America*, first published in 1557. The simple, pious tale, often reprinted and translated into many languages, is one of the earliest accounts of Brazil and perhaps the first Indian 'adventure story'. It describes the fears and tribulations of a prisoner who became the hapless author of a 'little classic' of American ethnology. The woodcuts follow the old custom of depicting successive events as though they had happened simultaneously.

1. Staden, serving as a gunner with the Portuguese during his second visit to Brazil, was quartered in a 'fortified house' on the island of Amaro. The Portuguese aim was to hold up the predatory Tupinambas on their way down from their own territory, further north. One day the tribe captured the dangerous warrior (recognizable by his beard) in the forest, stripped off his clothes and carried him away in one of their boats. Staden called imploringly upon God to succour him.

2. After rowing for three days the Indians arrived with their prisoner at their village, Ubatuba, situated not far from the sea, between the present-day cities of Santos and Rio. In accordance with an ancient ritual of torture, he was first beaten by the women and children, who then clipped off his eyebrows, put a feather belt round his waist and led him, dancing at a rope's end, between their long huts. As he pranced along, he was required to call out, in inviting tones, 'Here come I, your victuals!'

3. The prisoner was for many days in constant danger of death. The Indians had already lost several men in fighting against the Portuguese and would be bound sooner or later to take a bloodthirsty revenge on any white man within reach. But one day, when steady rain had been preventing the women from planting manioc in a patch of freshly cleared forest, Staden fell on his knees and prayed for help. The sun broke through the clouds—and from that time on the Indians were afraid of the stranger who had such a marvellous God to help him.

4. The village behind its protective palissade, garnished, as an awful warning, with the skulls of enemies killed in battle.

When about eight months had gone by, the Tupinambas sent their prisoner as a gift to the chief of a tribe in the vicinity of Rio. A French ship anchored there one day; the captain heard about the white captive and succeeded, by employing great eloquence and offering many presents, in procuring his release. After a sea voyage that lasted four months (right), Staden found himself back on European soil, in Normandy.

1

2

3

174

HANS STADEN'S HOMEWARD VOYAGE

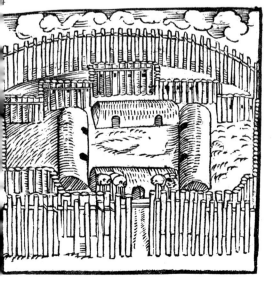

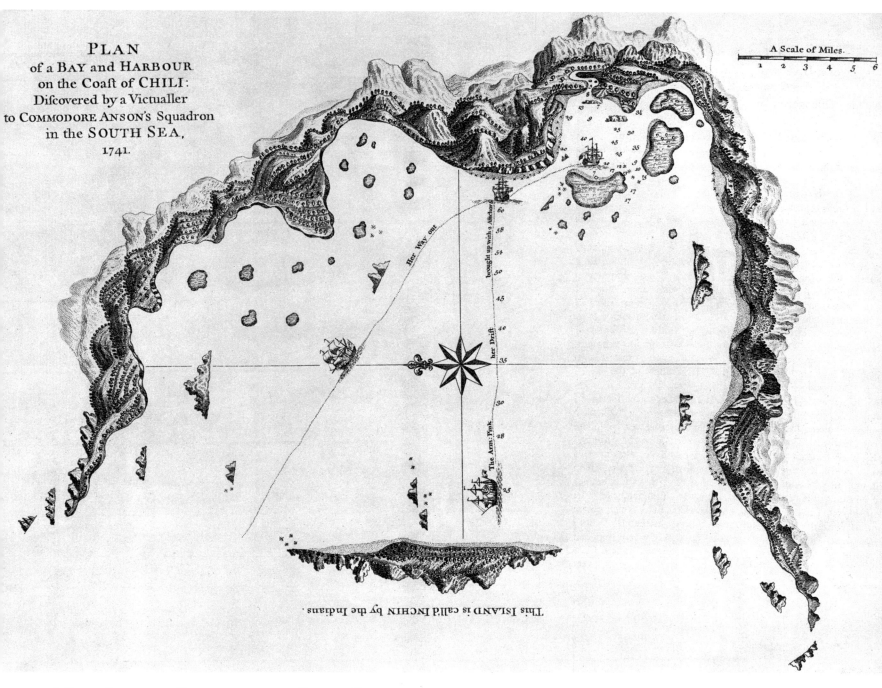

PLAN
of a BAY and HARBOUR
on the Coast of CHILI:
Discovered by a Victualler
to COMMODORE ANSON'S Squadron
in the SOUTH SEA,
1741.

A Scale of Miles.
1 2 3 4 5 6

This ISLAND is call'd INCHIN by the Indians.

A PIRATE SHIP FINDS A HIDING-PLACE ON THE COAST OF CHILE

◄ Two Spanish naval officers were seconded to La Condamine's expedition—Antonio de Ulloa and Jorge Juan. They assembled voluminous notes about the region of the Andes and published them in 1748 under the title of *Relación histórica del viaje á la America meridional*. They give, among others, a detailed description of the method by which the natives used to cross the rivers that rushed down through deep ravines from the cordillera to the Pacific. A thick rope hangs loosely between the double stakes planted on either edge of the cliff. A kind of leather hammock is suspended by two loops. By hauling on the rope, this can be pulled safely across to the further bank. Animals were lashed to a wooden support and secured round the belly.

*Above:* The popular British freebooter George Anson (1697 to 1762) made an interesting addition to the map of South America during a voyage of piracy and exploration he undertook in 1741. In May of that year his victualling ship *Anna Pink*, badly damaged in a storm, was swept past the island of Inchin (near the Chonos archipelago) and driven straight towards the coast of Chile, at the foot of the towering Andes. At the very last moment a passage was found through the rocks, and the company were relieved of all anxiety by finding themselves in a natural haven, well provided with water, wood, game and medicinal herbs. Two months later the vessel sailed out to join Anson's flagship and resume the patriotic sport of 'catching a Spaniard'.

THE 'BEAGLE' AT THE FOOT OF MOUNT SARMIENTO IN TIERRA DEL FUEGO

The *Beagle*, a three-masted vessel of 235 tons burden, equipped with lightning-conductors, ten guns and twenty-four chronometers, had been sent out to investigate the coasts of Patagonia, Chile, and various groups of Pacific islands, and to record time-readings by the chronometer during her progress round the world. She was accompanied by the little schooner *Adventure* whose mission was to map bays and rivers. The *Beagle* was at sea from 27th December 1831 to 2nd October 1836. She has a permanent place in the annals of natural history, for among her company, his cramped quarters barely sufficient for his specimens and books, was the youthful geologist and zoologist Charles Darwin (1809–82), recording daily, in a journal destined to become famous, the impressions he gained from regions so new to him.

His entries for 8th and 9th June 1834 describe the wild, desolate scenery of Cape Turn, at the foot of Mount Sarmiento (7,874 feet). Its snowy peak was swathed in mist, its rocky face descended almost vertically into the sea. From the far-distant heights glaciers flowed down to mingle with the waves—cataracts of blue ice, 'like great, frozen Niagaras'. 'The inanimate works of nature—rock, ice, snow, wind, and water, all warring with each other, yet combined against man—here reigned in absolute sovereignty', declares the journal. The immensity of the landscape made an equally strong impression on young Conrad Martens, a painter of the school of Turner and Cox, who won great praise from Darwin for his work with the expedition.

Darwin made long excursions on land, collecting a vast amount of material for research and developing his genius for creative comparison through this contact with plants, animals and minerals from half the globe. Even before he left the *Beagle* he had tentatively outlined a theory of the variability of species; but more than twenty years of silent study were to elapse before the publication of his book *The Origin of Species* (1859), which presented a new picture of 'this vast and wonderful world', rejected the Christian myth of the Creation, and described nature as a great, consistent drama, determined by the principle of 'natural selection' and proceeding inexorably from the emergence of the different species, through the successive phases of their evolution, to decay and extinction.

*Overleaf:*

Darwin formed an important collection of fossils in South America. In his diary he mentions the megatherium, the mastodon, the toxodon and other extinct animals, and remarks that in earlier epochs the region must have abounded in these enormous creatures. He also raised—at a time when palaeontology was just developing as a science, thanks to Agassiz, Pictet and others—the question of what kind of life had existed on earth before the arrival of man. Behind the picture of the universe brought home by the explorers, a dim, wavering outline of the prehistoric world had begun to take shape. Eleven years before the publication of Darwin's great book, the Viennese botanist Franz Unger (1800–70) who, working along his own lines, had reached similar conclusions to Darwin's about the variability of species, made a bold attempt to reconstruct the appearance of the world during various geological periods in the remote past. On his fanciful expeditions into prehistory he was accompanied by an artist—the painter Joseph Kuwasseg—whose drawings gave visual form to Unger's palaeontological visions.

Our illustration shows a battle between three saurians in a marshy forest during the Wealden period—part of the Middle Ages of prehistory. Ferns rise from cliffs of free stone; cycada ceous plants grow close to the ground or spread over the rocks and tree-trunks—the largest and most decorative of them is *Neuropteris Huttoni*. In the right foreground is a monocotyledonous tree, *Clathraria Lyellii*.

COOK'S FLAGSHIP 'RESOLUTION' ANCHORS IN CHRISTMAS SOUND AT THE END OF DECEMBER 1774

The continent of South America tails off into cold, forlorn rocks. In the background we see a chain of snow-covered mountains in Tierra del Fuego. Some large rocky islands with a growth of scrub yielding a meagre crop of berries, and a few starveling trees and bushes, constitute the furthest outposts, extending into the bleak waters of the Antarctic. James Cook described all this in his journal as 'the most desolate and barren country I ever saw'. But the solitude was enlivened by a number of creatures inured to its climate— gulls, ducks and several varieties of geese, not to mention the great bustard, the only living thing the artist has included in his picture, where it looks like the presiding spirit of the landscape come in disguise to investigate the strange vessel as it lies at anchor in an inlet beside the entrance to Christmas Sound.

Cook, as an experienced seafarer, realized at once that this place offered safe anchorage to ships from far and wide, where they could easily find supplies of fresh water, wood and fish. The name of the Sound commemorates a Gargantuan Christmas dinner on board the *Resolution*. A foraging party had been sent out and returned with a good bag of wild geese. 'Roast and boiled geese, goose-pye, etc., was a treat little known to us, and we had yet some Madeira wine left, which was the only article of our provision that was mended by keeping. So that our friends in England did not, perhaps, celebrate Xmas more cheerfully than we did.'

# The Opening-up of North America

Five hundred years before Columbus the first dim tidings of North America drifted into the Danish court, slipped through men's minds like a phantom vessel in some ancient saga, passed into legend and vanished into oblivion—till all had forgotten that from Iceland and Greenland, the furthest Arctic borders of the medieval world, Viking seafarers and fishermen sailing without the compass had reached the shores of Labrador, Newfoundland or places further south.

The first deliberate attempts to gain a footing in these regions were equally transient. The Portuguese under Cortereal, the English under the two Cabots and the French under Verrazano groped along the coast from Newfoundland to New Jersey without trying to found settlements. The Spanish Conquistadors did the same—with a few exceptions—further south; and the earliest efforts by the French and English to colonize Carolina were unsuccessful. Thus North America, later to be the emigrant's Eldorado, remained in those days the most despised of the continents where the Indians wandered unchallenged over their vast territories, Eskimos lived undisturbed in the snow-bound north, buffaloes roamed the prairie, beavers fished the rivers, and fox, deer and bear lurked in the dense forests.

Rumours of rich fishing-grounds off the north-east coast began to reach the ears of a few Western European fishermen during the sixteenth century, and in the course of their more or less surreptitious voyages they stumbled on a source of profit that was to provide the chief attraction for explorers until well into the eighteenth century. For as well as their booty of fish they brought home furs obtained by barter from the natives, which found a ready market.

This led, in the early seventeenth century, to the rapid and systematic opening-up of North America by French and English trading companies, encouraged by the sovereigns of both countries. The movement maintained its impetus fostered by certain characteristics of the two peoples in question—the cool, tenacious courage of the English and the brilliant verve of the French—until, in the nineteenth century, the great undertakings were completed.

Here the great unknown was summed up by the word 'West', conjuring up vast distances that embraced the rivers, lakes, forests and prairies of the interior and, far beyond them, the alluring coasts of the Pacific —at first believed to lie immediately west of the Mississippi, with China only a short sea-voyage further on. The steady advance into the interior followed two main directions which lay roughly parallel. The French, led by the far-sighted Samuel Champlain, an official of the Rouen trading company, started from the St. Lawrence and made their way from river to river and lake to lake until they were beyond Lake Michigan; they also turned south and explored the whole course of the Mississippi. The English advance was further north, across Labrador and Hudson Bay to the Coppermine River and finally to the Mackenzie River in north-west Canada; in their case the driving force was the Hudson Bay Company. The greatest feat was achieved in 1793 by a Scot, Alexander Mackenzie, who crossed the Rocky Mountains and reached the Pacific, establishing the first northern overland connection between the east and west coasts of the vast continent and between the world's two broadest oceans. The French and English set up an extensive network of forts and warehouses from the east coast to the Rockies—a range whose name, even on a modern map, seems touched with glamour by the exploits of those who first set eyes on it.

The story of North American exploration is inseparably bound up with the figures we meet in the pages of Fenimore Cooper, the daring pioneers—forest rangers, itinerant fur-traders and trappers—who pushed so steadily westwards into unknown territory.

While these great discoveries were being pursued in a westerly direction across the continent the British, after a few setbacks, were consolidating their New England colonies. In the course of the eighteenth century new features were added to the map of America's north-west coast by the Spaniards, the Russians, and most of all by an Englishman, Vancouver; and during the 1830s the long Arctic seaboard was explored, chiefly by Sir John Franklin's expedition, during which many lives were lost. Meanwhile there was intermittent warfare between rival tribes of Indians, between Indians and white men, and between the English and the French. In 1763 Canada fell to the English, in 1776 the young United States declared their independence. But exploration continued with undiminished vigour, collaterally with and regardless of political developments, and its aim grew steadily clearer—to secure this wonderful land of milk and honey as the home of a new, free race. President Jefferson fully realized the affinity between the feelings and outlook of the new American citizens and those of the pioneers, and went so far as to raise two civil servants—his private secretary, Lewis, and a Lieutenant Clark—to the dignity of explorers by sending them to find a route from the upper Missouri across the Rockies to the Pacific through western regions that were still largely unknown.

The warmest expression of fellow-feeling for explorers came from an American poet—Walt Whitman, who broke the bounds of conventional verse forms and wrote poems that had the breadth and surge of the sea. He was well fitted to describe the colourful abundance of the newly discovered continent and the feats of those who were blazing trails across it from ocean to ocean. He saw America as the cradle of the new, democratic nation of the future, which would for ever retain the impetus first given by the pioneers and explorers, perpetually moving, as it were, towards a 'Far West' that had long ceased to be a purely geographical concept. A nation that had set its sights high, and which would ultimately encompass all that was great and precious in the ancient traditions of Europe and Asia as well. Thus, he felt, Columbus's daring dream of building a bridge between Europe and Asia would come true at last.

### The Voyage of St. Brandan (I)

It is generally assumed that the Vikings were the first Europeans to set foot in North-East America, where they arrived in or about the year 1000. But in point of fact the Norsemen were undoubtedly preceded—at any rate in Iceland—by seafarers from Ireland, who forestalled them by more than two hundred years. These were Irish monks for whom the sea voyage was a pious venture, a supreme act of renunciation. They were seeking for remote islands on which to live as hermits, withdrawn into undisturbed communion with God. It is not improbable that one or another of them may have been driven on to the American coast.

Ireland had been converted to Christianity in the fifth century, and hermits quite soon began to resort to islands, there to live in contemplative asceticism. Dicuil, the Irish geographer, even declares that there were Celtic hermits on Iceland in 795. Christian legend wove its wondrous tales around these solitaries, who incidentally were explorers as well, adding themes from Celtic fairy-tales about the distant Islands of the Blessed and details from Nordic seafarers' sagas. The most hazardous adventures were attributed to the Irish abbot, St Brandan (480–577). A number of marvellous natural phenomena, such as icebergs and arctic volcanoes, were introduced to heighten the supernatural atmosphere surrounding his travels.

The elaborated Latin form of the legend—the *Navigatio Sancti Brandani*—made its way across to Europe as early as the eleventh century; French, Flemish, Norwegian, Italian and German translations were made in the course of time. A popular version, in prose, was among the favourite reading-matter in Germany in Gutenberg's day. This is preserved in the Heidelberg Codex pal. germ. 60, from which our illustrations are taken. In 1927 Richard Benz made it available to present-day readers in a free adaptation, incorporating the passage from the *Navigatio* which describes the Island of Smiths.

*Above:*

On one occasion the ship in which St Brandan and his twelve monks were travelling was blown into the Sea of Glue, where many vessels lay stuck fast, their crews dying on board. Here the supernatural became intermingled with the wonders of nature: the monks heard the bitter wailing of great numbers of souls which were being carried off by the devil; only three virtuous spirits were found, and those were borne away to heaven by the Archangel Michael.

*Below:*

In the far north they came to a stony island without a leaf or a blade of grass. Sailing closer, they saw a noisy party of smiths working at a blazing forge. One misshapen creature, with flames darting from his body, ran down to the shore with threatening gestures, carrying a huge lump of red-hot iron in a pair of tongs. He hurled this at the ship, but it fell into the sea which began to hiss, bubble and steam. St. Brandan made the sign of the cross and bade his companions row away as hard as they could, for the smiths were now swarming down to the beach, throwing their fire-balls at the ship, and the air was thick with clamour, steam and stench; hell had identified the hostile vessel. The exhausted monks had much ado to make their escape. They had come close to the gate of hell—or to one of the Icelandic volcanoes.

## THE VOYAGE OF ST. BRANDAN (II)

*Above:*

After eight years of tossing on the waves, far from their native Ireland, St. Brandan and his companions landed on a delightful island where the trees were always green, the air balmy and the springs of water cool. They climbed a strange mountain and came to a plot of greensward with a fountain playing in its midst. Drinking vessels and a golden pitcher hung in a tree beside the fountain, birds sang among the branches, and the choicest food lay ready on a table. The inhabitants of this paradise had men's bodies, but pigs' heads and dogs' paws. They were the angels who, when Satan rebelled against God, had been apathetic and neutral, serving neither God nor the devil. Now, with this carefree land for their home, they lived in the direst distress, for they might never look upon the face of God.

*Below:*

In the ninth year of their voyage the Saint and his company were encircled for forty days by the body of a huge fish, which held its tail in its mouth. Their vessel was in sore peril, for it was the usual frail craft of the Middle Ages—rudderless, steered only by an oar, with a small quarterdeck and a single mast, broad in the beam and always liable to capsize in a storm. Soon after this experience they reached home again and were welcomed with joy. During the voyage St. Brandan had written their marvellous adventures in a book which he now carried into his monastery. The monks followed him in and laid the book on the altar of the Virgin Mary. 'Then they heard the voice of God, speaking words of welcome to him and saying: "If it be thy desire, Brandan, now mayst thou come unto me." Then St. Brandan made him ready to hear Mass, and right piously did he partake thereof and sing. And when Mass was over, and he had spoken the blessing, St. Brandan vanished from before the altar and bore up his soul to God.'

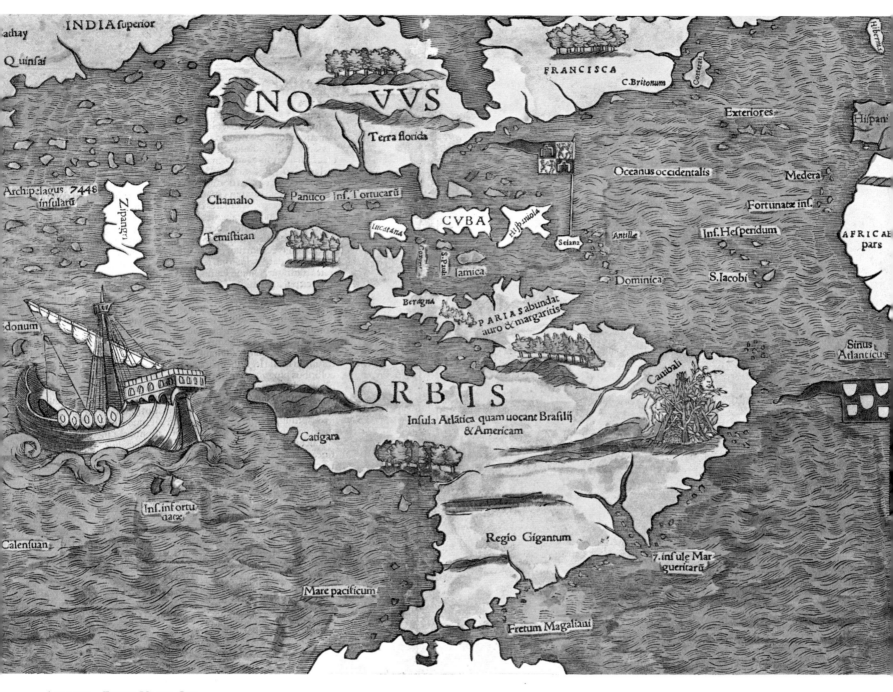

The map image contains the following labels:

INDIA superior
athay
Quinsai
Archipelagus 7448 insularū
Zipangri
Chamaho
Temistitan
donum
Inf. infortunacæ
Calensuan
Mare pacificum

NO VVS

Terra florida

FRANCISCA
C. Britonum
Cortezu
Exteriores
Hispani
Oceanus occidentalis
Medera
Fortunatæ inf.
Inf. Hesperidum
AFRICÆ pars

Panuco Inf. Tortucarū
lucatana
CVBA
Hiſpaniola
Seiana
Antille

Cozumel
S. Pauli
S. Pauli
Iamica
Dominica
S. Iacobi

Beragna
PARIAS abundat auro & margaritis

ORBIS

Catigara
Insula Atlātica quam uocant Brasilij & Americam

Canibali
Sinus Atlanticus

Regio Gigantum
7. insule Margueritarū

Fretum Magaliani

AMERICA—FORTY YEARS OLD

The cartographer Sebastian Münster (1489–1552) lagged behind most other map-makers of his day in the technical clumsiness of his wood-engraved maps and his neglect of scientific and mathematical methods. But he had an unusual gift for absorbing and passing on the latest information brought home by the explorers who were then pressing hard on one another's heels. Thus, though the ship he shows on the left side of his map is still of the old-fashioned late medieval type, he reveals a very accurate knowledge of the discoveries made in Central America, despite the exaggerated dimensions he gives to that region. He still believes Yucatan to be an island, but he has already heard of little 'Dominica' in the West Indies. Acquaintance with reports on the first voyage round the world is indicated by his marking the mouth of the River Plate, the land of the Patagonian giants *(Regio*

*Gigantum)* and the Straits of Magellan. The bay he shows in the north was discovered *before* the time of Hudson, whose name it now bears; Münster seems inclined to mistake it for a waterway cutting almost right across north America. Zipangu (Japan), the archipelago of 7448 Pacific islands, and 'Catay' (China) with the city of Quinsay marked in it, all known from Marco Polo, lie close to the west coast of America, like vestiges of Columbus's great dream. Münster indicates the division of the world decreed in the Treaty of Tordesillas, by showing the Spanish flag to the west and the Portuguese flag to the east of an invisible line in his picture.

The first version of this map (without the ship) appeared in Münster's *Novus Orbis* (1532), forty years after Columbus landed on Guanahani; this coloured copy is taken from Münster's new edition of Ptolemy, published in 1540.

I. First Penetrations into Carolina. A. The French discover Broad River in 'Florida' (Carolina)

After their highly profitable conquests in Central and South America, the Spaniards left the east coast of the continent, from Florida northwards, uncolonized and unguarded. In 1562 the French Court, advised by Admiral Coligny—a Huguenot and therefore anti-Spanish and anti-Catholic—sent two ships to gather information about this neglected strip of coast. The commander of the expedition, Jean Ribaut, reported with amazed enthusiasm on this 'peerless land, as yet untouched by the plough'. The French anchored near the mouth of what is now Broad River, and named the spot Port Royal *(Portus Regalis)*. They sailed up the river in a small boat, through forests of oak, cedar and other trees; maize was stacked in the shade of the trees, the scene was enlivened by glimpses of deer and turkeys. Vines bore grapes of unprecedented size. A few natives who were roasting a young wolf on a wooden spit took to flight; but they showed no sign of hostility. There was even rumoured to be gold

and silver in the Appalachians. But the dream of establishing a *douce France* in this region came to nothing. The first settlers backed out, and Fort Caroline, built in 1564 at the mouth of May River, was captured only a year later by the Spaniards who had become aware of the threat to their sea communications.

The attempts made by the Huguenots to colonize 'Florida' and the first efforts of the Englishman John White to establish a settlement in North Carolina (see page 190) were alike doomed to failure. But they served to guide others, such as the New England Puritans in 1620, who came to these new lands armed with greater physical and moral energy. They also yielded much new information, particularly as each expedition was accompanied by an artist who took part in the historical events. The French in 1564 had Jacques Le Moyne as their cartographer, and John White, the leader of the English expedition, made his own pictorial records.

B. The French build Fort Caroline at the Mouth of May River (now St. John's River), 1564

Everyone joined in the work—aristocrats and sailors, craftsmen and soldiers, white men and Indians—felling trees, digging a moat, piling the soil into embankments and putting up dwellings and store-houses. At the first attempt they built the houses too high and they were blown down by a series of storms. So then they kept their buildings low. The bakery stood on the left bank of the river, at a safe distance from the living-quarters with their highly inflammable palmleaf thatch. But this disciplined architecture was not matched by self-discipline among the settlers. As time went by a number of Europeans deserted, and the friendly relations that had been established with the Indian chiefs were destroyed in many cases by the colonists' rapacious demands for gold.

It is clear that in this instance the engraver has allowed himself a certain artistic licence.

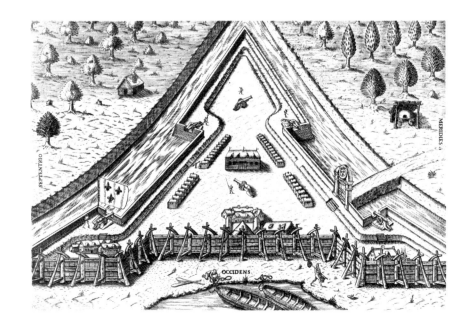

189

C. How the Indians of South Carolina hunted Alligators—according to Jacques Le Moyne

The Indians used to put up watch-posts on the river bank—huts with many peep-holes in their walls. When the watchman gave the alarm, the hunters came hurrying and tried, with their united strength, to drive a long, sharp-pointed stake far down the animal's gullet. By this means they forced it on to its back and then belaboured the soft belly with clubs and shot arrows into it until the creature was dead.

D. *Page 191:* The Indian Village of Secota on the Pamlico River as John White saw it. In the second half of the sixteenth century England, too, began to put out feelers across the ocean. Elizabeth I found eager crews for her stripling fleet among an aristocracy yearning for activity, a merchant class bent upon world-wide trade, and an under-employed peasantry. Courtiers such as Sir Humphrey Gilbert and his half-brother Walter Raleigh fitted out expeditions and fixed the first targets, which included the east coast of North America. The first attempts to found colonies were made in 1584 and 1587 on the island of Roanoke, in what is now North Carolina; both expeditions were sent out by Raleigh, the second under the leadership of John White. They failed because they had with them too many adventurers lusting for gold and too few genuine colonists. It was not until 1607 that a durable settlement was established, on James river. However, the first abortive attempts produced an immortal piece of ethnographical description—White's report and his water-colour illustrations to it. To the latter belongs this delightful bird's-eye view of Secota, which shows everyday happenings and festive events in a kind of Indian Lilliput. Tobacco plants and sunflowers grow in many gardens (E); there is a pumpkin-bed (I); maize is sprouting, carefully planted out (H); thickets are left as game reserves (top, left). A watchman (F) is stationed to scare the birds out of the maize-fields by making a din. There is a special place for festivities, where the inhabitants meet to dance, waving rattles made from gouds (C), after which they gather for a feast (D). K is a place reserved for council meetings; a fire burns there. B is a place of prayer; A is the chiefs' burial-place, L a river.

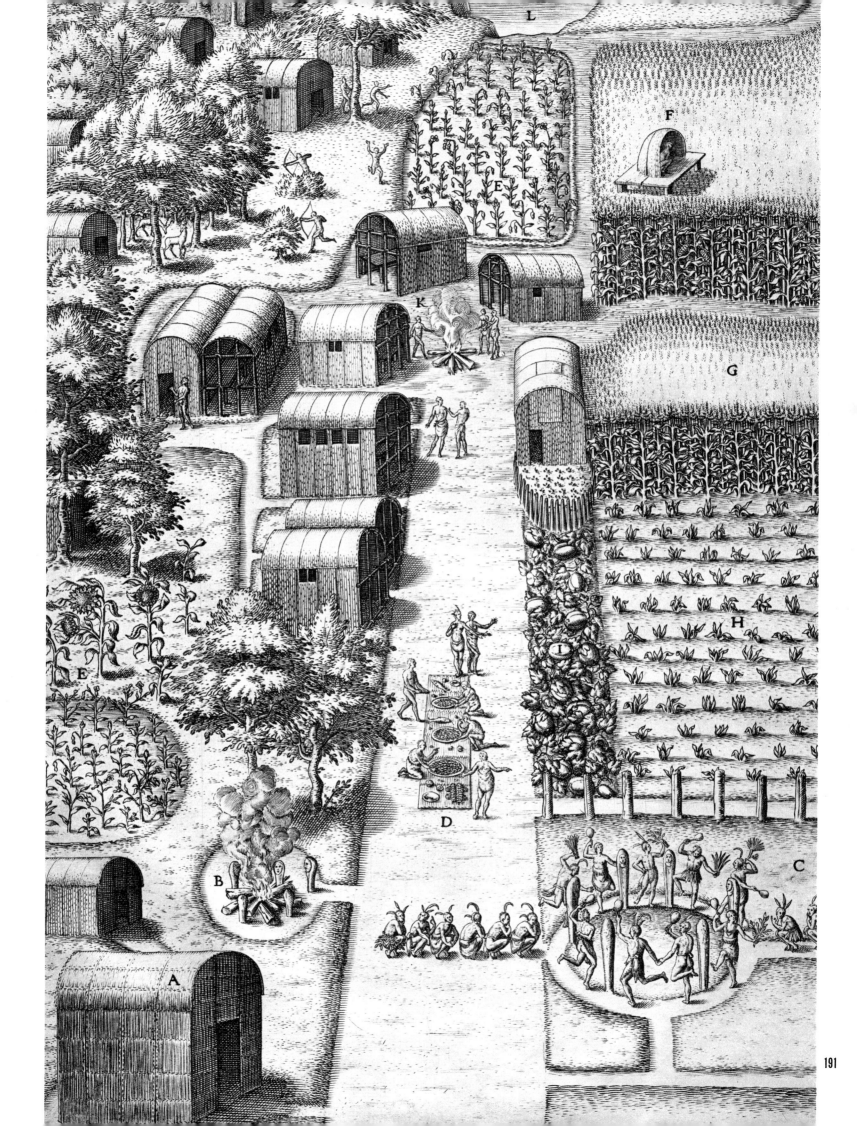

II. Advancing from the St. Lawrence and Hudson Bay to the Pacific. A. Hennepin and two Companions taken Prisoners by the Sioux

*Above:* In 1679–82 the intrepid Belgian Franciscan friar Louis Hennepin, with two companions, travelled down the Mississippi to a point approximately below the present-day Memphis. He was sent by Cavalier de La Salle, who was haunted by the vision of a powerful French colonial empire extending right to the mouth of the great river, and followed in the footsteps of Father Marquette, the Jesuit who had gone as far as Arkansas. Hennepin and his company fell into the hands of the Sioux, who took them by boat, in great discomfort, to their own territory on the upper Mississippi. The redskins stole the missionary's vestments; they left untouched a chest which, to their disappointment, contained only books and papers; they came to blows over a few rolls of tobacco; and they covered their eyes before a chalice that glittered in the sunshine, because they took it to be inhabited by a spirit. During the months that elapsed before the group was released, Hennepin mastered the Sioux language.

*Next page:* Samuel Champlain (1567–1635), the founder of Quebec, gave a stirring definition of the qualities needed by an explorer in North America. He declared that only those who would plight themselves body and soul to the country, settle down in it and learn from its first inhabitants, were destined to open up its unknown regions. One such was Hennepin, the Franciscan friar who gazed in 1679 at Niagara —discovered only a year earlier—and beyond it into enticing, unexplored territory towards Lake Erie. The tremendous Falls, with their thundering waters (the man on the left has his hands over his ears), are like nothing else in the world; far below and far above them the current is already so swift that, as the doughty monk relates, travellers by canoe were obliged to lift their boats out of the water and carry them along the zigzag path seen to the left of the Falls. Hennepin spent many happy years among the Indians, teaching them, learning from them and exploring their country.

B. The Earliest View of Niagara. (After Hennepin)

*Overleaf:* C. Lake Athabaska in North-Western Canada, January 1772. It is situated on a stretch of land levelled out by the glaciers of several Ice Ages, and covered with moorland, tundra, forest, lakes and rivers that made it the Eldorado of the animal world. There is nothing to break the force of the arctic winds, and the lakes are frozen thick in the long winter months. The English merchant-explorer Samuel Hearne saw a host of islands lying before him here, and he took delight in sketching the delicate tracery of fir, poplar and birch against the grey wintry sky. At the same time he noted with sober satisfaction that these waters were full of trout, pike, perch and barbel, and that all kinds of fur-bearing animals swarmed on the dry land. He had been sent out from Fort Churchill by the Hudson Bay Company to report on the region lying between Hudson Bay and the Coppermine river.—Lake Athabaska was also a point touched at by the explorers who made their way north-westwards from Montreal and the Great Lakes. As early as 1734 La Vérendrye's sons had penetrated in this direction as far as the vicinity of Lake Winnipeg. After the French lost Canada to England in 1763, the British set a tremendous pace in the exploration of the unknown western territories towards the Rocky Mountains. Hearne noted in his journal that the American continent was much more extensive than people had supposed. Alexander Mackenzie (1763–1820), the Scotsman who was the first to cross the vast expanse from coast to coast (in 1793), established his base camp on Lake Athabaska (see page 197). Before setting out for the Pacific he admitted to being somewhat overwhelmed by the magnitude of his task—which was to link the world's two mightiest oceans by a land route stretching right across North America, so that the products of America itself and of the other continents might find easier and speedier passage to and fro than the Straits of Magellan could offer.

193

D. Furs were the Most Highly-prized Product of North America in the First Centuries of its Discovery

A *battue* among the Iroquois, described by Samuel Champlain, who gave the decisive impetus to the exploration of Canada. The Indians, yelling and striking animal bones together to make a noise, drove the game into the space formed by two convergent stockades closed in at the narrower end by a fence behind which the hunters, armed with spears and arrows, waited for their prey. The Iroquois also used baited traps in which the animal ran itself into a sling fastened to the down-bent branch of a tree; the jerk released the branch, the animal was swung into the air and was thus easily captured.

# An Adventure during the first Crossing of the Rocky Mountains. From Alexander Mackenzie's Diary

*13th June 1793 (a little beyond the spot where the waters in a wild mountain region began to flow westwards, towards the Pacific):*

At an early hour of this morning the nine men began to cut a road, in order to carry the 26 feet long canoe and lading beyond the rapid, and by seven they were ready. That business was soon effected, and the canoe reladen, to proceed with the current, which ran with great rapidity. A small group continued walking on shore.

We pushed off, and had proceeded but a very short way when the canoe struck, and notwithstanding all our exertions, the violence of the current was so great as to drive her sideways down the river, and break her by the first bar, when I instantly jumped into the water and the men followed my example. But before we could set her straight, or stop her, we came to deeper water, so that we were obliged to re-embark with the utmost precipitation. One of the men who was not sufficiently active was left to get on shore in the best manner in his power.

We had hardly regained our situations when we drove against a rock which shattered the stern of the canoe in such a manner that it held only by the gunwales, so that the steersman could no longer keep his place. The violence of this stroke drove us to the opposite side of the river, which is but narrow, when the bow met with the same fate as the stern. At this moment the foreman seized on some branches of a small tree in the hope of bringing up the canoe, but such was their elasticity that, in a manner not easily described, he was jerked on shore in an instant, and with a degree of violence that threatened his destruction.

But we had no time to turn from our own situation to inquire what had befallen him; for in a few moments we came across a cascade which broke several large holes in the bottom of the canoe The wreck becoming flat on the water, we all jumped out and held fast to it; to which fortunate resolution we owed our safety, as we should otherwise have been dashed against the rocks by the force of the water, or driven over the cascades.

In this condition we were forced several hundred yards, and every yard on the verge of destruction; but at length we most fortunately arrived in shallow water and a small eddy, where we were enabled to make a stand, from the weight of the canoe resting on the stones rather than from any exertions of our exhausted strength...

We called to the people who had meanwhile walked on shore to come to our assistance, and they immediately obeyed the summons. The foreman, however, was the first with us. He had escaped unhurt from the extraordinary jerk with which he was thrown out of the boat, and just as we were beginning to take our effects out of the water, he appeared to give his assistance.

Our two Indian companions on shore, when they saw our deplorable situation, instead of making the least effort to help us, sat down and gave vent to their tears. I was on the outside of the canoe, where I remained till everything was got on shore, in a state of great pain from the extreme cold of the water, so that at length it was with difficulty I could stand.

The loss was considerable and important, for it consisted of our whole flock of bullets, and some of our furniture; but these considerations were forgotten in the impressions of our miraculous escape. Our first inquiry was after the absent man, whom in the first moment of danger we had left to get on shore, but in a short time his appearance removed our anxiety...

All the different articles were now spread out to dry. The powder had fortunately received no damage, and all my instruments had escaped. Indeed, when my people began to recover from their alarm and to enjoy a sense of safety, some of them, if not all, were by no means sorry for our late misfortune, from the hope that it must put an end to our voyage, particularly as we were without a canoe, and all the bullets sunk in the river...

I listened to the observations that were made on the occasion without replying to them, till their panic was dispelled and they had got themselves warm and comfortable, with a hearty meal, and rum enough to raise their spirits.

I then addressed them by recommending them all to be thankful for their late very narrow escape. I also stated that the navigation was not impracticable in itself, but from our ignorance of its course, and that our late experience would enable us to pursue our voyage with greater security. I brought to their recollection that I did not deceive them, and that they were made acquainted with the difficulties and dangers they must expect to encounter before they engaged to accompany me. I also urged the honour of conquering disasters, and the disgrace that would attend them on their return home without having attained the object of the expedition. Nor did I fail to mention the courage and resolution which was the peculiar boast of the Northmen; and that I depended on them, at that moment, for the maintenance of their character. I quieted their apprehension as to the loss of the bullets by bringing to their recollection that we still had shot from which they might be manufactured. I at the same time acknowledged the difficulty of restoring the wreck of the canoe, but confided in our skill and exertion to put it in such a state as would carry us on to where we might procure bark, and build a new one.

In short, my harangue produced the desired effect, and a very general assent appeared, to go wherever I should lead the way.

From Alexander Mackenzie, *Voyages on the River St. Lawrence and through the continent of North America to the Frozen and Pacific Oceans* (1801).

GEORGE VANCOUVER

Along the west coast of North America all was quiet for a long time. It was an artificial quiet, under cover of which the Spaniards were moving up from California and the Russians down from the Aleutian Islands, drawing closer to one another in the search for bases that would help them to extend their trade empires. The rest of the world learnt of this with astonishment in 1784, through Cook's report on his voyage of exploration in the North Pacific. He shook the English and the leaders of the young United States out of their complacent apathy, urging them to find out as rapidly as possible what belonged to whom and to discover, at long last, the exact contours of the coastline and the way in which its different sections joined up.

On Cook's last two voyages a young Englishman named George Vancouver had travelled with him. In 1791 the English sent Vancouver, with two ships, to chart the course of the west coast. He completed the task in four years. With diplomatic assistance, Spain was admonished to keep within the borders of California; the nonoccupied coast was declared to be free of access to all; and Vancouver surveyed the entire stretch, meticulously and conscientiously, from latitude 30 degrees to latitude 60 degrees. The work took him far into the north, to the rocky shores, wooded mountains and great snow-capped peaks beyond which the seafarers could sense the boundless forests and prairies that spanned the continent like another ocean, still largely unexplored. Before Vancouver's survey was completed Mackenzie's bold east-west expedition had already set out from Lake Athabaska; and in 1805 a second party, led by Lewis and Clark, reached the mouth of the Columbia river, further to the south, up which Vancouver had sailed for a considerable distance.

III. Exploration of America's Western and Northern Borders. A. George Vancouver discovers Eddystone Island

The scene depicted above lies to the north of Vancouver Island, not far from Point Nelson. When Vancouver's big ships could not make their way through some maze of islands lying close inshore he would send out a well-equipped gig, fitted with an auxiliary sail and carrying enough provisions for several weeks, to investigate the unknown bays and channels. It was thus that on 9th August 1793, travelling up a narrow inlet, he came to a rock that looked from a distance like a ship in full sail. Pine trees and many different shrubs were growing in its clefts. It reminded Vancouver of the Eddystone Rock near Plymouth, and he gave it the name of New Eddystone. He wrote that they breakfasted at its foot and were visited by unarmed natives who landed from canoes. A week later they were back on board the flagship.

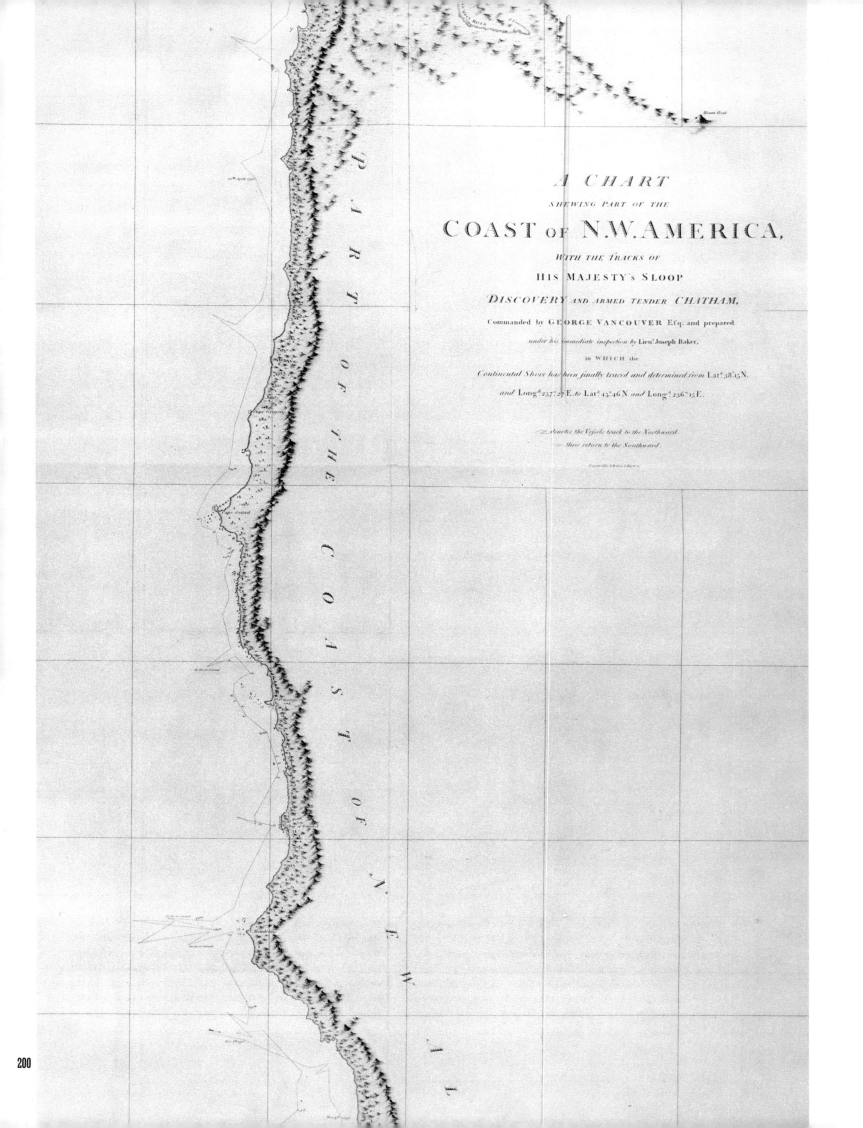

A CHART

SHEWING PART OF THE

COAST OF N.W. AMERICA,

WITH THE TRACKS OF

HIS MAJESTY's SLOOP

DISCOVERY AND ARMED TENDER CHATHAM,

Commanded by GEORGE VANCOUVER Esq. and prepared

under his immediate inspection by Lieut Joseph Baker,

in WHICH the

Continental Shore has been finally traced and determined from Latd 38°15 N.

and Longd 237°27 E. to Latd 43°46 N. and Longd 236°15 E.

⟶ denotes the Vessels track to the Northward.

⟶ their return to the Southward.

C. A Russian Trading Settlement on Norfolk Sound near the North American Coast

◄ B. Part of the West Coast of North America, showing all the promontories and bays and some mountain stretches; at sea, but never far from land, Vancouver, the conscientious surveyor, has traced his course and noted the figures of the soundings he took. This is the New Albion section, extending northwards from the vicinity of San Francisco to the mouth of the Columbia. The long, narrow strip of familiar ground between the trackless expanse on the right and the vast ocean on the left is depicted with as much care as though the map-maker had been working for some historical diploma, and the result is full of charm. Months would pass here without a ship being sighted, and weeks without a human being appearing on the beach. Some of the names remind us of Vancouver's passion for identifying any feature that was at all striking, even on a comparatively neglected stretch of coast. Discovery Bay was named after his flagship, Hazel Point because hazel bushes grew thickly there . . .

As the eighteenth century drew to a close it became a matter of common knowledge that Russian fur-traders and agents of the Tsar had followed the tracks of Bering (see page 106) to Alaska and were now working their way south down the American coast. They set up trading posts such as the one shown above, as far as Vancouver Island. Gregory Shelekov, a trader whose will-power drove all before him, became known as the 'Russian Columbus'. In 1798 his monopoly was transformed into the Russian-American Company directed by Alexander Baranov.—In the foreground of the picture the fort stands on a mound, the flag with the Russian Eagle flying above it; on the right, outside the fortifications, are the baths and the craftsmen's living-quarters. To the left, on the point projecting into the sea are warehouses, in front of them the landing-stage. Here the skins of beaver, seal, bear and otter were loaded into ships, to be sold at fantastically high prices on the western side of the same ocean.

D. The Second East-West Transcontinental Thrust across the Rockies: Lewis and Clark on the Columbia River (1805)

The flag is an important feature of this picture: it proudly displays a circle of thirteen stars, one for each of the States that in 1803 had taken over from Napoleon the territory between the Mississippi and the Rockies. In 1804 President Jefferson had sent out an expedition to discover the best route, by mountain passes and waterways, from the Missouri to the Pacific Ocean, and to incidentally assert the title of the young States to a stretch of that coast. Both leaders wear Indian dress (Lewis is standing), and in the boat with them sits Sacajave, a most helpful member of the Shoshone tribe whose territory included the mountain passes that white men were now to cross for the first time. In front of her is her baby son. The laughing Negro behind them is Clark's servant, York.—After an extremely arduous journey the party reached the mouth of the Columbia River, and by mid-August they were back on the upper Missouri.

E. *Right:* PROSPECTORS. Many pioneers followed in the tracks of Lewis and Clark, to look for hunting grounds and stake mineral claims. Routes for migration and trading were established. In Colorado, with its wealth of mineral ores, these prospectors spared neither man nor beast in their fortune-hunting, which was a kind of small-scale exploration.

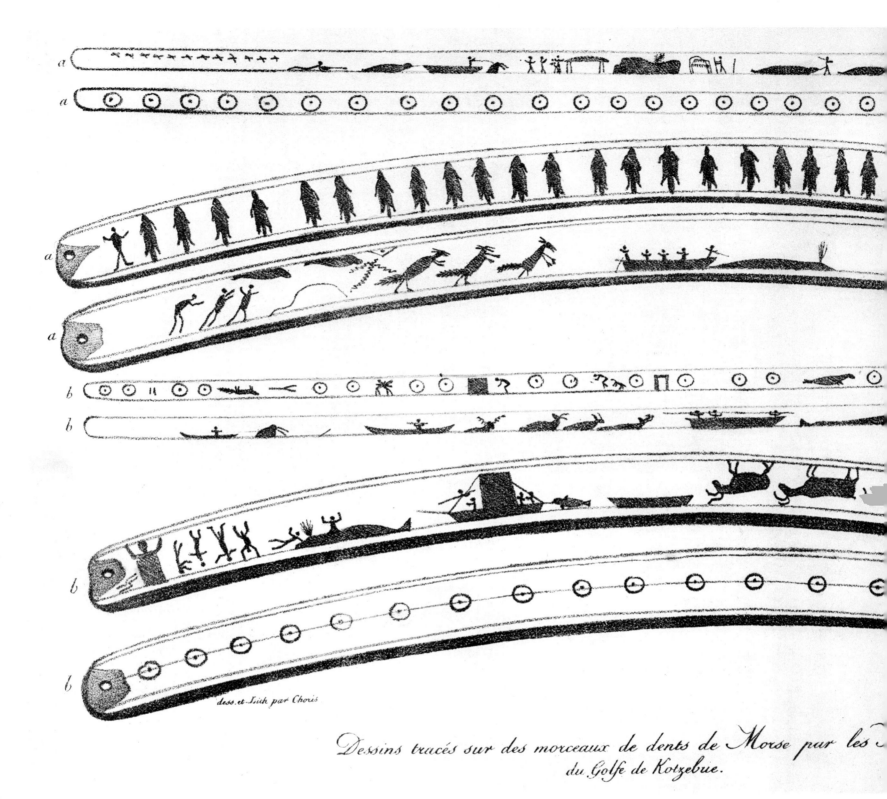

*a*

*a*

*a*

*a*

*b*

*b*

*b*

*b*

*dess. et Lith par Choris*

*Dessins tracés sur des morceaux de dents de Morse par les du Golfe de Kotzebue.*

F. Eskimo Life depicted on Walrus-tusks—a Find in the Vicinity of Kotzebue Sound

In 1815 Otto von Kotzebue, then in Russian service, was despatched to investigate the possibility of a northerly route to the east, across the Bering Strait, and to spend the winter season in collecting geographical and ethnological data on some of the islands the Dutch had discovered in the South Pacific. The journey was cut short in 1818, because the leader developed tuberculosis. It had achieved its best results in Alaska, discovering the great Sound that now bears Kotzebue's name. The poet Adelbert von Chamisso sailed with the *Rurik* to undertake research on natural history. He later published a selection of notes on the subject, and a journal which has a permanent place in German literature.

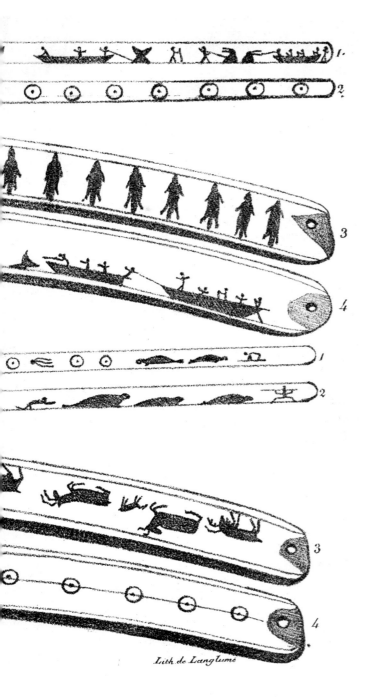

Lith de Langlumé

tans

*Left:* Two pieces of walrus tusk, on all four sides of which an Eskimo artist has illustrated scenes from the life of the 'Americans' (as the Eskimoes were often called in those days). 1 (a), to left and right, shows seal and walrus hunts (the walrus can be identified by its long tusks); in the middle we see equipment for drying fish. 3 (a) displays a handsome row of fox-skins; the foxes themselves, with their bushy tails, are to be seen on 4 (a), to the left of centre, looking like animals from some fable. To the right, whales are being hunted by boat; one of them is blowing. On 3 (b) a sailing boat is towing the catch home; on the left some Eskimoes, in festive mood, are merrily turning somersaults. A herd of reindeer can be seen arriving on the right.

G. AN ELABORATELY CARVED PIPE from Queen Charlotte Island off the north-west coast of America—also brought back by von Kotzebue's expedition

205

H. JOHN FRANKLIN'S EXPEDITION MAKES A PORTAGE TO AVOID SOME RAPIDS

While in the east, west and south and in many parts of the interior the map of North America was being steadily completed, long stretches of the endless Arctic coastline were still wrapped in mystery. Apart from Hudson Bay and the route that led to it, little was known, as late as 1800, except about the mouths of the Mackenzie and Coppermine rivers and the northern corner of Alaska. The map of this bleak coastal region remained very incomplete until, in 1818, the English resumed the search for the North-West Passage (see page 347) and began to weave their way through the labyrinth of the Arctic islands. From 1819 to 1822—except when winter confined his party to a fort—John Franklin was exploring this region with the help of four Englishmen, sixteen French

Canadians and ten Red Indians. Only nine men returned to York Factory, in Hudson Bay, from an appalling journey of 4,870 miles; the others had died, mostly from hunger, cold or exhaustion.

*Above:* In September 1819, a month after the expedition set out, Franklin's party is dragging its heavy boat—built for coastal waters—along the bank of Trout river to avoid some rapids. The river pours foaming over rocks to Lake Knee, 16 feet below. Three such portages had to be made that day, during which the party travelled only three miles. In the evening, worn out, they reached their shelter—a ruined building, once a depot of the Hudson Bay Company.

I. The Stone Indians catching Bison in the Winter

Franklin witnessed this scene in the neighbourhood of his winter camp, on the Saskatchewan. The aim of the beaters in this hunt was to drive the animals into a round, fenced-in pen with an embanked entrance to prevent them from making their escape. Beyond this was a funnel-shaped enclosure fenced with stakes and hurdles; these were carved into human shapes, to scare the animals from breaking away. Mounted Indians drove the buffalo into the funnel. Once the bewildered animals were penned in, other Indians jumped up from behind the fence and slaughtered them with arrows or rifle-shots. The man in the tree is hanging up some strips of buffalo meat as an offering to the Great Spirit. In the background is the village of the Indians.

L. Fort Franklin, near Great Bear Lake

K. *Left:* Franklin's Expedition completed its Exploration of the Coppermine River, continued eastwards along the coast from the river mouth during the summer of 1821, reached Hood river, and turned inland to follow its course towards the distant Lake Athabaska. Not far from the coast they found their way blocked by the Wilberforce Falls. Inspecting the landscape from the top of a hill they realized they could not hope to get any further with their big boats, for the river was both rapid and shallow. So the thirty-one men built smaller, lighter boats on the spot and went on their way in these, to meet their tragic fate. Food gave out, the weather grew bitterly cold, and as there was no moss to be found they could no longer light fires to warm themselves and dry their clothes. They were finally reduced to chewing the leather parts of their clothing. Twenty-two of the party lost their lives before hospitable Indians came to the rescue. A few explorers were treacherously murdered—the victims of cannibalism—by one of the Indian members of the expedition; these included Hood, who had made the picture of Trout river reproduced on page 206 and drawn the view of the Wilberforce Falls jointly with his companion George Back (to whom we owe the picture of the buffalo hunt).

During a second journey (1825–27) Franklin and Back explored the long Arctic coastline from Mackenzie westwards to Point Beechey and eastwards to the Coppermine river. Franklin quickly had a half-ruined fort belonging to the North-West Company repaired to serve as winter quarters; it stood on a knoll near the south-western arm of Great Bear Lake, which teemed with fish. In the centre of the fort were the officers' quarters, with the men's quarters set at right angles and to the right of them, and the storehouse to the left with an annex for the interpreter's family. The Union Jack was run up proudly over the completed building. Franklin had fifty men under his orders. He kept them occupied in hunting wolves, foxes and reindeer, fishing, and felling trees; a few illiterates learnt to read and write; two of the best men on snowshoes went to and fro with dog sledges to maintain contact with far-distant posts on the Slave Lake and the Mackenzie. The scientific tasks included magnetic observations, temperature readings and the study of the Northern Lights. This continued till the day when wild geese were seen on their flight northwards, the first sign of returning life in the Arctic, and the expedition began to make ready for departure to the coast.

IV. Pioneering Journeys in the Interior of North America. A. A Male Canadian Lynx (after Audubon)

In 1803 John James Audubon landed in North America—an eighteen-year-old French lad, the mystery of whose origin has never been cleared up. From Europe he brought with him remarkable artistic talent, trained and encouraged by the great painter David, and a vehement, romantic love of nature. America offered him unlimited scope—the whole tremendous range of its fauna, hitherto scarcely investigated, and their habitat, from Labrador to Louisiana. He spent thirty-five years in seeking them out, travelling on foot, on horseback or by canoe, helped by his wife, struggling to bring up his children, feeling himself at one with the new settlers, trappers and forest rangers whom he had learnt to admire, when he first encountered them along the Mississippi, for their courage in tackling pioneer conditions in this wilderness. He made thousands of drawings and hundreds of water-colours, birds being his favourite subjects. When publishers in Philadelphia refused to print his work he went to London and there, in 1827, discovered the brilliant engraver Havell, who made the etchings for the four great volumes of his *Birds of America* (1827–38)—'le plus magnifique monument que l'art ait jamais élevé à la nature' said Cuvier.

*Above:* This *Lynx canadensis* is taken from *The Quadrupeds of America*, a work produced by Audubon in later life, in collaboration with his two sons. His style was keen and vigorous; his revolutionary aim was to show animals full of life and in their natural surroundings. He has been thrillingly successful with this lynx, which seems ready to bound at any moment out of the thicket where it lurks in hiding. The lynx, with its thick coat, has nothing to fear from the hard winters north of the Great Lakes. Its characteristics are all displayed here—the thick-set body and short tail, the great paws, the whiskers, the triangular tufts of hair on the ears, and the big, brilliant eyes which chiefly delighted the artist —the eyes of a beast of prey.

B. This Magpie-like Bird was thought by Audubon to be ►
the Columbia Jay *(Garrulus ultramarinus)*, though other naturalists take it for the *Calocitta Colliei*. The female is shown above, cracking nuts, and the male below. The most remarkable feature of this bird is its long tail feathers, two of which project a good way beyond the others; with the silken, blue sheen of its plumage it is a delight to the eye.

C. Pioneer Trappers in the Forests of Quebec Province

The log-cabins of the trappers, those pioneers of North American exploration, had a poetry all their own. It is not surprising that Adalbert Stifter, the woodland poet, felt his heart go out to them when he found them described in Fenimore Cooper's tales of the American trappers and their world. These men, especially the French, learnt a great deal from the Indians—how to make a canoe from birch-bark and caulk the seams with resin ('A canoe weighs less than a tobacco-pipe', said Champlain), how to make weather-proof clothing out of skins, how to use snowshoes and the lasso, how to make pemmican, the staple travel diet which would keep almost indefinitely, from dried meat pounded up with buffalo grease; and so forth.

The log-cabins were trading posts, too, where woollen cloth, tobacco, kettles, knives, guns and ammunition were bartered for the skins of the great forest animals, and much was learnt about the districts from which the Indians came for this purpose. When, after months of absence, a trapper brought his booty downstream to the collecting-point he would hand over geographical information at the same time.

D. American Homage to America: the Poet William ▶ Cullan Bryant and the Painter Thomas Cole gazing at the Catskill Gorges in the Forest along the Hudson.—The picture of the trapper's log-cabin belongs to the history of the *physical* exploration of North America. A. B. Durand's painting *Kindred Spirits* (1849) records a no less important aspect of exploration—the spiritual integration with the landscape thus discovered. The great achievements occurred in the eastern part of the continent in the 1840's, when a circle of painters and poets living near the Hudson Valley, who had been influenced by the Romantic movement in Europe, came more and more to realize that the process of discovery would never be really complete until people began to feel themselves deeply and strongly at one with the landscape, entering into its very spirit. 'Go not abroad in search of material for the exercise of your pencil while the virgin charms of our native land have claims on our deepest affections', wrote the painter of this picture. A sincere, heart-warming reverence for American nature radiates from his and Cole's landscape paintings.

V. Early Views of the Unknown Regions West of the Mississippi. A. The Mouth of Fox River as Karl Bodmer saw it

In 1832–34 Prince Maximilian of Wied-Neuwied (1782 to 1867) visited the prairies and rock-strewn wastes around the headwaters of the Missouri. He travelled in the boats of the fur-trading companies and used their forts as his bases. His interest extended to all aspects of nature; but the outstanding quality of his travel book was that it described the manners and customs of the Indians on the great prairies at a time when their old way of life was still unchanged, before they were crowded out of their own lands by swarms of settlers. Karl Bodmer, the Swiss artist who accompanied the expedition, tirelessly filled one sketch-book after another with drawings that reflect the grandeur and spaciousness of the scenes he recorded in the old Far West.

*Above:* During its long outward journey, in 1832–33, the expedition made its winter quarters at New Harmony, Indiana, not far from the confluence of the Fox river—seen in this picture—and the Wabash river. The atmosphere breathes a kind of primeval, sylvan poetry. Ancient oaks and hickories line the river banks; the plane-trees are a curious sight,

with their huge trunks, often quite hollow, dividing overhead into thick branches with dazzling white bark. A tremendous and varied bird population makes its home here. Hawks sit motionless, watching; blue jays swoop down to the river's edge, ducks up end themselves in the water. But the farm animals on the opposite bank are the first representatives of a new order of things; they show that settlers are hot on the heels of the fur-traders and hunters and that man is taming ever-wider stretches of the wilderness.

B. The Indian Villages were surrounded by Sacred ▶ Places, denoting their reverence for the benevolent spirits and their terror of the powers of evil. Their burial-grounds, where the dead lay on trestles, tied up in blankets and facing towards the east, were regarded as the most propitious places for communicating with the other world. The two scarecrow-like figures raised on the tall poles are made of skins, grass and brushwood, and represent the sun and moon. An Indian woman is praying and lamenting in front of them, as it was customary to do, in a loud voice, for hours at a time.

## C. In the Hut of a Mandan Chief

The roof of the hut rests on four supporting posts joined by beams; it is made of osier mats with hay and earth scattered over them. In the middle of the hut is a hollowed-out hearth. Baskets, leather bags and clothing hang from the posts; oars, weapons and other implements are propped round the walls. The horses have a place to themselves in these winter quarters, and the Mandan Indians share their living-space not only with their families but with their lean, wolfish dogs. Bison-hides and bear-skins, perhaps spread over a convenient hump of the ground, are used to sit on. Smoking their long-stemmed clay pipes, the Indians sit whiling the time away.

*Overleaf:*

D. Minitari Indians wintering on the Upper Missouri. The winter village is simply a collection of earth huts built in the lee of a wood. Men and women alike wear robes of bison-hide; the former are responsible for putting up the huts, making weapons, hunting and fighting, the latter for everything else. The young men go stripped to the waist, to harden themselves. The game being played in the foreground is intended to sharpen the wits and induce a fighting spirit. The players are equipped with spear-like poles; a small hoop is rolled along the ground, and the players hurl their poles at it as it moves. The winner is he whose spear-point penetrates it.

E. Battle outside Fort Mackenzie: 28th Agust 1833 (after Karl Bodmer)

Fort Mackenzie was a fur-trading post. The Piekan Indians had set up their tents in front of it, and not far off was the camp of their enemies, the Cris tribe, who had also come to barter furs. After a night of carousing and singing, the Piekans were wrapped in deep sleep when, towards dawn, they were suddenly attacked by about a hundred Cris and Assiniboins who had made common cause against them. In the twinkling of an eye a savage full-scale battle was launched, while the garrison of the fort, in some alarm, climbed on the roofs of the warehouses and workshops, inside the stockade, ready to open fire on the combatants. In the centre fore-ground lies a man who has been scalped by two of the enemy, while several braves are trying to help a wounded companion to safety. In the end the Piekans, routed, were let into the fort, whereupon they immediately began to shoot at their assailants from the roofs.

Later the fighting shifted to the neighbouring heights, and on the following day it calmed down—the Piekans having received reinforcements. One of them, 'Distant Bear', reported proudly when all was over that not a single bullet had hit him, because Bodmer had made a drawing of him a few days previously.

F. *Below:* A DANCER BELONGING TO A LEAGUE OF WARRIORS KNOWN AS
'THE DOGS'. On festive occasions the Indians delight in gorgeous cos-
tume. This brave, in fearsome war-paint, wears a towering headdress of
magpie's, owl's and raven's feathers and gives an impression of fierce,
warlike power which is heightened by the bow, arrows and rattle (made
from animals' hooves) that he carries. Strings of glass beads hang round
his neck; among them dangles the pipe of peace, made from the wing-
bone of a swan. A wolf's tail, the symbol of courage in battle, hangs from
his ankle. The red cloth falling behind him to the ground shows that he
is one of the tribe's leaders in time of war.

*Overleaf:*

G. ANIMAL LIFE ON THE UPPER MISSOURI. An enchanting sight met the
eyes of the Wied-Neuwied explorers as they came round a bend of the
river on their way back. A herd of bison, over a hundred strong, was
sunning itself on a sandbank at the mouth of Wincher's Creek. Hardly
sixty paces further off was a scene that might have come straight out of
a fairy-tale: a small herd of 'elk' were disposed around a powerful buck,
standing on another sandbank. The rowers had shipped their oars and
the boat was gliding softly downstream, carried by the current. At the
last moment the buck stationed on the cliff to the left scented danger,
bounded away, and started a general stampede. But in those few minutes
Karl Bodmer, with his artist's eye, had formed an unforgettable picture
of the primeval scene; and he later inserted it in his *Pictorial Atlas,* thus
helping to strengthen the deep-seated, inextinguishable feeling for their
country that was growing up in many Americans.

H. The Rugged Scenery along Diamond River (1858)

The first discovery of the Colorado canyon, by the Spaniard Vasquez de Coronado in 1540, was not followed up, and it remained *terra incognita* until the new-born American State, pushing westwards, sent an expedition into its almost impenetrable depths. It was Joseph C. Ives and his trusty companions who worked their way up the Colorado on their primitive steamboat, *Explorer* (see page 228). Here we have a geologist's paradise on the Diamond river.

I. *Right:* The steamer could get no further than the point where the canyon emerges from the Black Mountains. On 10th March 1858 Ives set out with a small party to continue the journey in a rowing-boat. Walls of dark rock rose perpendicularly on either side to a height of 980 feet. The noise of the water was deafening. They often came to rapids which could only be negotiated, in this confined space, by wading up them and dragging the boat behind. At last, on the third day, the precipitous cliffs drew apart, giving a view over more open ground in the vicinity of the Mormon Road. The expedition let itself be carried back by the force of the current as far as the steamer, and subsequently explored many of the valleys running into the Colorado.

*Overleaf:* K. Government Geologists at Work in the Grand Canyon (1879–90). In 1879 the United States Geological and Geographical Survey began to give active encouragement to exploration of certain regions in the Far West which had not yet been opened up. One of the results was C. E. Dutton's survey of the Grand Canyon. William Holmes, the geologist (centre), made a number of drawings there including this view, which looks eastwards from Point Sublime in the Kaibab district. From a depth of more than 4,900 feet, gigantic walls of rock stretch as far as the eye can see, traversed by great horizontal bands—the natural friezes and mouldings formed by the geological strata. These clefts had been made and shaped by water. Rivers had eaten through the rock, with endless ramifications; edges had crumbled and collapsed, creating jutting buttresses recessed with alcoves; volcanic action probably accelerated the process; rainwater had furrowed the cliffs with innumerable vertical channels; stone had been slowly weathered away. The Grand Canyon had become a landscape of erosion which has no parallel elsewhere. To the left, a few mountain pines stand defiantly in this rainless region.

225

L. Ives's Expedition aboard the 'Explorer' passes Chimney Peak on its Way up the Colorado

*Explorer*, an iron boat, was made in eight sections which were transported from the shipyard on the Atlantic coast, across the Isthmus of Panama, to the mouth of the Colorado river. On Christmas Day 1857 the eight parts were assembled and the engine started up. The boiler was so immense that it hardly left room for the members of the expedition; what with that and the rest of the cargo the boat was almost up to the gunwales in water. For cooking and sleeping purposes the party always had to land. Wood for fires could be gathered on the banks. The pilot stands on the cabin roof, receiving a steady stream of information from the man in the bows who is taking soundings—this is a shallow stretch, where the boat might easily go aground—and calling out instructions to the engineer who has to regulate the steam pressure. The outlines of the Canyon are already appearing among the mountains beyond the barren river-banks which are sparsely populated by Indians.

Later, *Explorer* took some of the party back to Fort Yuma (about twenty-five miles below the spot shown here), and was left there—already a veteran of North American exploration. Though doubtless not in the front rank of the immortal ships of history, with *Victoria*, *Discovery* or *Astrolabe*, she has a good claim to immortality. Though extremely difficult to handle in a strong current and always threatening to run aground in shallow water, she did remain afloat; and she reached her goal. She and her doughty crew offer a touching example of the courage and determination that went with the pioneer spirit—the unconquerable energy that characterized all the explorers, great and small, to whom we owe the opening-up of North America.

# THE PACIFIC

Until the early eighteenth century the picture of the world that was slowly being revealed by the great explorers consisted almost exclusively of Asian and American scenes. In the year 1500, 25 per cent of the earth's land surfaces was known to Europeans; by 1800 territories subsequently discovered had raised the figure to 60 per cent. A respectable rate of progress; but between 1600 and 1800 new discoveries had increased the area of 'known' seas and oceans from 52.5 per cent to 92.1 per cent of the total surface. This was due chiefly to the long voyages undertaken on the mightiest of all oceans, the Pacific, by a succession of explorers, greatest among whom was James Cook. They had been preceded by the few sixteenth-century navigators who had followed Magellan and charted new courses across that lonely expanse—and at an even earlier period by those brilliant seafarers, the 'Stone Age men' of Polynesia who, guided by migrating birds and by the stars, are believed to have sailed in their frail craft from the Marquesas and the Friendly Islands to remote spots such as Easter Island.

Scarcely 250 years ago, the Pacific still confronted explorers with three baffling questions: was it closed by a bridge of land in the far north, or was there an 'open passage'? What was the precise geographical distribution of the bewildering number of islands with which its surface was studded? And what of that measureless, mysterious *Terra Australis,* a persistent legend for more than a thousand years?

The Pacific lay in the half of the globe which in 1494, at Tordesillas, had been assigned to the Spaniards. It therefore behoved them, the conquerors of Central and South America, to cross that ocean and establish a sea-route between Mexico or Peru and the Philippines. Many lives were sacrificed and great privations endured in the attempt, until success came with the discovery that the prevailing westerly winds could bring a ship back from Manila to Acapulco in five or six months. Some of the Spaniards who went on to look for the legendary Terra Australis, found, instead, the Solomon Islands and the New Hebrides—and promptly lost them again, for the technique of calculating positions was not yet equal to the task of placing islands accurately on the map.

Cook, La Pérouse and others introduced a new style of exploration. Their aim was to make a comparative scientific study of the whole Pacific area, its flora, fauna and human population. Whenever one of their great three-masted vessels set sail it took along a team of naturalists, astronomers and draughtsmen. They were quick to adopt the new-fangled chronometer, invented in 1735—a magical instrument which at last made it possible to calculate geographical positions with accuracy. All that was needed was to carry two chronometers, one still recording the time of the port from which they had sailed, the other the time—determined by the sun—of the newly-discovered territory; the difference between the two would give them the distance they had travelled to east or west. From now on the explorers' outlook was dominated, as their journals testify, by sheer delight in scientific discovery for its own sake—though it is none-the-less true that the great eighteenth-century navigators were fully conscious of the economic and political importance of the South Sea islands, and that their nineteenth-century successors were all too ready to involve those islands in the far from idyllic atmosphere in which the great European powers were conducting their struggle for supremacy.

No other part of the world, however beautiful, made such a poetical impression on its discoverers as did the Pacific islands, which were hailed as the true Earthly Paradise. Many sailors tell how the approach to these tropical isles was announced, long before they came in sight, by the perfumes wafted from their myriad blossoms; they never tire of describing the scene that became a permanent feature of Europe's most nostalgic dreams—the rugged, forest-clad mountains soaring abruptly out of a deep blue sea that broke in gentle ripples on the white sand of a palm-fringed beach; the bamboo huts, the squawking parrots, the tranquil, brown-skinned natives approaching in canoes laden with fruit. Cook and the others all tell of mournful partings, weeping friends left behind on the shore—and deserters from the crew, hiding in the woods till the European ships had sailed away.

But it was a paradise where hell might easily break loose. The proudest three-master became a mere den of misery under the torrid sun of the tropics, when scurvy smote the crew and men lay dying (Cook was the first to combat scurvy by introducing food containing vitamins). Drinking water became brackish, food went bad, starvation threatened. There were tropical storms with veritable cloudbursts, there were treacherous coral reefs where ships ran aground. And while the natives in some places were friendly and hospitable, others would kill in a flash—as they killed Magellan, Cook and La Pérouse.

But for all that the islands still cast their spell. For one thing, the great century of Pacific exploration was also the century of humanitarian concepts. A philanthropical streak ran through it; the expeditions took domestic animals, iron tools and seeds from Europe to the far lands; explorers talked about the 'Noble Savage' and used their firearms only as a last resort. Rousseau's standard streamed from the masthead. It had to be admitted that these primitive, naturally virtuous communities included a number of cannibals and incorrigible thieves; but people agreed, on the whole, with Georg Forster when he said that for every scoundrel in the Pacific islands Europe could show fifty.

*Overleaf:*

MAGELLAN SAILS OUT INTO THE PACIFIC, through the western extremity of the Magellan Strait, where the bleak shores of Patagonia in the north and Tierra del Fuego in the south begin to recede, the ship moves to the long, slow surge of the Pacific, and the seafarer coming from the east has his first glimpse of its boundless, shimmering waters. Magellan, an experienced Portuguese navigator who had taken up service with the Spaniards, set out from Spain in the middle of August 1519, with a fleet of five vessels, to search the southern portion of the newly-discovered American continent for a western passage to the legendary treasure-grounds of China, India and the Moluccas. Only three days' voyage separated him from his goal, when snowstorms obliged the fleet to lie up for winter (March 1520). In October and November 1520, with the three vessels that had survived, he sailed in five weeks through the labyrinth of the straits that now bear his name—the first European ever to do so. The subsequent voyage across the Pacific costs the lives of many of his men, and when it was over Magellan himself met his death—killed by natives during a skirmish in the Philippines. The expedition originally numbered 270 men. When the last remaining ship got back to San Lucar, the Spanish port from which the fleet had set sail 1,124 days earlier, she was leaking at every seam, her pumps continually working; and her complement was twenty-two!

This picture is an allegorical tribute to that pioneering voyage round the world. For the first time there had been a systematic attempt to establish by actual experience the contours of certain essential features of the globe, its size and the way in which land and water were distributed over its surface. The eastern route into the Pacific had been discovered, and the period of European mastery of the oceans could now begin. The splintered mast is a reminder of perils endured. Apollo hovers near the ship to chant the praises of the heroic explorer who, equipped with compass, dividers and armillary sphere, is placidly calculating his position. Above, on the right, is the God of Winds; on the left the Roc—a bird from the Arabian Nights—is flying away with an elephant. On the northern shore a Patagonian giant, seated, is using an arrow to produce vomit; on the opposite coast burn the fires from which the country took its name. (Engraving by Th. de Bry, after Stradanus.)

ISLANDS OF THE PACIFIC AS GUILLAUME LE TESTU REPRESENTED THEM IN 1556

The titles of many sixteenth- and seventeenth-century travel reports begin with the words 'The Marvellous History . . .' and the maps made by Guillaume Le Testu, the French navigator and cartographer (1509–72), are marvellous *painted* histories. They were intended for the instruction and diversion of the French Court, and their title to be regarded as masterpieces of map-making is based on aesthetic rather than scientific grounds. Le Testu had travelled a great deal, but for what he had not seen with his own eyes he relied on the maps and descriptions of earlier or contemporary geographers—not always dependable,—or simply on his own imagination. Thus he sprinkles the Molucca Sea, south of the Sinus Magnus (the Gulf of Siam, bordered to the west by the Malayan Peninsula), with the countless little islands that Marco Polo had made so famous. Turning the map so that

the 'Chinese' coast, in the north, is at the top, we recognize Java among the big islands at the bottom, and towards the middle, Celebes, the Solomon Islands, and whatever else geographical gossip had brought to Le Testu's ears. His maps are peopled and have a lively atmosphere: we see two natives in a sailing-boat; higher up there is a dynamic-looking group comprising dolphins, a sea bird and what may be flying fish. But on Le Testu's seas the real sovereign is invariably a proud European ship—the new Portuguese galleon with her three masts, the bold lines of her forecastle and quarter-deck, her port-holes for guns and her beautiful, spreading sails. She serves as a symbol that the Portuguese from Europe and the Spaniards from their American bases were now beginning to carry their voyages of exploration into the zone of the Pacific islands.

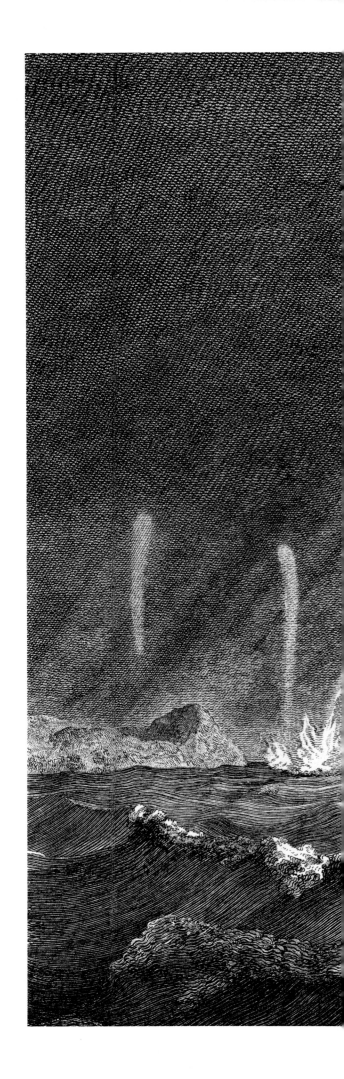

## James Cook

James Cook was born in 1728, the son of a poor farm-worker at Marton, in Yorkshire. His subsequent achievements were the result of the unswerving resolution with which he set about training himself for the sea, and the point of perfection to which he carried that training. It all began by his running away to sea at the age of fourteen and a half, when he was apprenticed to a tradesman, and joining the crew of a collier. He worked his way up, learning everything there was to learn about handling a ship. In the long winter months he studied navigation—almost unaided—and thus discovered how to keep a ship on her course. From the age of twenty-six onwards he took part in naval operations against the French in the Gulf of St Lawrence—and learnt how to defend a ship against enemy attack. In 1762–67, making a survey of the Newfoundland coast, he learnt how to map the earth's features with scientific accuracy; his maps long remained the most reliable of all. And on this same voyage, with a small survey vessel under his command, he learnt how to handle subordinates. As a naturalist, he was inevitably handicapped by his lack of scholarship; but he compensated for this by using his eyes—the all-seeing eyes of a genius—and by a power of logical thought and inspired deduction that plays like a searchlight over the whole colourful range of material, from stars to chips of stone, that is covered by the notes in his journals.

His first expedition (1768–71) was an official one, like the two others that succeeded it. It took him to Tahiti and then round the world, by way of New Zealand—which he recognized as consisting of two islands—and the dangerous east coast of Australia, which he was the first to chart. A year later he solved the ancient problem of the *Terra Australis*. With two ships, he spent three successive summers in the Antarctic (1772–75), investigating the vast southern areas between Africa and Australia, Australia and South America, and South America and Africa, sometimes sailing beyond the Polar Circle and tracing the famous zigzag lines across the map of the South Seas which denote the most glorious voyages undertaken by any navigator since Magellan. He laid a geographical ghost by proving that there was no such thing as an unknown continent outside the Polar Circle. Cook's last expedition (1776–80) dealt with important questions relating to the north-west coast of America and led to fresh discoveries in the Pacific (including the Sandwich Islands). Like Magellan, Orellana and many others, he died while opening-up new territories; in his own way he was one of the greatest figures of that age of neo-humanism.

## In Danger off the New Zealand Coast

On 17th May 1773, during his second circumnavigatory voyage aboard *Resolution*, Cook was making for his usual anchorage, in Charlotte Sound, on the north coast of southern New Zealand. He had been cruising for 117 days, chiefly in icy Antarctic waters, with one break in Dusky Bay, New Zealand; and now his goal was close at hand. Suddenly, at four o'clock in the afternoon, the wind rose and the sky darkened. Cook gave orders to furl all sail. A wild natural spectacle was just beginning, dangerously near at hand. Breezes blowing from different directions began to ruffle the surface of the water. Foaming waves reared up in several places, and whirling columns—'spirals of water or air or both'—rose from their peaks to meet the louring clouds. After a time these air-shafts or waterspouts broke loose at the lower end and were gradually sucked up, still spinning, into the clouds. Then the tumult gradually subsided, the sky cleared, and the crew breathed again and unfurled the sails.

VISIT TO THE ISLAND OF AMANOOKA

◄ A GLIMPSE OF PARADISE on Huaheina, in the Society Islands, of which Tahiti is the largest. These fertile, mountainous islands, with their confiding inhabitants, had been discovered by an Englishman, Wallis. Cook investigated them more closely, on his first and second voyages. The principal feature in this picture is a pandanus-tree. To the right we have to visualize a 'House of the God'—a vaulted structure made of wooden hoops, roofed in and raised on pillars, where the emblem of the god lay carefully wrapped up. Tupia, a native in Cook's party, at once made offerings here to the island's gods, so that they would not be angry at being disturbed by foreigners. When Cook came on land, five pisang saplings, the emblems of peace, were ceremoniously carried on board his ship; and when he said farewell at the end of the few days' visit, which had been one long, hospitable feast, the ruler of the island embraced him amid tears.

*Above:* In May 1777 Cook had himself rowed to this island with a few officers and men. The island had been discovered by Tasman, and Cook had already visited it on his second voyage. Now he took a closer look at it. It fully lived up to the reputation of the Friendly Islands, to which group it belonged, and there was a wholehearted exchange of presents. There were lively barter transactions too—yams, fruit, pigs and hens being traded for hatchets, sail-cloth and beads. Merchandise of this kind can be seen piled up in the open space outside the huts. Under the tall palm-trees beside the sea is the observation post where, with the help of the sextant, the exact position of the island was calculated. Beneath the trees on the right we see a stallion and mare—newcomers to this part of the world, brought on land for a change of scene. Cook later gave them to the people of another island, for breeding experiments.

## COOK IN THE ARCTIC

On his third voyage, with *Discovery* and *Resolution*, Cook sailed conscientiously into every large inlet along the west coast of Alaska, always hoping that one of these fjords, instead of coming suddenly to an end, would prove to be an open passage leading north-eastwards, right across North-West America, into the Hudson Bay region and would thus solve the old problem of the North-West Passage. He also wanted to find out how much of this territory, with its wealth of fish and furs, was already in the hands of Russian or even Spanish traders. How had the Eskimo-like coast dwellers come by the beads and knives he had seen in their possession?—Our illustration shows one of these far-reaching Alaskan inlets, Prince William Sound. On 12th May 1778 the menace of a storm, together with on-creeping fog, had decided Cook to leave the open sea and wait for better weather in the lee of a cliff in the bay, which had many creeks. A leak was patched too, and when the fog lifted the naturalists set out in two boats to explore the neighbourhood. Birds were shot for food. The shore was wooded at some points; where there were no trees the ground was covered with snow, from two to three feet deep. The mountains further inland could be seen above the tree-tops; they were naked, snow-capped rock. Inquisitive natives rowed past in kayaks, one or two to a boat; but relations got no further than a little elementary barter.

*Below:* COOK IN THE ANTARCTIC (JANUARY 1773)

During the three winters of 1772–74, the flagship *Resolution* several times ventured far into the South Polar Sea. Cook found no sign of the gigantic South Atlantic continent which many geographers still believed to exist, though the explorers saw plenty of icebergs and drifting ice-floes, sometimes in such quantities that they had to retreat before them. During pauses in the voyage the naturalists in the party (the two we see here are probably Reinhold Forster and his son Georg, who was later to win celebrity) used to shoot albatross, stormy petrel and other specimens for their collections, from their positions in the row-boat, while the sailors were bringing in drinking-water in the form of blocks of ice. Cook, however, took all this as the starting-point of one of the trains of deduction for which he was famous. Where did the ice come from? Since it didn't taste salty it could not be frozen seawater; but there was much to suggest that it had been broken from a layer of tremendous thickness under which there might perhaps be dry land. And that must be where the birds nested, too. Consequently, there might be a land mass in the Antarctic, far within the Polar Circle. The strange shapes taken by the ice (bottom left) proved that wind and waves wrought greater destruction there than warmth did—so, after a stormy season, it should be easier to break a way through the barrier of ice, towards that land mass.

*Overleaf :*

EASTER ISLAND. On 13th February 1774, returning from his second deep thrust into the Antarctic, Cook landed on the sandy shore of Easter Island—fifty-two years after Jacob Roggeveen, a Dutchman, had discovered that barren spot, lost in the ocean. Cook and his party, in their turn, were immensely intrigued by the mystery of the stone figures—frequently mentioned, even in these early years, and already beginning to collapse—whose gigantic heads, under their enormous hats, stared so fixedly out to sea. The explorers found skeletons in the vicinity of some of these figures, and came to the conclusion that they marked the burial-places of certain families. Hodges, Cook's artist, has placed a Polynesian spearman, like a messenger from another world, in his eerie, almost surrealist landscape.

COOK'S DEATH

On 17th January 1779, on his way back from the Arctic, Cook dropped anchor in Kealakekua Bay, on the Island of Hawaii. Both his ships were in need of repair. As on his previous visit, he was welcomed with the rites due to a god; for the natives believed him to be the gentle New Year divinity who, when he left the island, had promised to return one day in a ship with a little forest growing on it. The king of the island and its powerful theocratic priesthood took charge of him. Local produce and other gifts poured into the ships; the people literally emptied their stores. Finally, on 4th February 1779, the divine vessels sailed out of the bay. But two stormy nights did them further damage, and Cook reluctantly decided to turn back. This time there was not a soul on the beach; but the king and the priests, with an effort, repeated their due homage. One day some natives stole one of *Discovery*'s boats. Cook set up a watch, but gave strict orders that nothing should be done to antagonize the people, who were already sufficiently on edge. He was just about to begin negotiations with the king when a messenger arrived with the fatal news that his men, forgetting Cook's orders, had

fired on an escaping canoe and killed one of the local chiefs. The natives were beside themselves at this. Cook retreated to the beach, where his marines were lined up. Stones were thrown, spears were hurled, Cook fired, his men followed suit; and now the frenzied mob, perhaps stirred up by agitators, swept forward irresistibly. In the ensuing tumult Cook was trying to get the firing stopped when he was hit from behind by a stone and stabbed by one of the native daggers he had described with such precision in his journal. Amid a deafening hubbub the fallen divinity was torn to pieces.

On 20th February a friendly priest came out to the flagship, bringing what he declared to be Cook's bones; at sunset they were lowered into the waters of the bay, while the guns fired a salute. Peace was made with the king, who was also grief-stricken at Cook's death, and the ships, with a new commander, weighed anchor on 22nd February and set out for home. This picture went all round the world. It was made by John Webber—more accurately Johann Weber, a Swiss artist who had accompanied England's greatest explorer on his last voyage, as draughtsman to the expedition.

GYMNODACTYLUS PHYLLURUS, A VARIETY OF CHAMELEON FROM THE PACIFIC AREA

Characteristic features: large eyes, the eyes of a nocturnal creature, whose pupils contract to slits in daylight; a big, triangular head; protective scales, like thorns, covering the whole body; flat, leaf-shaped tail; prehensile paws. Found by Baron H. Y. P. Florentin de Bougainville (1781–1841), who sailed round the world in 1824–26 with two ships, on one of the numerous expeditions led by French officers which dominated the history of South Pacific exploration after the death of Cook.

The fauna of the Pacific islands and Australia became famous because of the extraordinarily great number of strangely-shaped animals like this *Gymnodactylus*.

*Overleaf:*

In the century when monarchies were still supreme, explorers received written instructions from their king's own hand, like generals before a battle. This painting by Nicolas-André Monsiau, belonging to the collections in Versailles Palace, shows La Pérouse receiving his orders in this way from Louis XVI in 1785. He was put in command of two corvettes,

*Astrolabe* and *La Boussole* (their names reflect the contemporary enthusiasm for mathematics), with picked crews, and with a group of distinguished scientists under his authority as well. He was to sail round Cape Horn and up to the north-west coast of America, there to investigate the representatives and potentialities of the fur-trade with China; he was to improve the mapping of the islands lying between Kamchatka and Japan; and finally he was to clear up the mystery still surrounding Australia, New Guinea, and various groups of islands. The aims were scientific as well as economic and political, and it was by no mere accident that the orders concluded on a philanthropic note: 'Le sieur de La Pérouse... défendra [à ses équipages]... de jamais employer la force pour enlever aux habitants ce que ceux-ci refuseraient de céder volontairement.'

Directions of this kind sometimes assumed the size of a small book and the character of a scientific treatise, particularly when leading scholars were called in. In certain outstanding instances such instructions belong to the most informative documents of their period.

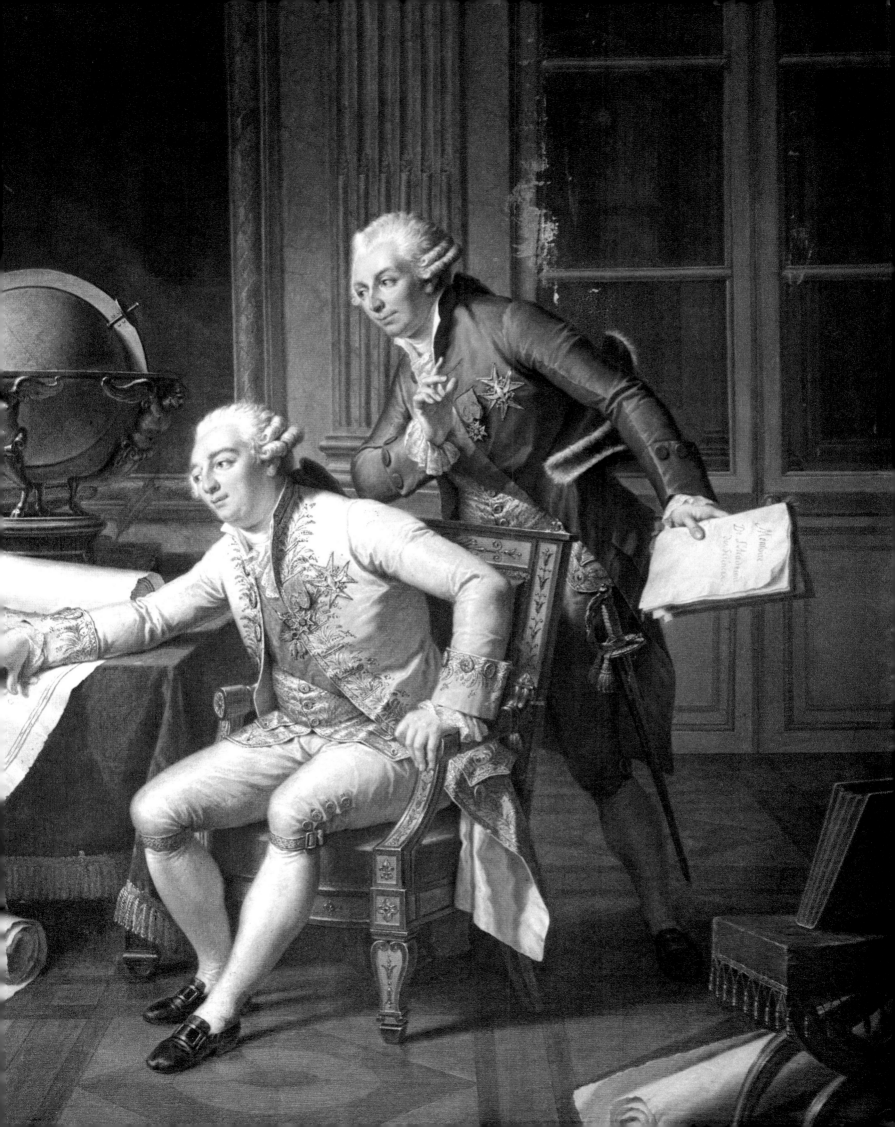

Mémoire De l'Académie des Sciences

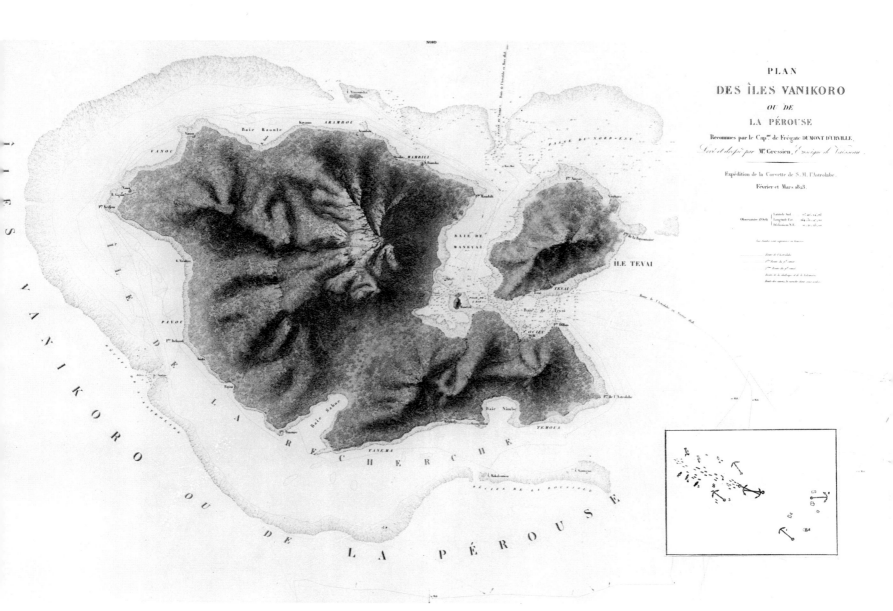

THE VANIKORO ISLANDS, ON WHOSE REEFS LA PÉROUSE'S EXPEDITION WAS WRECKED

At the end of January 1786 La Pérouse reported, from Botany Bay in Australia, that he intended to sail northwards with his two corvettes calling at various groups of islands, and to return through the Torres Strait to France. This was the last that was seen or heard of his expedition. Not until 1827 was it discovered—by Captain Dillon, a British merchant seaman—that both the explorer's vessels must have sunk in the Vanikoro archipelago, north of the New Hebrides. In February 1828 a Frenchman, Dumont d'Urville, reached the spot Dillon had indicated. The largest of the islands was surrounded by a 36-mile reef, through which there was only one opening, to the east; and inside this first circle, close to the shore, lay another. D'Urville found a narrow passage and anchored for several days in the lee of a tiny island, Maneva. The naturalists who were with him explored the whole area; Gressien, one of his officers, made a fine map; and the leader himself, guided by a native, found a place where, looking down into the clear, shallow water, he could dimly see the outlines of rusty anchors, lead plates and gun-barrels—the last vestiges of the ill-fated expedition.

The ships were presumed to have run aground during the night, the first not far from the native hamlet of Puiu, the second near a place called Vanu. The entire crew of the second vessel had perished; some survivors from the first had settled down among the natives for the rest of their lives; others, trying to get away in self-made boats, had vanished without trace.—The two pictures next described were brought home by the expedition sent out under the leadership of d'Entrecasteaux to search for La Pérouse, in 1791–94.

*Left:* A variety of *banksia nivea,* found growing in the sun-parched sands of the Australian coast; a distinguishing feature is the deeply serrated leaf, with its silvery underside.

*Overleaf:* The mountainous Admiralty Islands. Natives in pirgaguas—some of which have out-riggers and sails—are approaching the boat sent out by d'Entrecasteaux, passing close to some small reefs (on the right). The captain of one of the outriggers, standing on a kind of wooden platform, holds a shapely jar which he is bringing as a present.

DUMONT D'URVILLE'S CORVETTE 'ASTROLABE' IN CARTERET BAY (COCOS ISLAND), NEW IRELAND

The most eminent French explorer in the South Seas was Dumont d'Urville (1790–1842). In 1826–29, as leader of the *Astrolabe* expedition, he sailed round the world, returning with priceless collections of plants and animals, greatly improved maps of the ocean, and a wealth of ethnological material. It was he who first classified the innumerable islands in three groups—Melanesian, Micronesian and Polynesian—according to the races inhabiting them. Another point to the credit of Dumont d'Urville was his choice of Louis-Auguste de Sainson as the expedition's artist. De Sainson produced not only the boldly conceived plates for the folio volumes of the official report (see pages 252-3) but also the sketches for the lively little steel engravings—four are

reproduced here—illustrating his commander's most popular work—*Voyage pittoresque autour du monde* (1834)—in two volumes, full of zestful delight in adventure and exploration, from which are taken the four illustrations reproduced here.

*Above:* The sheltered anchorage of the *Astrolabe* between 7th and 19th July, 1827. The scientists collected and sifted the material for their researches from the sultry tropical forest, all about them; soundings were made in order to chart the bay, which had been discovered by Carteret, and the sailors busied themselves collecting wood and fresh drinking water to take aboard ship. The artist was enchanted by the bizarre shapes of the plants on the shore.

## Pacific Scenery

*Above:* A gay, fertile place with palms and bananas, on the main island of Hawaii. The River Wai-Akea, which rises in the wild forest-covered mountains here flows gently into the nearby bay.

*Centre:* Pitcairn Island, discovered by Carteret in 1767. Its interior is a veritable Garden of Eden, but from the sea it looks inhospitable, with its precipitous coast and rocks surrounded by foaming breakers. Dumont d'Urville landed in the sheltered corner where the rowing-boat can be seen. Pitcairn was the refuge chosen in January 1790 by some of the sailors from the *Bounty* who had been driven to mutiny by the harsh cruelty of their captain, William Bligh. They set fire to the ship on this coast, after setting their detested captain adrift on the open sea with the eighteen members of the company who had not deserted him, and landing the remainder of the crew, by their own wish, on Tahiti. But the Lotus-eaters' paradise to which they had looked forward was short-lived, simply because they behaved towards the natives like a collection of Captain Blighs.

*Below:* A waterfall on the island of Celebes. After running through the rice-fields near Lake Tondano the River Manado has carved a narrow passage through a barrier of basalt and falls thundering into a pool, round which innumerable species of plants grow luxuriantly in the hot moist atmosphere. The Dutch Governor has had a small pavilion built from which to admire the view—a flimsy-looking erection perched on tall stilts.

*Overleaf:*

On 28th June 1827, the *Astrolabe* ventured through a narrow gap in the reef dividing the rough waters of Tasman Bay from the calmer surface of Admiralty Bay, on Cook Strait, New Zealand. On the previous day Dumont d'Urville had stood on the bluff seen on the right, with its growth of tree-ferns, and had made a careful study of the dangerously narrow passage, while his company noted the directions of currents and winds. At the very moment of the dangerous manoeuvre, when the ship lay immediately in front of the opening, the wind dropped suddenly; the vessel would no longer answer to the helm, and was carried by the current towards the reef. She heeled over to the left and the horrified crew thought she would inevitably run aground on the treacherous rocks. At the last second, however, a breeze began to blow again; and though the ship was carrying only a few sails, wind and current together sufficed to float her, undamaged, out of the perilous shallows. Soon she was sailing safely over the friendly waters of Admiralty Bay.

## The Voyage of Madame Freycinet

One day the Paris newspapers informed their readers in chorus that: 'The corvette *Uranie* under the command of M. Freycinet has set sail from Toulon harbour to undertake a great voyage of exploration round the world. Officers and men are in the best of spirits, and France expects important results from the voyage, which is expected to last at least three or four years.'

The report continued: 'The first day of the voyage was marked by a noteworthy incident. At the very moment when a violent squall struck the corvette, which was then rounding Cape Sépet, a small figure was observed sitting on the look-out bench on the wet deck, shivering slightly, with face in hands, and waiting for someone to notice and lead it to shelter; for the rain was falling in torrents with wild gusts of wind. This young and pretty person was Madame Freycinet, who had slipped on board, disguised as a sailor. The commander was thus obliged, willy-nilly, to carry along this courageous traveller, who, as a loving wife, would not allow her husband to confront alone the dangers and hardships of this voyage.'

Now none of all this was true, or at any rate it was a mixture of truth and falsehood. It is true that *Uranie* had sailed and had run into a violent storm just off Toulon; but Madame Freycinet was on board with her husband's consent and, though on deck, had been seated in a sheltered position.

So soon as the first squall had abated, the Captain sent for the officers and introduced their fellow traveller to them.

The thought of a pretty woman alone among so many men of often unpredictable moods, a delicate, fragile being among these iron-hard natures who must withstand so many battles against the wild elements; a soft, timid voice, like the notes of a harp, drowned by rough, loud voices which must make themselves heard above the crash of waves and the hum of the wind in the rigging—everyone who reflected on such an uncommon situation was filled with concern...

After we left Gibraltar, Madame Freycinet again donned woman's dress. She seldom walked on the bridge, but when she did appear there the officers gallantly withdrew to the weather side, while behind the mast the not very edifying songs died on the singers' lips and even the roughest sailor bit back those oaths of fifteen or eighteen syllables that delight the fiends in hell. Observing the iron restraint placed on all these fiery tongues, Madame Freycinet would smile sweetly under her trim bonnet.

When some poor sailor lay below decks in the grip of dysentery or scurvy, Madame Freycinet would never fail to enquire after his progress, and with the permission of the ship's doctor she sent pots of preserves to the sick men.

When the ship put in at more civilized ports Madame Freycinet would accept the homage of the local authorities as a woman of the world, who knew how to return a courtesy. It goes without saying that during difficult sojourns in regions where the populace was of the lower sort and some ugly scenes might be seen, she had to remain on board; this cloistered

THE AMERICAN EXPEDITION LED BY WILKES ON THE HIGHEST PEAK OF AN ISLAND IN THE FIJIS

The American Government sent out its first large-scale round-the-world expedition in 1838–42—chiefly in order to establish, in the eyes of the European Powers, its claim to share in the important tasks still awaiting explorers in the South Seas and the Antarctic. The leadership of the expedition was entrusted to a naval officer, Charles Wilkes (1798–1877), already well known as a cartographer. In 1840 the expedition was sailing among the Polynesian islands, where ethnographical material was assembled and improvements were made in the existing maps, especially of the Fiji group. Wilkes climbed with some companions to the highest point of Waialailaithake, one of the most rugged of these islands, and christened it Observatory Peak. It was a difficult climb over the volcanic rock, for the explorers carried equipment and weapons, and were uncomfortably aware that they were being spied on by unseen natives—reported to be of ferocious disposition. But they finally departed from the 'craggy rock' unharmed, and with valuable scientific booty.

existence might easily have seemed irksome to her, had she not prepared herself for this voyage with a firm resolution to accept deprivations and sacrifices.

And what was her reward for so much discomfort, hardships and danger; for so much suffering? What fame did she win?—A rock bears the name of the patron saint of the gentle companion of our trials; that rock is marked on the most recent and detailed nautical maps; all of us stood by when it was christened *Ile-Rose*. May seafarers greet it with respect!...

And finally the corvette met her day of doom, when, in the Falkland Islands, flying before the wind, she was suddenly brought up with a jolt—aground on a reef below sea-level, which had stripped off her copper keel, so that twelve hours later she lay on her side and could never be righted again. This day of misfortune was one of sore trial for us all.

Sorrowful, suffering, yet calm and resigned, without a word of complaint, Madame Freycinet waited for death, which threatened from all sides. The water rose, the pumps laboured without avail, we could number the hours of life that yet remained to us.

Madame Freycinet had gathered in her cabin some fragments from the wreckage. She kept careful guard over the damp ship's biscuits rescued from the submerged hold, and looked on without a tremor as the open kegs of powder were carried by, passing close to the cauldrons of burning pitch and the lighted lanterns. Madame Freycinet was a truly brave woman.

Storms at sea and dangerous tropical diseases had failed to vanquish her, but cholera in Paris succeeded. Our poor fellow-voyager, that resolute woman, that selfless wife, that kind, helpful creature, has departed for ever from the planet she so recently traversed from end to end.

Abridged translation from: J. Arago, *Souvenirs d'un aveugle: Voyage autour du monde*, Vol. 3, Paris, 1839.

THE SOUTH SEA EXPEDITION (1817–20) LED BY FRIGATE-CAPTAIN LOUIS-CLAUDE DE FREYCINET (1779–1842)

'Our predecessors have left us a monstrous amount to set to rights,' declared the French navigator, Freycinet, in a phrase worthy of a historionomer. But he was merely looking at the matter from the standpoint of his own research programme, which differed from that of the great Pacific explorers, Cook, La Pérouse and Dumont d'Urville. Freycinet was a forerunner of the nineteenth century, which soon began to distrust the sweeping philosophical theories of certain Romantic ideologists and the all-embracing type of exploration, and to call for more restricted and painstaking investigation of individual problems. Moreover, Freycinet, who had won his spurs as a member of Captain Nicholas Baudin's expedition to South Australia (1800–04) was inclined to lay the chief stress on physical geography, terrestrial magnetism and meteorological research. Two doctors—Quoy and Gaimard —and a pharmacist and botanist, Gaudichaud, accompanied him, however, to ensure that life in its various aspects would not be unduly neglected. The doctors brought back with them, among other discoveries, some important disclosures about leprosy and the antidotes employed against it by the natives. The prevailing feeling of the company on board Freycinet's flagship *Uranie* was a benevolent friendliness towards 'primitive' peoples. Looking at the pictures, which are packed with ethnological information, one realizes that they radiate a warm sympathy—dating back to the time of Rousseau—for man in the state of nature. This is to a great extent due to the expedition's official artist, the theatre director, playwright and novelist Jacques Arago (1790–1855). In contrast to Freycinet, who later retired to his estate in France, where he spent in contemplation the years until his death in 1842, Arago's love of adventure remained with him throughout his life. At the age of fifty-nine, when his sight was failing, he went to California and there, with help from others, plunged with feverish energy into the search for gold; and when death overtook him it was, appropriately enough, during a voyage to Brazil. Certain of the pictures he made for Freycinet's expedition were not passed for publication, because they included someone whom Freycinet had smuggled on board in direct contravention of French naval discipline—his wife, who bore the hardships of the long voyage in a way that excited general admiration (see pages 255 and 256).

Freycinet's 'Uranie' off Rawak Island (January 1819)

The bay is fringed with virgin forest—humid, sultry, with parrots screeching in the tops of its tall trees. The astronomers have set up their observation tent among some deserted huts on the beach. Meanwhile the geologists and botanists are rambling about the interior, and the neighbouring islands are being prospected and mapped. The usual picturesque animation has sprung up around the *Uranie* as she lies at anchor. Natives—Papuans with ugly faces and shocks of fuzzy hair—are paddling to and fro. The local dignitaries, most of whom are Moslem, can be identified by their dress, a kind of robe and a turban. The branch carried in the boat is a peace-token. While fever- and dysentery-stricken sailors lay sweltering between decks (Freycinet lost one man in ten during this circumnavigation), an occasional distinguished guest, e. g. the chief of a neighbouring island, had to be entertained in the staterooms on the afterdeck.

NATIVES OF OMBAI ISLAND, IN WAR-DRESS, DISPLAY THEIR SKILL WITH THE BOW

On 2nd November 1818 four scientists from the *Uranie*, accompanied by a few sailors, landed on Ombai Island, not far from Timor. With slight reluctance the natives led them to Bituka, one of their villages which lay hidden in the valleys of the interior (indicated by the rising smoke). Two of the men were persuaded to put on their war-dress—made of skins sewn with shells or pieces of bone—and display their skill at archery, which they did in the style of William Tell, by shooting arrows just clear of the fashionably up-swept coiffure of another member of the tribe. The arrows were tipped with bone, wood or in some cases iron. After four hours a gun-shot, the agreed signal for the return, was heard from the *Uranie* and the party rowed back to the ship.

IN THE INTERIOR OF RAWAK ISLAND. On the left is a palm-thatched 'mortuary' containing the bones of an important member of the tribe; the skulls arranged in front of it are the trophies he won in battle. The opening allows fruit, fetishes, weapons and so forth to be reverently passed through to the dead man, for his use in the other world. On the right we are shown Papuans roasting fish on a grill made of the green ribs of palm-leaves. In the centre of the picture an islander is twirling a stick which he holds upright, its tip resting in a hollow scooped out of a small board; the friction sets fire to sawdust and brings dry palm-leaves to a glow, and finally they burst into flame. The European onlookers may be Freycinet and the artist Jacques Arago himself.

*Right:* TWO IDOLS ON RAWAK. Many of the leading figures on Rawak were Moslems, but the original population still revered their ancient idols. The French visitors were impressed by the high quality of the wood-carving.

*Overleaf:*

EXPLORERS IN ONE OF THE BAMBOO-AND-PALM-LEAF HOUSES ON TIMOR ISLAND. Above is a kind of loft; outside is a projecting roof, to give shade. The simple furniture consists of benches and mats, with one rare feature—a chair. Protected against the damp rising from the ground, the occupants sleep on a low platform covered by a mat. The rolled end of the mat serves as a pillow, though the luxury of a cotton 'sofa-roll' is not unknown. A rather complicated form of backgammon is being played. The sarong, a long strip of cotton cloth, is the principal article of women's dress. They like to put flowers in their hair, which is piled high and held by a bamboo comb or a kerchief. Hanging on the wall is a cloth bag containing everything needed for the preparation of a betel 'chew'; its four corners are decorated with tortoise-shell rings. Some of the sympathy felt in Rousseau's day for distant island peoples, living in close touch with nature, still lingers in this scene. With a critical side-glance at Europe, Freycinet praises the healthy, unsophisticated way of life followed by the Timor islanders, who lived on rice, maize, mangoes, bananas and other fruit and seldom tasted meat.

RUINS OF ANCIENT BUILDINGS ON TINIAN ISLAND

At the end of April 1819 some of the scientists from the *Uranie* were taken in piraguas to visit Tinian Island, in the Marianas —a bleak spot, where life seemed extinct except for a sparse growth of plants. Yet they were puzzled and fascinated to find, in a region of wooden buildings, these orderly rows of stone pillars, with their hemispherical, flat-topped 'capitals'. Had they once supported a roof? Or an upper floor, reached through a central opening? How old were they? An archaeological problem had suddenly presented itself in the South Seas, where everything falls so rapidly into decay.

*Right:* THE ROMANCE OF EVERYDAY OBJECTS IN THE CAROLINES. These objects include necklaces (1–4)—the third bears a row of flowers; fishhooks (9–12); implements for baling water out of the piraguas (5, 6); a shell used as a fog-horn to warn boats out at sea (7); a dancer's staff (13); beauti-fully made wooden vessels and boxes (14, 15, 19–21); a sun-hat made of palm-straw (18); two pieces of magical apparatus: one (16), an instrument made from two long bones of the ray-fish, decorated with strips of palm-leaf, used to induce contrary winds to change their direction; the other, (17), a large 'pai' shell, similarly decorated, with which the medicine man would make circular movements above a slight wound, while he murmured healing spells; a picture-letter (8) sent by a Rota Island chief to the Spanish Captain Martinez with, above, a gesture of greeting, below, a branch used as a token of peace, on the left, arranged in three rows, the large, small, and unusually-shaped shells which were handed to the strangers and, opposite, the 'payment' charged for them—three large and four small fishhooks, two axes and two pieces of iron. Iron was considered a priceless metal by a Stone-Age economy.

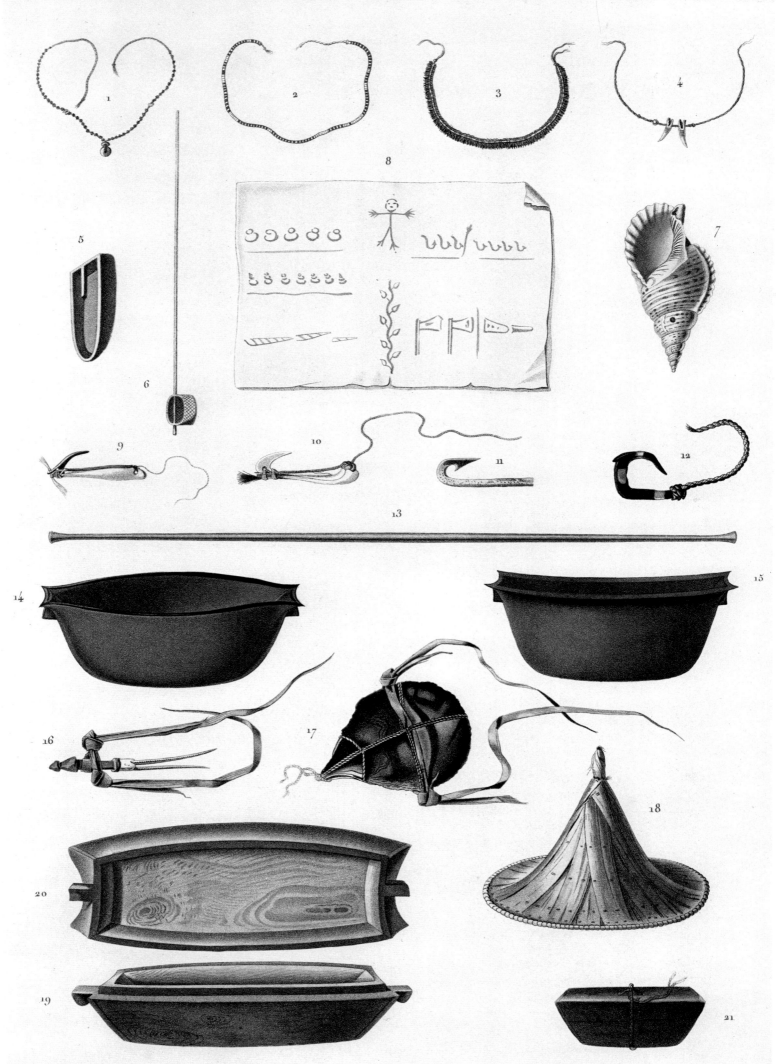

### Two Sloops of von Krusenstern's Expedition looking for a Landing-place on Nukuhiva Island in the Marquesas

During the eighteenth century most of the ambitious round-the-world expeditions which visited the Pacific islands came in English or French three-masted vessels. Explorers from these two countries discovered aspects of nature hitherto unknown, and their respective governments laid the foundations of the policy they were to pursue in this region in the following century. After 1800 Russia too sent out expeditions round the world, usually under Baltic commanders, with the same twofold purpose and, more particularly, to explore the northern coasts of the Pacific and certain groups of South Sea islands which had not so far been adequately investigated. A.J. von Krusenstern's expedition lasted from 1803 to 1806, Otto von Kotzebue's voyage on the *Rurik* from 1815 to 1818, Count Feodor Petrovich Lütke was exploring from 1826 to 1828, and so forth. This illustration records an episode from von Krusenstern's voyage to the Pacific. After a rainy night the clouds broke up, and in the cold light of early morning the island of Nukuhiva appeared ahead, ringed by naked, sheer-falling cliffs of irregularly-heaped volcanic rock. Hardly a tree or bush was to be seen, though grass grew on some less precipitous slopes. The Spaniards had discovered this group of islands in 1595, and recently Cook and other navigators had explored it more thoroughly, so von Krusenstern knew that the interior of Nukuhiva offered warm, well-watered valleys where coconuts, bananas, sugarcane and yams usually grew in abundance—although in periods of drought numbers of the population were liable to die of starvation.

The telescope failed to reveal any of the—unusually handsome—islanders on the shore, so two sloops put off to inspect the coast. The harbour of Tayo-hoaë, where the ship finally anchored, is behind the boat with the sail. 'A short time later, to our great satisfaction, we saw a boat approaching at last; it was flying a white flag and in it were eight naked men.' One of the eight proved to be an English sailor named Roberts who had stayed behind on this island some years ago. Von Krusenstern remained here for ten days. Roberts and a Frenchman who had also been living for years among the islanders acted as interpreters and provided information about the country and its people. The visit was altogether very profitable. A storm suddenly blew up just as the ship was sailing away, and prevented the Frenchman from returning to his family on land. He was carried back on the ship to the world of white men, far from the remote island where he had made his home.

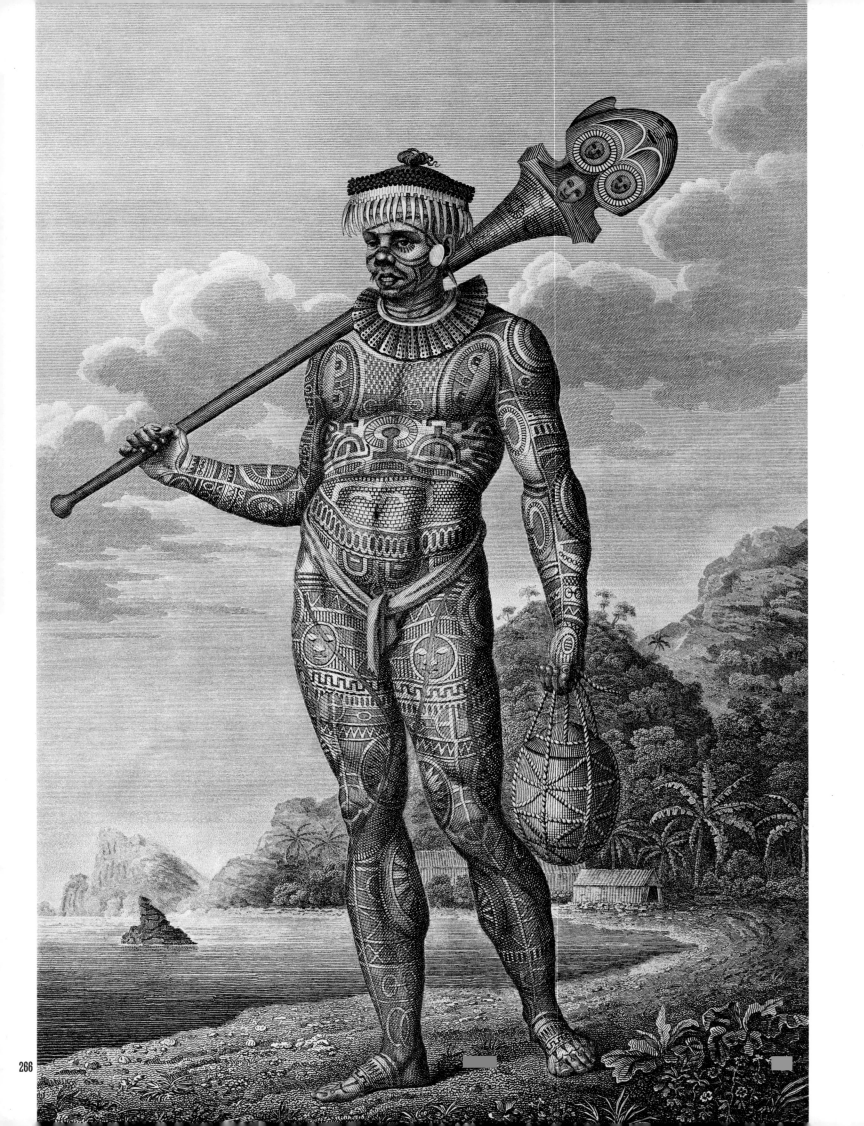

TATTOOING AS A FINE ART ON NUKUHIVA ISLAND

Explorers took an ever-growing interest in the highly individual forms of art practised by the South Sea islanders. Both these pictures of tattooing (the word is of Tahitian origin) were made by Krusenstern's expedition. On the left is an islander of high rank, distinguished from his fellow-countrymen by the extravagance of the absolutely symmetrical tattooed design that covers him from head to foot. He carries a calabash and a heavy club of casuarina wood, decorated at the top with carved heads, and wears a white shell in his ear. His semicircular collar of smooth wooden disks studded with red beans shows him to be a priest.

*Above:* A skilled tattooer at work in the hut of a female client, whose husband is bringing the artist a pig's head for his fee. A number of sailors on the expedition took the opportunity of visiting such an unusual beauty-parlour and submitted to this rather painful treatment, in which the skin is scratched to produce the pattern, and the colours are rubbed in.

THE CORVETTE 'CHALLENGER' LYING OFF ST PAUL'S ROCKS (29TH AUGUST 1873)

It was not only the Pacific islands, but the great ocean itself that presented explorers with a constant succession of problems. It prompted the boldest speculations. Did life exist in its apparently inaccessible depths? If so, in what form? Would it be possible to map the ocean floor? What was its history? The pioneering feat in this direction, which went far beyond the soundings to which efforts had been restricted in the eighteen-thirties, was achieved by the British ship *Challenger* whose most rewarding field of activity was the Pacific. In 1872–76 a party of botanists, chemists, zoologists and geologists, led by the biologist Charles Wyville Thomson (1830–82), made a voyage of 69,000 miles through the southern oceans. This marked the beginning of modern oceanography. The most up-to-date sounding apparatus, trawl-

nets and drift-nets were used, and the most extraordinary creatures were brought up from the depths.

*Above:* The ship, using both steam and sail, arrived in the vicinity of Bahia Bay and was moored by a cable in the lee of the small, rocky islands of St. Paul, round which run the wild breakers of the southern equatorial current. To make landing easier, a rope was stretched across to the steep cliffs, and the company hauled their boats over in turn. Soundings showed that the rocks fell sheer into very deep sea; astronomical calculations established the exact position of the island on the map, for it constituted a great danger to shipping, especially at night. Thomson was anxious that a lighthouse should be built there without loss of time.

*Right:* THE UPPER AND MAIN DECK OF THE EX-
PEDITIONARY SHIP 'CHALLENGER'. The corvette had
been specially fitted up with chemical and bio-
logical laboratories, both lit from above, a chart-
room and—as a great innovation—a photo-
graphic laboratory. Note the three masts and the
funnel for the steam-engine, the three lifeboats and
the technical equipment for deep-sea research—
especially the hempen ropes, thousands of feet in
length, rolled up in their containers and the various
drums and rollers for guiding the tow-line and
preventing it from running out beyond control.

*Below:* THE BIOLOGISTS' WORKING QUARTERS ON
BOARD 'CHALLENGER'. A bewildering array of
test-tubes adorns the walls; below, secure in deep
sockets, are bottles containing the different liquids
used for preserving the specimens; beyond are
rows of drawers, some of them tin-plated to make
them air-tight repositories for pressed plants,
which must be protected from damp sea-air. There
are even harpoons for whale-fishing (above, left).
The table in the middle is screwed to the floor; in
front, on the right, stands a binocular microscope.
In the groove running across the microscope table
we see an inkstand and a quill pen—for the notes
which will one day add to the world's common
fund of scientific information.

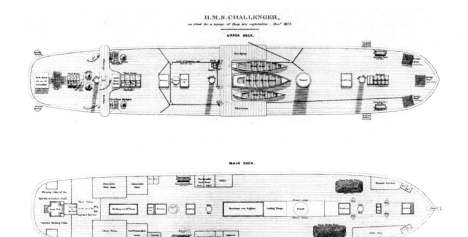

# The Discovery of Australia

◄ Four Samples from the Sea-bottom seen through 'Challenger's' Microscopes

What is there at the bottom of the sea? was one of the chief questions asked by the *Challenger's* naturalists. They discovered that in the South Seas, over an area of millions of square miles, the sea-floor was piled high with calcareous shells formerly inhabited by minute, primitive creatures, while the presence of higher forms of life was indicated by splinters of fishbone, starfish prickles and other vestiges that had sunk to the bottom. Minerals were also found. Above, on the left, is a specimen dredged up from a depth of 150 fathoms on the Agulhas Bank, near the Cape of Good Hope, magnified thirty-five times. The light-green, white and brownish patches represent the calcareous cells, while the dark green specks are grains of a mineral, glauconite.

Above, on the right, is a similar specimen taken from a depth of 410 fathoms in the vicinity of the Australian coast, magnified thirty-five times. The expedition discovered about ten thousand new varieties of protozoa shells, most of them multicellular husks with pin-point openings, through which the tiny creature—little more than a slightly differentiated speck of protoplasm, protected by a shell—extends its minute protuberances or pseudopodia, into the surrounding water. The majority of these foraminifera consisted of globigerina (collections of globules of different sizes—see central region of picture). Some minute vitreous particles of volcanic origin are mixed up with the rhizopods.

Below, left, is a sample of coral sand from the Great Barrier Reef, North-East Australia, taken from a depth of 155 fathoms, magnified twenty-five times. The reddish colour is produced by clay containing iron. It was the expedition's drift-nets that solved the problems of the actual habitat of the unicellular creatures whose shells, with their amazingly delicate structure, are shown again here in great numbers. They were found to live not far below the surface, multiplying themselves by fission at a very rapid rate. When they die, their shells sink down to the bottom of the sea like a shower of dust, and have piled up in some places, in the course of millions of years, to a depth of several hundred yards. The expedition succeeded in establishing the general contour of the ocean depths.

Below, right, is a sample from the South Pacific, taken from a depth of 1,450 fathoms, magnified twenty-five times. This was found to include 55 per cent of calcareous shells of foraminifera—globigerina, pulvinulina, rotalida, textularida and so forth; 10 per cent of silicious remains of radiolaria, lituolida, etc., and 6·4 per cent of vestiges of more advanced marine animals, together with traces of augite, feldspar and other minerals.

For fifteen hundred years it was assumed that Ptolemy had been right about the existence, to the south of the known world, of a vast unknown continent with the South Pole as its central point. Even at the beginning of the modern age many people still believed that Africa, America and the York Peninsula were long tongues of land running northwards from this 'Terra Australis'. The first inkling that this might be a fallacy arose in the minds of bold seafarers who began to suspect that Africa, America and Australia were not, in fact, parts of the great southern continent: Diaz, rounding the Cape of Good Hope, found no trace of land to the south; Magellan discovered the Straits which bear his name connecting the Atlantic and the Pacific; whilst in 1642 the Dutch navigator Abel Tasman sailed past Australia all unawares and discovered nothing but the south coast of Tasmania. It was Cook, on his second voyage, who finally demolished the most fantastic legend in the history of exploration, dismissing the idea with a characteristically sober pronouncement: 'As to a southern continent, I do not believe any such thing exists unless in a high latitude.'

In the seventeenth and eighteenth centuries a number of expeditions—Spanish (Torres), Dutch (Hartog) and French, but more frequently British—venturing into the 'emptiness' of the South Pacific between 113 and 153 degrees east, charted various unconnected stretches of coast which were gradually linked up to form the outline of Australia. The culminating feat was the mapping of Australia's south and east coasts, the Torres Strait and the Gulf of Carpentaria, by an Englishman, Matthew Flinders, in 1801–03. It was at his suggestion that the territory now at last recognized as a fifth continent was given the name so long borne by the mythical southern land-mass.

Long after the Australian seaboard had become comparatively familiar the interior remained a land of mystery, envisaged as a barren plateau with deserts in the west and marshes and virgin forest in the north. As one geographer put it, Australia, whose coast was seething with life, had a heart of stone.

The European immigrants, in their undaunted determination to succeed as colonists, pitted their will against hostile nature. It was the search for land on which to settle that incited them to penetrate into the interior, and exploration began when two groups of men, both convinced that Australia, for them, meant present freedom and future prosperity, joined forces to open it up. The leaders were hardy immigrants and their followers came in part from among the convicts sentenced to transportation to Australia by the British penal authorities. These came in rapidly-increasing numbers from 1788 onwards, egged on by the promise that part of their sentence would be remitted if they joined an expedition.

The first efforts were directed to the south-eastern regions, with their mountains, rivers and unsuspected grazing grounds; in 1836 Thomas Mitchell, full of confidence in the future, gave the name 'Australia felix' to what is now the province of Victoria. In 1844–45 Ludwig Leichhardt made his way across Queensland in the north-east. Next came attempts to cross the continent from south to north. This was a formidable undertaking, and many lives were lost in the merciless drought of the barren interior before, in the early 1870's, the famous overland telegraph cable finally linked the south coast with Port Darwin in the north. Many of its isolated maintenance stations served as starting points for the expeditions (led by Giles and others) that now took on the hardest task of all—the attempt to cross the untravelled and largely desert region in the west.

The pewter plate shown on the right evokes the Dutch contribution to the early discovery of Australia. Their daring advances from Java and Malacca into the open Pacific brought the Dutch ships within sight of the north coast of Australia. But since 1611 the captains in the service of the Dutch East India Company had been following a new route between the Cape of Good Hope and Batavia, the centre of their expanding trade empire in the Pacific. Instead of sailing northwards along the east coast of Africa and then crossing the Arabian Gulf to India they struck right out from the Cape into the Indian Ocean, sailed for four thousand miles, and then turned north towards Java—thus saving several months. Occasionally, however, while still on the eastward course, before being able to turn northwards, they came to Western Australia. It was in this way that in October 1616 the *Eendracht,* an Amsterdam ship commanded by Dirk Hartog, came to a group of islands lying south of the North-West Cape, one of which is still called 'Dirk Hartog Island'. The crew landed, stayed three days, and left, nailed to a post on the shore, a flat pewter plate bearing an account of their visit. Eighty years later, when long stretches of the west coast were already familiar to sailors, another Dutchman, William de Vlamingh, landed on the island and replaced the original plate by another, engraved with a copy of the first inscription and a note of his own visit (see caption).

THE MOST REMARKABLE PEWTER PLAQUE IN THE HISTORY OF EXPLORATION ►

The pewter plaque bearing the announcement of two Dutch visits to Hartog Island (see text on left), attached to a stake on the deserted beach, was exposed to wind, rain and sun for more than a hundred years, before Freycinet, in 1801, landing on the island as a member of a French expedition, found it already half-buried in the sand, and nailed it to an oaken post. And it was not until 1818, when he landed in the nearby Shark Bay in the course of his own voyage round the world, that he brought the plate away—a document recording one of the earliest attempts to solve the great Australian mystery. The draughtsman was keenly alive to the magic of such a relic, surviving from that distant period in the history of exploration.

The inscription runs as follows: '1616. On 25th October the Ship *Eendracht,* from Amsterdam, arrived here. Gilles Miebais, merchant, of Lüttich; Captain Dirck Hatichs [Hartog], of Amsterdam. On the 27th day of the same month she set sail again for Bantam' [Java], [here follow two names].

'1697. On 25th February the ship *Geelvinck* arrived here from Amsterdam. Captain Willem de Vlamingh of Vlielandt [other names follow].... With her were the Hooker *Nyptangh* [Master Gerrit Colaart, of Amsterdam...] and the Galliot *Weeseltie,* Commander Cornelis de Vlamingh, of Vlielandt.... We sailed hence again with our Fleet, to make further search of the Southland [Terra Australis]; bound for Batavia.'

=:16:16=

DEN 25 OCTOBER IS HIER
AEN GECOMEN HET SCHIP D EENDRAGHT
VAN AMSTERDAM DE OPPER KOPMAN GIL=
LES MIEBAIS VAN LVCK SCHIPPER DIRCK HATICHS
VAN AMSTERDAM DE 27 DITO TE SEIL GEGHN NA BAN=
TVM DE ONDER COEPMAN JAN STINS DE OPPER STVIER=
MAN PIETER DOORES VAN BIL ANNO 1616 =—

1697 DEN 4 FEBREVARY IS HIER AEN GEKOMEN HET SCHIP
DE GEELVINCK VOOR AMSTERDAM DEN COMANDER ENT SCHIP=
PER WILLEM DE VLAMINGH VAN VLIELANDT ADSISTENT JOAN=
NES BREMER VAN COPPENHAGEN OPPERSTVIERMAN MICHIL
BLOEM VANT STICHT BREMEN DE HOECKER DE NYPTANGH
SCHIPPER GERRIT COLAART VAN AMSTERDAM ADSIST' THEO=
DORIS HEIRMANS VAN DITO OPPER STIERMAN GER=
RIT GERITSEN VAN BREMEN TE GALIOOT HET
WEESELTIE GESAGH HEBBER CORNELIS DE VLAMINGH
VAN VLIELANDT STVIRMAN COERT GERRITSEN
VAN BREMEN EN VAN HIER GEZEYLT MET ONSE
VLOT DEN VOORTS HET ZVYDLANDT
VERDER TE ONDERSOECREN EN GE DIS=
TINEERT VOOR BATAVIA =—

12

AN UNEXPLORED COAST LIES AHEAD OF 'INVESTIGATOR'

In 1801 a British naval officer, Matthew Flinders (1774–1814), received orders from his government to proceed, with *Investigator* and her crew of eighty-two, on an expedition taking in the whole south coast of Australia, the east coast from Port Stephens to Cape Palmerston, the full length of the Barrier Reef, the Gulf of Carpentaria, and the territorial waters in those regions. In carrying out his tremendous task he was the first to establish beyond a doubt that Australia was not composed of two or more large islands, but constituted a fifth continent.

*Watering Gully*
*N.W. one mile*

On the remote and desolate coast north-west of Port Bowen, Queensland, past whose rocks and scrub Cook had once sailed unheeding, Flinders discovered, on 24th August, 1802, a small, well-hidden inlet with a stream running into it (Watering Gully). He sent a few men ashore with casks and they lingered to take soundings before returning to the ship. They brought back their casks full of fresh spring water, and a supply of wood for the cook's galley from the pines which had already been observed here and there, through the telescope, from the distant vessel. In his report the leader mentions the artist of the expedition, William Westall (1781 to 1850), then only twenty-one years old, saying that his picture will enable any seaman to find the little landing-place without difficulty. Among Westall's duties was that of drawing views of points along the coast. Many of these, such as the one reproduced above (considerably enlarged), are not merely topographical documents, but really convey some of the poetry and seductive charm sensed by the explorers in the untrodden land that rose, mysterious and silent, from the mirror-like surface of the ocean.

KANGAROO ISLAND OFF THE SOUTH COAST OF AUSTRALIA

While mapping the southern coast, the *Investigator* anchored off Kangaroo Island, which Flinders had already visited in 1798, when he and Bass had sailed for the first time round Tasmania and thus proved it to be an island. Kangaroos, ostriches and seals were gathered in the deep peace of a forest-fringed bay, at one of the few spots where there was a spring of fresh water. Even the matter-of-fact Flinders had difficulty in tearing himself away from this place where, as he remarked, the Golden Age seemed still to endure.

THE FLINDERS EXPEDITION MEETS DISASTER ON ITS HOMEWARD VOYAGE

After more than a year of toilsome exploratory sailing the *Investigator* had become unseaworthy, so Flinders and his men began their voyage home from Port Jackson with the *Porpoise* and its little escort vessel the *Cato*. On 17th August 1803 both ships ran aground on a sandbank near a coral reef (foreground). Many books, maps, drawings and plant specimens were lost. The party used the ships' canvas to make tents, hoisted the Union Jack upside-down as a distress signal, and settled down to wait for help, under a stormy sky where light and darkness seemed to fluctuate like the fears and hopes in their own minds. Flinders and a few men rowed back to Port Jackson—a distance of about 800 miles—and returned with another ship. By 11th October 1803 everything was stowed on board again; but Flinders was not to set eyes on his native land till June 1810, for he was captured by the French off Mauritius and held as a prisoner of war. The publication of his book, *Voyage to Terra Australis,* was consequently delayed until 1814. On the day it appeared, he died.

An Expedition takes a Holiday

During his voyage round the world, the French explorer H. Y. P. Florentin de Bougainville (see page 243) decided to give his ship and crew a rest, while he himself, with a few companions, went inland to visit the hospitable Cox brothers on their big estate at Regentville, Camden County—on the borders of what was then a newly colonized area. On 8th August 1825 the guests, with a party drawn from the estate, travelled some distance by boat up the Waragamba, a river flowing down from the mountainous district of Argyle County. The force of its seething waters could be judged from the great boulders washed down by the current, a splintered tree and an overhanging cliff, washed clear, beneath which stood a natural table. The excursionists enjoyed an informal picnic in the 'furnished grotto'.

In mid-September 1818 Louis-Claude de Freycinet's *Uranie* (see page 256) anchored off the west coast of Australia and an armed party went ashore. Over the hill-top appeared a group of natives who hurried towards the explorers, brandishing long spears. Were they friends or enemies? Two of the Frenchmen indicated the visitors' peaceful intentions by courageously advancing towards the wild men with a dancing gait. This elicited similar behaviour from the aborigines; prancing forward, they held out their spears with inviting gestures, and the Europeans sealed the agreement by affixing their presents—coloured neckerchiefs and bead necklaces. In return they were given some weapons. More and more natives came hastening up, and the atmosphere grew tense. Arago, the artist, saved the situation. He moved slowly forward, clicking a pair of castanets. Immediately one of the Australians took up the rhythm, tapping it out on the haft of his spear as though obeying a pre-arranged signal, and one of the older men began to dance. At sundown the natives withdrew.

*Below:* The Expedition's Distilling Apparatus. Freycinet was the first explorer to take distilling apparatus on a voyage round the world, in an effort to solve the vital problem of drinking water aboard ship. The transformation of sea-water was a tedious process, so whenever a party went on land it took one set of distilling equipment, collected wood and prepared a supply of water which was poured into casks, while the other apparatus was working on the ship.

ABDUCTION SCENE NEAR PORT JACKSON

The Freycinet expedition witnessed some extremely bar-barous abductions, which were customary in South Australia. The young aborigines usually took their wives from other tribes, either by striking a bargain with a girl's parents or simply by carrying her off. In the latter case the victim would be fallen upon in an unwary moment by a mob of young men who grabbed her by the arms—so roughly that a shoulder was often put out of joint—and while she struggled to defend herself, beat her over her head and shoulders with their clubs or boomerangs until she was stunned. She was then dragged away into the neighbouring forest and given over to the tender mercies of her kidnappers; after which one of them would take her as his wife.

*Right:* AN AUSTRALIAN COCKATOO (PLICTOLOPHUS LEAD-BEATERI). This bird is easily recognized by its magnificent crest of feathers and its exceptionally strong beak, with which it can crack the hardest nutshells and also, when tree-climb-ing, lever itself up. It is found in vast numbers in the Aus-tralian bush and eucalyptus forests, and the glorious colours of its plumage delight the eye, although planters have not a good word to say for it. 'Undoubtedly the most beautiful of all cockatoos', declared the great ornithologist Otto Finsch.

The English artist John Gould (1804–81) could render the beauty of birds to the very life. He began his career as a taxidermist for the Royal Zoological Society's museum, but later gained world-wide renown as an ardent ornithologist, tireless in hunting for specimens and painting them. In the course of his long life he published forty-one volumes with 2,999 plates; many of them are of great artistic value. He visited Australia in 1838–40, after he had already published his *Synopsis of the Birds of Australia,* which was based on a unique collection of stuffed birds. This picture is an enlarged reproduction from that work.

VIEW FROM JELLORE LOOKING NORTH AND NORTH-WEST OVER THE UNEXPLORED INTERIOR OF NEW SOUTH WALES (1828)

This is a page from the sketchbook of Thomas Livingstone Mitchell (1792–1855), a Scot who made four expeditions into New South Wales between 1831 and 1846, when he was in charge of the Australian Ordnance Survey. During these journeys he established the course of the River Darling and looked for a route from Sydney across South Australia to Port Phillip on the southern coast; he also investigated the possibilities of an overland route to the Gulf of Carpentaria in the north. Mitchell's work began at a time when, with the exception of Africa, the interior of Australia was the largest tract of unknown territory in the world. In 1828, making his first preparations, he gazed out from Jellore across the untrodden ridges and valleys stretching like a billowing ocean to where the Blue Mountains closed the horizon and, while

he gave names to a few prominent landmarks, he felt that the forbidding task ahead of him might prove too much for any topographer. The expanse of naked rock was criss-crossed by a maze of steep-sided ravines, while here and there dense forests seemed to block the way completely.

But Mitchell struggled forward, sometimes following the course of rivers, sometimes setting up his apparatus on a mountain peak and trying to distinguish the features of the landscape from that point of vantage. He travelled with oxcarts, collapsable boats and a flock of sheep (as a perambulating meat-supply); some of his companions were convicts who had volunteered as a means of earning their freedom. Sometimes the expedition came across mistrustful natives, but its worst enemy was the notorious Australian drought. However, the way did not lead entirely through uninhabitable wilderness; Mitchell also found what every explorer of Australia hoped to discover in the interior—grasslands, fertile soil, groves of trees, a Promised Land for settlers. He writes of this 'Australia Felix' with prophetic ecstasy: 'This highly interesting region lay before me with all its features new and untouched as they fell from the hands of the Creator. Of this Eden it seemed that I was only the Adam; and it was indeed a sort of paradise to me, permitted thus to be the first to explore its mountains and streams—to behold its scenery—to investigate its geological character—and, finally, by my survey, to develop those natural advantages all still unknown to the civilized world, but yet certain to become important to a new people.' (See page 286.)

ABORIGINES FROM THE REGION OF SYDNEY PERFORMING A WAR-DANCE

The American expedition led by Charles Wilkes (see page 255) spent some time in Australia on its way round the world. Among the episodes recorded by A. T. Agate, the official artist, was this dance, which took place at night by the flickering light of a camp fire. The spectators sang or beat time on their shields, while the dancers, who had drawn skeletons on their bodies with chalk, emerged eerily like phantoms from the thick forest into the firelight and worked themselves gradually into a frenzy, some of them hurling their boomerangs. Then they vanished into the darkness as silently as they had come. This was a favourite dance, performed not only to mark the close of battles but also as an entertainment in time of peace.

Pl. 36.

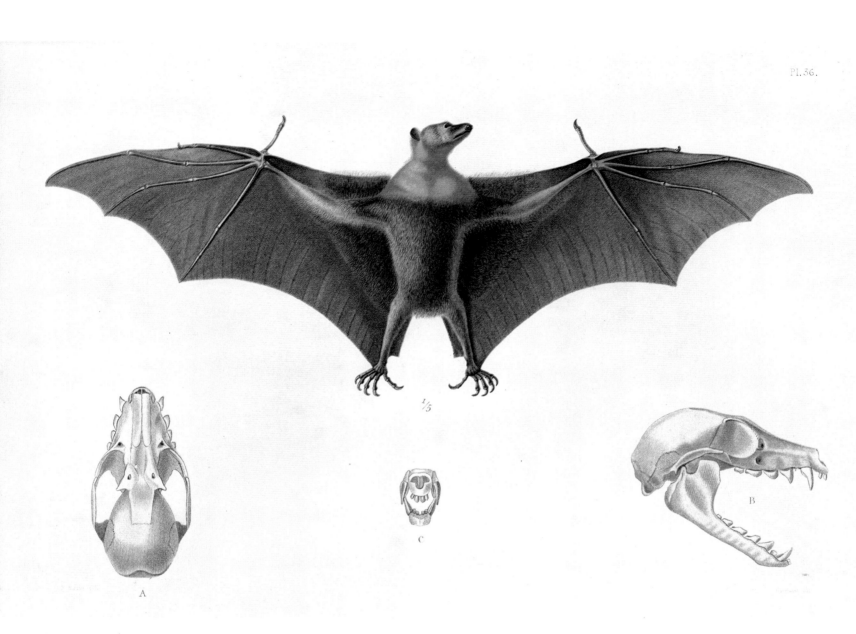

A Flying Fox (Pteropus poliocephalus) from New South Wales

As the explorers penetrated further into the interior of Australia, it began to seem like a veritable zoo of fabulous animals —kangaroo, duck-billed platypus, lyre-bird and so forth. The creature shown above—one of the cheiroptera, with a head like that of a fox—astonished de Bougainville's company, too, during his exploration of the South Pacific islands in 1824–26. They were particularly impressed by its size—one they measured had a wingspan of 35 inches—and made an accurate record of its characteristics, noting the claws on the thumb and first finger, the short, bald ears, long, pointed snout, hairy body and rudimentary tail. The cranium is seen from below (A); in profile (B); and from the front (C).

A Tree serving the Same Purpose on Land as the Crow's Nest of a Ship at Sea

Two pictures based on drawings made by Mitchell during his last great expedition (1845/46) to explore the north-western territory in the direction of the Gulf of Carpentaria. *Above:* Scanning impenetrable forest from a tree-top. *Right:* After toiling on foot and horseback through a labyrinth of oppressively narrow river valleys, Mitchell emerged with joyful surprise into one of the beautiful landscapes which sometimes rewarded the explorer in Australia. At the top of a pointed hill among scattered trees rose what looked like the ruins of some ancient watch-tower built by human hands. Across the foreground wound one of the narrow drains in which his party had so often sought in vain for a drop of refreshing water. Mitchell called the place 'Tower Almond', after a castle that stood, as lonely as this crag, in his homeland.

near Dr Baynton's. Crossing an ancient Crater 25 August. L. Becker

ROBERT O'HARA BURKE'S EXPEDITION CROSSING THE CRATER OF AN EXTINCT VOLCANO. From the sketchbook of the naturalist L. Becker.

## Robert O'Hara Burke's Journey from South to North Australia

The Royal Society in Victoria promised considerable backing to any explorer who would discover a route across Australia from south to north—from Melbourne to the Gulf of Carpentaria. Robert O'Hara Burke (1820–61), a senior member of the Melbourne police force, got together a party of twenty for this purpose, including a doctor, an astronomer, a geologist and the naturalist and painter Ludwig Becker. He hoped to cross the waterless tracts which would have to be traversed by using Afghan camels to help out the horses that drew his covered waggons. On reaching his base camp at Cooper Creek, about half-way across the continent, he decided to wait for his rearguard to catch up with him. The first picture (left) shows the expedition crossing the crater of an extinct volcano not far from Cooper Creek. Burke reckoned that the journey from there to the Gulf of Carpentaria and back would take three months. Impatient at the delay caused by the tardy rearguard, he set out northwards on 16th December 1860, leaving a few of his followers at the camp with orders to go on waiting. On the morning of 20th April 1861, these too—afflicted with scurvy and with no sign of relief from the rearguard or of Burke's return—left the base camp in the direction of Melbourne. Their leader, Brahe, buried some supplies for Burke at the foot of a tree and carved the one word, 'DIG!' in its bark. On the evening of the same day Burke and his companions reached the camp, utterly spent—one of them had died of exhaustion on the way, and it was his burial that had caused the fatal day's delay in their return to Cooper Creek. Burke had reached his goal on 11th February 1861; but his expedition ended in a series of tragedies, all connected with the tree marked 'Dig!' Burke dug up the provisions and left a message in the hole, explaining what had happened during his expedition to the coast. But he gave no indication of the route he next intended to follow (through dangerous territory along the River Darling), and left no visible sign of his passage. After a month of desperate hardship he decided to make good this omission, and sent Wills, the doctor, back to the fatal tree. Wills duly buried the new message, but forgot, in his turn, to mark his visit. He returned only to find Burke dying of exhaustion.

Meanwhile Brahe had gone back to the deserted base camp; but as there was nothing to suggest that anyone had passed that way, he had not dug up the cache. The same thing happened when a rescue party reached Cooper Creek on 13th September 1861—some two and a half months after Burke and Wills had died, for lack of help, in the arid wilderness. Two days later, purely by chance, this new expedition found the sole survivor of Burke's party, a man named King. He was half-crazy and reduced to a skeleton, but had made shift to live among the natives, occasionally doing them service with a shot from his flintlock, while his scanty ammunition lasted.

# AFRICA

◄ One of the Marvels of Australia: The Blow Hole at Kiama (1848)

A spit of rock protrudes into the Pacific at the southern end of the harbour of Kiama in New South Wales, 125 miles south of Sydney. Immediately above water-level there is an opening in the rock so that, when the ocean rises, the water is forced with enormous power through the passage behind. At the end of this it gushes up through a rock-crater with such pressure that it rises high into the air, like a fountain.

Far out to sea is a ship—a trader linking ambitious Australia with the rest of the world, via routes which have now (1848) been known for many years. Expeditions are no longer sent out to Australia. The explorer is remembered only by his two legacies: the country itself, which he was the first to open up for those whom, in his mind's eye, he already envisaged laying out streets, cultivating the land, building towns and harbours; and his written descriptions of the territory he had added to the map of the world.

On old maps Africa looks like a frame around a half-empty canvas. Even in the late eighteenth century the world knew little of the 'Dark Continent' except its coastal fringe and here and there a strip of land—on the Congo or the Zambesi, or in Abyssinia, for example—though the picture became clearer as the eye travelled northward, from the lonely Cape of Good Hope towards the Mediterranean whose shores had been colonized by ancient peoples, and finally to Egypt, the scene of the earliest independent high civilization on African soil. The interior south of the Sudan remained a mystery until well into the nineteenth century. European imagination accordingly ran riot there—no other continent was so richly filled by fabulous tribes, beasts and rivers.

From the ninth century onwards, fanatical Arab Moslems took possession of the desert belt and expanded the already established trade between the Mediterranean coast and the Sudan. Considerable information about these territories had been recorded by their geographers, but unbelievers were not admitted to them and very rarely did a foreign merchant make his way across country into some forbidden city. In the sixteenth century the Portuguese established themselves on Africa's western and eastern coasts; later the Dutch began to colonize the South; and in course of time the French from Senegal and the British from Gambia tried to secure a share of the trade in gold, skins, valuable woods and so forth; but even then the actual interior of the continent was not penetrated.

The other great continents, whose possibilities were more attractive, lured the explorers away from Africa with its scorching central deserts. And when they finally turned their attention to it they were indeed confronted with other deadly obstacles besides those endless wastes of sand. There were great expanses of fever-ridden marsh and forest; travellers who survived the dangers with which nature beset them easily fell victim to Moslem rivals or hostile Negroes. It has been estimated that 374 explorers lost their lives in Africa between 1800 and 1894—a casualty list almost as long as that of Arctic exploration.

At the end of the eighteenth century European explorers turned to the gigantic task of 'making up for two thousand years of lack of curiosity' about Africa, as Marcel Griaule puts it. The great movement began in the north-east and north-west of the continent. The manner in which Napoleon's Egyptian campaign laid the foundations for the present-day picture of Egypt may be seen from pages 296 to 305; in the north-west and, a little later, in the neighbouring desert lands, the impetus came from England. In 1783 Britain lost her economic footing in the United States, and Africa, with its limitless possibilities, began to attract explorer and merchant alike. The African Association—forerunner of the Royal Geographical Society—was founded in 1788 and began to despatch investigators into what were still blanks on the map. Many of these pioneers were impelled not only by curiosity and by economic and political considerations, but also by a passionate determination to free the continent from the clutches of the Arab slave-traders.

In 1795 the Association sent Mungo Park, a young Scottish doctor, to chart the elusive course of the Niger; in the eighteen-twenties it sent Denham and Clapperton along the ancient caravan routes which crossed the immense desert of North Africa, as far as Lake Chad. The further details added to the picture of the desert belt by Caillié and later by Nachtigal and others are described on pages 312 to 320. The most important figure among the early explorers of the territory between the Mediterranean, Lake Chad and the Niger was Heinrich Barth, a German working in the spirit of Humboldt. Acting on behalf of England in the years 1850–55, he concluded trade agreements with local chiefs.

But it was David Livingstone, above all, who excelled in keenness of observation, intelligent understanding and a heartfelt compassion for the black population in their wretchedness. He crossed the continent from coast to coast; he explored the lake regions; he disproved the theory, held since the time of Herodotus, that the interior was one vast desert; and he dreamt of the day when Africa would take its place in world trade and in the great currents of humanism and Christianity. He was not only Africa's greatest explorer, but its most unselfish champion (see pages 321 to 331). His discoveries were supplemented by the achievement of Henry Morton Stanley, who travelled right down the Congo. A number of less spectacular achievements allowed the picture of the southernmost part of the continent to be gradually filled in between the seventeenth and nineteenth centuries (see page 332 f.).

Livingstone and Stanley also turned their attention to the ancient problem of the sources of the Nile; but it was two other Englishmen, J. H. Speke and S. Grant, who found the final solution, replacing the vague, though basically correct description offered by Ptolemy (see page 336).

Now that these tremendous tasks were completed, there still remained a host of smaller regions of the interior to be investigated. Many nations did fine work here, but in the latter part of the century there was a growing tendency for the continent to become the scene of political rivalry among the great powers. This was the beginning of the era of the 'scramble for Africa'.

THE SOUTHERNMOST POINT OF AFRICA AND THE ▶
VISIONARY TERRA AUSTRALIS

In 1487 Bartholomeu Diaz sailed round the Cape of Good Hope, the first European to accomplish this feat. Sixty-nine years later, Guillaume Le Testu (see page 231) completed his *Cosmographie universelle,* a work that radiates delight in the visibly widening world. He still believed unquestioningly in the existence of an Antarctic continent, the Terra Australis. Le Testu furnishes this southern expanse with animals, rivers, trees, and strangely-bedizened human beings and the sea around it with monstrous creatures; he adds a Portuguese galleon, the proudest ship of that period, sailing west in all its glory. The masts of some galleons were over 90 feet high; the third and shortest mast often carried a triangular lateen sail. The high forecastle and quarter-deck, from which the lower level, amidships, could be raked with gunfire, served as final defence-posts against enemy boarding parties: the Portuguese galleon was both a transport vessel—often with upwards of five hundred human beings crowded on board—and a floating fortress. With these ships it became possible, for the first time, to set up a world-wide trade network.

The lavishly-decorated disks are a striking feature of this chart; some of them show the compass needle, pointing north, in the form of a stylized lily. They are placed, in most cases, at points where a number of orientation lines run together, often at completely arbitrary intervals. The distance from one to another can be ascertained by consulting the scale on the left-hand border of the map. Le Testu gives the distance between two figures as nearly 46 miles, making the earth too small by at least one-third, as was customary in his day. To set a course by the compass with the help of these orientation lines was no simple matter.

TERRE                    DV CAP DE BONE
                        ESPERANSÉ

Cap de bonne esperanse

MER   OCEANE

TERRE        AVSTRAL

293

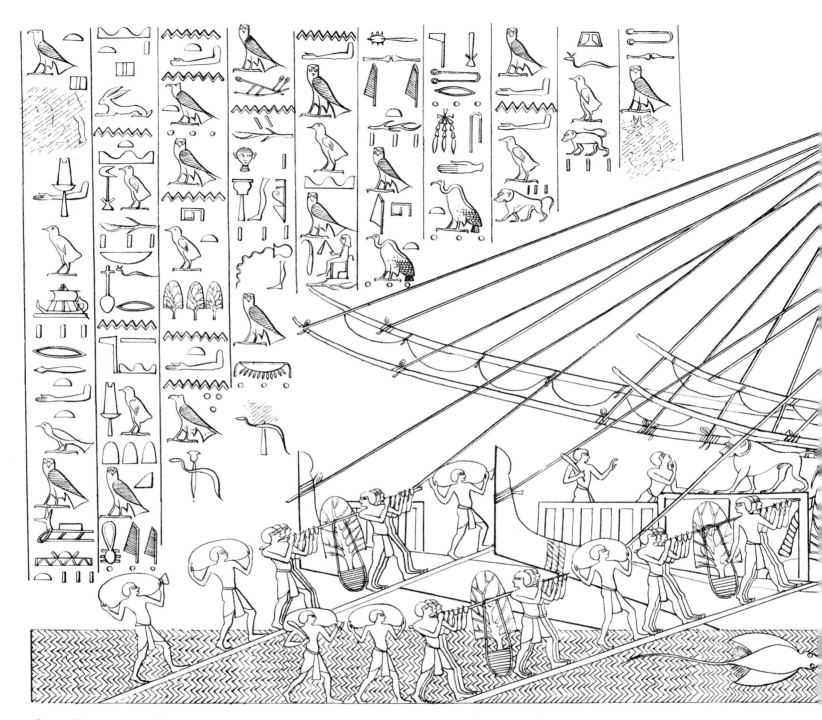

QUEEN HATSHEPSET OF EGYPT SENDS A TRADE DELEGATION TO THE LAND OF PUNT (1493/92 BC)

The earliest expedition mentioned in African history dates back nearly 3,500 years. It was sent out by Queen Hatshepset, the ambitious, of Egypt, to establish trade relations with the Somali coast. One of the precepts she handed down to her successors of the Eighteenth Dynasty was an injunction to widen the political frontiers and intensify the trading activities of the empire. Her spirited career is reverently depicted in rows of reliefs in the precincts of the gigantic temple of Dêr-el-bahri, near Thebes. These two Egyptian ships are

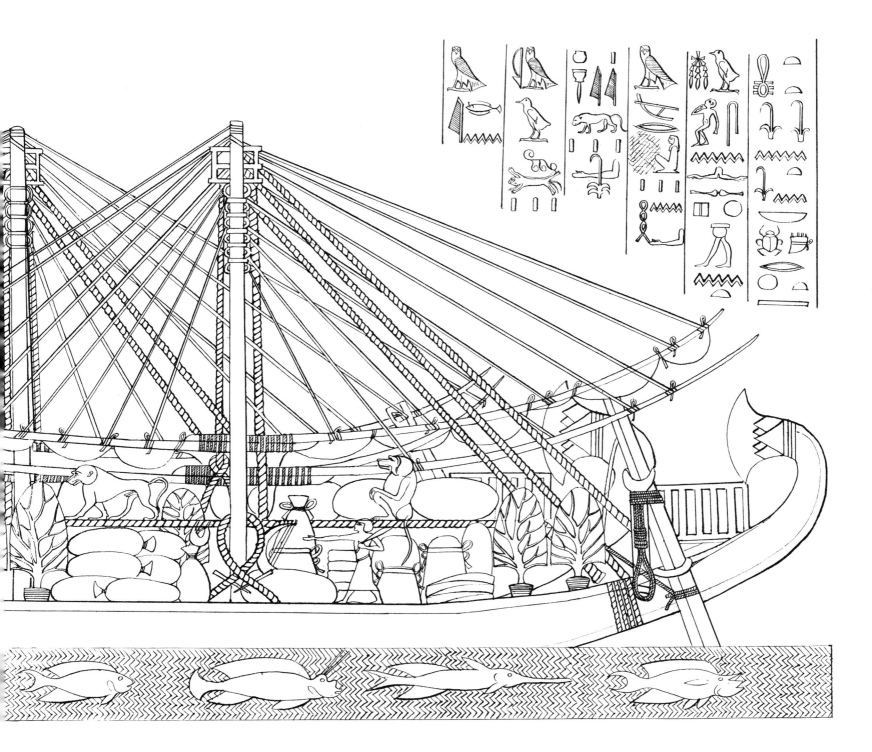

shown taking up a cargo for Egypt in the legendary incense land of Punt (somewhere in the region of the Somali coast). The voyage across the Red Sea and beyond was a venturesome affair for these vessels, which relied partly on rowers and partly on sail. Here the top yard has been lowered from its position at the masthead to its place of stowage, just above the main yard, and the pair of heavy steering oars at the stern hang idly in the water. The low gunwale rises gracefully to the perpendicular stem and the bold curve of the stern, and there is a platform, or bridge, fore and aft of the vessel. The inscription informs us that the cargo consisted of resin for incense, ivory, firewood, leopard-skins, apes and so forth, in exchange for which the Egyptians had brought the products of their craftsmen. Teams of six men are dragging baskets full of the much-coveted incense trees over the gangway. The reports brought back by these seamen extended their countrymen's geographical horizon almost as far as the equator.

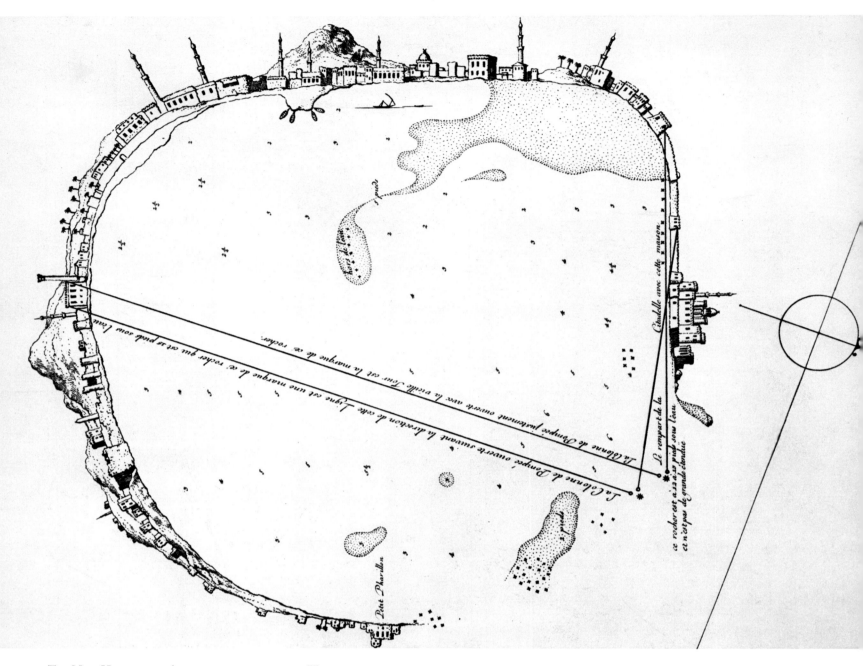

THE NEW HARBOUR OF ALEXANDRIA SHOWING THE HAZARDS IT PRESENTED

*Above:* The first coherent map of Egypt was made in 1737/38 by the Danish cartographer F.L.Norden (1708–42)—a highly original personality. His 'fish's-eye view' of the new harbour at Alexandria carefully indicates the dangerous shallows and the safest way in. In ancient time the Pharos— one of the seven wonders of the world—stood on the right side of the entrance to this harbour.—*Right:* One of the twenty-nine sections of Norden's map of the Nile Valley, showing where the inhabited land meets the barren desert. *Below:* The old City of Cairo, on the site of 'Babylon', originally a settlement for Assyrian prisoners of war. In the river we can just see the southern tip of the island of Rôda, with the famous Mikjas water-gauge of the Nile. Memphis, the chief city of the Old Kingdom, was situated near the village of Gizeh. Both banks of the river are lined with villages, arable land, palm-groves and the minarets of mosques. The cross at Deir Etiin marks a Coptic church.

*Overleaf:* IN THE REALM OF THE DEAD—THE SUBTERRANEAN MAUSOLEUM OF SETI I, NEAR THEBES. The first man to make a systematic search for the ancient Egypt which lay concealed was G.B.Belzoni (1778–1823), who began his career as a 'strong man' in a circus. One of his red-letter days was 18th October, 1817, when he tunnelled through the pile of stones and earth shown above on the left, into the subterranean monument, about 330 feet long, whose contents bore witness to the Egyptian desire to live for ever, with the help of the gods, in the other world. A pit, 33 yards deep, intended to collect any rainwater that might seep in, was bridged by a plank, on the far side of which the explorer passed an enthroned statue of Osiris, God of the Underworld, with Isis, his consort, on his left and the Sun God on his right. Belzoni came later to a gallery, its roof supported by two columns, and unfinished sketches on its walls. In the principal chamber, with the winged Sun God, he found the (empty) alabaster sarcophagus.

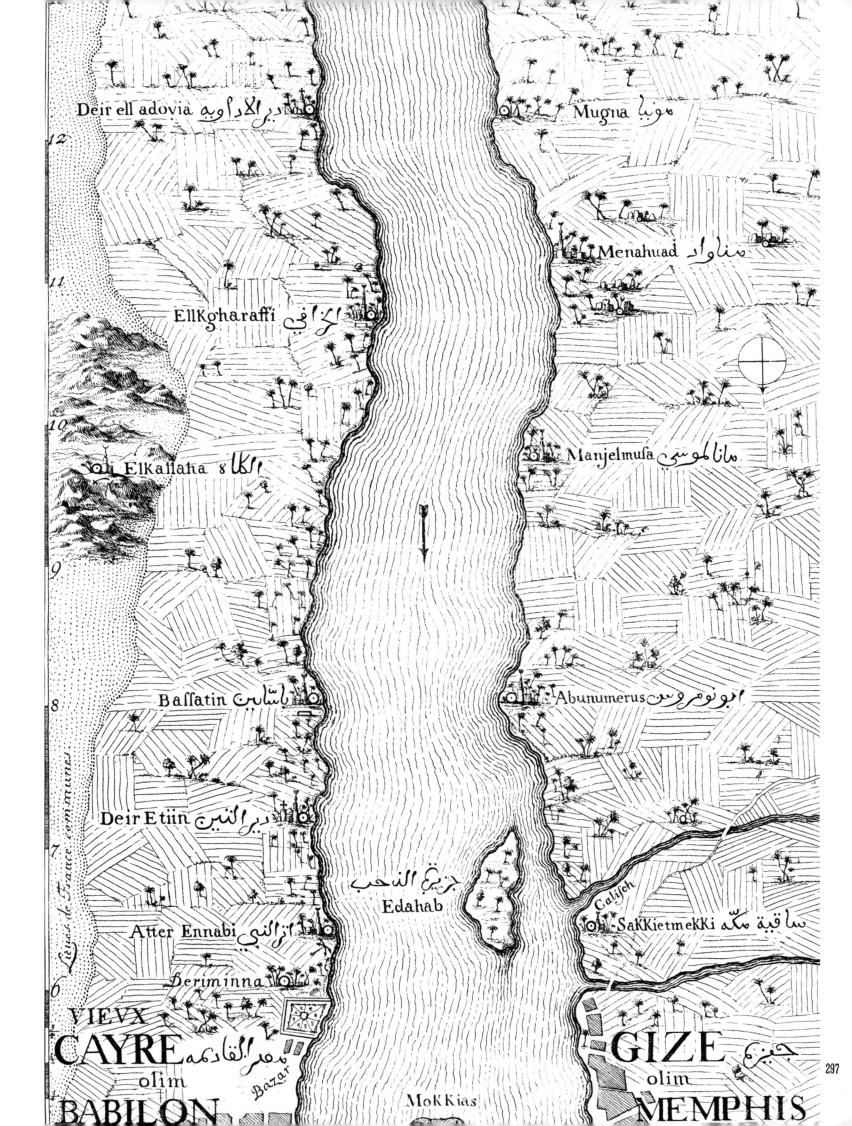

Deir ell adovia مدير الادوية    Mugna موبيا

Menahuad مناواد

EllKgharaffi الخرافي

Elkallaha 8 الكلا

Manjelmufa مانا الموسي

Ballatin باسّاتين    Abunumerus ابونومرس

Deir Etiin دير النبي

جريج النحب
Edahab    Calisch

Atter Ennabi ازر النبي    SakKietmekKi ساقبة مكّه

Beriminna

VIEVX
CAYRE مصر القادمه
olim    Bazar
BABILON

GIZE جبزه
olim
MEMPHIS

MoKKias

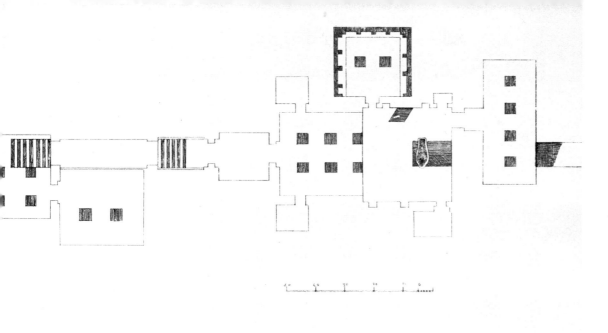

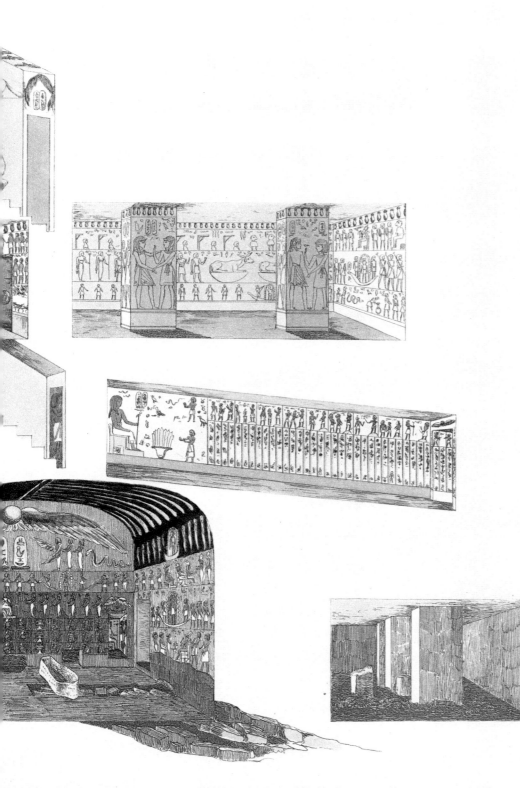

PHARAOH RAMSES II AND HIS CONSORT QUEEN NOFRETIRI GUARD THE SMALL CLIFF TEMPLE OF ABU SIMBEL

Few archaeologists who visited the scene of Africa's most ancient civilization during the early nineteenth century penetrated far enough beyond the first cataract of the Nile to reach the place on the left bank—Abu Simbel, in Nubian territory—where two subterranean temples had been carved in the solid rock by the daring architects of the Nineteenth Dynasty. The best drawings of these extraordinary carvings were made by Franz Christian Gau (1790–1853), a German architect who had settled in Paris. *Above:* The façade of the Small Temple, dedicated by Ramses II (1293–25 BC) to Hathor, Goddess of Love and to his own consort, Nofretiri,

who had been raised to divine rank. Buttresses, niches, and statues of the King and Queen—three of each, all over 30 feet high—were carved by the Egyptian sculptors in the cliff-face. The young princes and princesses are shown as tiny figures beside their towering parents. Dedicatory inscriptions are carved round the statues, whose size dwarfs the camels below. The Queen, in her role of mother, holds in one hand the hieroglyphic symbol for 'life'. *Right:* The dimensions of the Great Temple are even more fantastic. Gau drew one of the four statues, 66 feet high, of Ramses II which stand at the entrance. Beside his knee we see the artist himself.

*Overleaf:* TIMELESS ART IN ANCIENT EGYPTIAN BAS-RELIEFS. In the early days of Egyptology the principal work of reference was the *Description de l'Egypte,* published in twenty-four volumes between 1809 and 1813, which described the highly successful scientific results of Napoleon's disastrous Egyptian campaign (see page 304) and gave the first accurate pictures of many ancient Egyptian monuments which were still standing in the open. But amazing masterpieces lay buried in sand or hidden in caverns, awaiting future seekers; and even more important, the numerous hieroglyphic inscriptions so carefully copied by the French archaeologists had yet to be deciphered. It was Jean-François Champollion (1790–1832) who, shortly before 1820, found the key to this enigma and thus penetrated the secret of the most ancient cultural monuments the world had yet discovered. It was not till 1828/29 that he actually visited Egypt, and the huge folio volumes containing the inscriptions he had copied out there, together with a host of reproductions of reliefs, drawn on the spot, did not begin to appear until after his premature death. They depicted a rich, fascinating universe, an inexhaustible range of timeless, primeval human lore, presented with a classical, stylized restraint that seemed to anticipate the finest period of Greek art. Four examples will serve to illustrate this.

*Above:* Ramses III has just concluded a victorious campaign. The defeated party are carrying a dead comrade-in-arms back to his home, on a hill where herdsmen live. A messenger is breaking the news to the man's young widow, who makes sorrowful gestures. From ed-Derr, Nubia.

*Left:* Two prisoners of war, an Asian from Mesopotamia and a Negro. They are painted on the soles of Pharaoh's shoes, as symbols of the perpetually downtrodden. From a burial chamber at Kurna, near Thebes.

*Above, right:* Egyptian potters working at their wheels. From Beni-Hasan.

*Below, right:* Four priests carrying a sacred boat, in which a king kneels before a shrine. On the right is the hawk-headed Sun God, at the prow of the vessel is the head of Isis, and above is the winged disc of the sun. Found on the island of Philae where a Temple of Isis once stood.

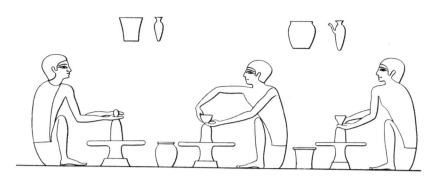

ZAOJÊ VILLAGE ON THE NILE IN LOWER EGYPT

Napoleon's rash Egyptian campaign (1798–99) opened with a series of brilliant victories; but after Nelson had destroyed the French fleet at Aboukir matters went from bad to worse, with Napoleon leading the thirty-eight thousand soldiers of his army to defeat, sickness and death. But, for the swarm of geometricians, mineralogists, astronomers, orientalists and historians—one hundred and seventy-five in all—whom he had also brought, the final outcome was triumph and lasting benefit. Their gigantic *Description de l'Egypte* paved the way for a more comprehensive presentation of ancient and modern Egypt, which gradually effaced the confused picture which had lingered on for centuries; and their map of the country (1807) was a masterpiece. An appetizing foretaste of these marvels was given in *Voyage dans la Haute et la Basse*

*Egypte,* by Dominique-Vivant Denon, an artist who, for all his fifty-one years, had gone right through the campaign, imperturbably sketching alongside General Desaix and his troops, and had penetrated into Nubian territory.

Denon was a man of the world and a connoisseur of good living. As an aristocrat, he had lost his estates twelve years earlier in the French Revolution, but this had impaired neither his brilliant draughtsmanship nor his insatiable thirst for adventure—whether amorous or geographical. On his return to France, Napoleon made him Director-General of French Museums. In Egypt his interest embraced not only the country's ancient art but its modern life as well, and in between-times he recorded episodes of the campaign with the accuracy and verve of a born journalist.

Even in this (considerably enlarged) picture of a peaceful Egyptian village on the Nile, two piles of guns and a sentry remind us that the country was under foreign occupation, and the unusual number of boats on the river may indicate military activities rather than those of the local fishermen. The houses are built of clay, mixed with chopped-up straw and baked in the sun. Denon, who had a vivid imagination, was thrilled by the thought that the whole village might be reduced to a mud-pie by a heavy rainstorm—though such an occurance was hardly conceivable in the Nile valley. The little turrets are dovecots. Cakes of dried ox- and camel-dung, to be used for fuel, are heaped into low ramparts on the flat roofs. The bundles in the foreground are stems of dhurra *(Sorghum vulgare),* Africa's most important cereal.

A Troop of Striped Mongooses on a Deserted Termites' Nest

For the gifted naturalist Wilhelm von Harnier (1836–61) drawing was a form of exploration. He met his death on his great journey up the White Nile and the notes in his journal were never published, so the principal results of his expedition are his pictures. Accompanied by a hunter and a taxidermist from Europe, and with an escort of fifteen armed Dongolese, he left Khartoum in 1860 on board a Sudanese merchant vessel, intending to study the world of men and animals of the primeval forests and grasslands along the White Nile, between latitudes 15 degrees and 4 degrees north. He built a special village for his expedition in this region.

One of his liveliest drawings (prepared for colour reproduction, like the rest, by the painter J. M. Bernatz) shows a company of striped mongooses *(Herpestes)*; small, bushy-tailed, playful carnivorous animals which bustle along, snuffing about with their sharp-pointed noses. From earliest times they have been renowned for their heroic duels with poisonous snakes. The ancient Egyptians regarded them as sacred, and dead mongooses were embalmed and buried in consecrated ground, like kings. Near the trees in the distance is a group of water-buck, and a shadow-bird *(Scopus)* gazes down from his perch upon the lively scene.

A Herd of Buffalo in the Primeval Forest of Nubia

Wilhelm von Harnier's passion was to study every kind of living creature at the closest possible quarters. It was this that led to his death. On 23rd November, 1861, he wounded a charging bull buffalo, and the infuriated beast trampled on him. It was a *bos caffer* similar to those shown in the above picture, which he had drawn only just before. This is the rainy season; sullen-eyed buffaloes, with the characteristic huge swellings at the roots of their horns, are standing in the cool water. They tolerate the heron on their backs to be rid of the parasites it destroys. Below, left, is a kingfisher; above, an eagle perches on the branch of a tamarind.

ONE OF THE MOST MAGNIFICENT BOUNDARY-STONES IN THE WORLD (enlarged detail)

For a long time the frontier between Egypt and Nubia was situated near the First Cataract, where the Nile flows through a wild, rocky landscape and over a ledge of granite boulders. One of the later Pharaohs, Psammetichus II, had his name and various inscriptions carved here, on a cloven rock of granite, north-east of the island of Philae. This was not long before 525 BC when Egypt lost independence and became a Persian province; so we see here one of the last of the enduring monuments erected by the ancient Egyptian rulers, who pitted their royal will against the destructive forces of time.

# An Explorer battles with the Sahara

After the Denham-Clapperton and Heinrich Barth expeditions, the most important of the explorers to cross the Sahara by the ancient caravan route from Tripoli to Lake Chad was a German doctor, Gustav Nachtigal (1834–85). He went to the Chad region to take a gift from the King of Prussia to Sultan Omar of Bornu, and the mission developed into a journey of exploration lasting six years.

In 1867 he set out on a daring venture, to investigate the rugged, desolate mountains of Tibesti, about which nothing was then known. Ragged, weak, abandoned by his native guides—who had turned out to be extortioners among whom even his life was in danger—he toiled back across the Sahara towards Mount Tummo and safety. The remaining members of the expedition—five Arab camel-drivers and his Italian servant, Giuseppe—were with him on this last desperate march, some incidents of which are described below in his own words.

Nachtigal spent nine months in recovering from these hardships at Kuka, the residence of the hospitable Omar and a great market for the Sudan. From there he made trips round Lake Chad and to Timbuktu, and also sought information about Baghirmi, the country of Moslem Negroes which lay further east. In 1874 he returned to Europe by way of Wadai, the eastern desert and Egypt.

We could see Tummo ahead of us, to the north-west, but it looked discouragingly far off. Its well-known shape was only faintly visible through the misty vapour that always hangs over the desert as the sun climbs up the sky, and we reckoned that several days of painful travel must elapse before we could reach it. The scorching sun was a torment; our feet sank deep into the sand that filled the hollows between the ridges; I saw no hope of ever getting to Tummo; after only a few hours my strength was so completely exhausted that I felt convinced I should soon succumb.

Before the day was far advanced, Giuseppe and I noticed a kind of hesitancy in the movements of our companions, who were a little ahead of us, with the camels. This was not one of the short pauses that occur sometimes because a camel's load has been shifted; the whole train could be seen to be slowing down appreciably. We went up to them in great anxiety, and our fear that something serious had happened to one of the camels proved only too justified. The animal belonging to the Tubu youth had become 'Battâl'—unfit for work. This discovery was indeed grievous, but I was so overwhelmed by my own sense of physical unfitness as to be secretly relieved at the necessity of making a long halt so early in the day.

There was no hope of getting the camel any further in the increasing heat. If it was to render any service it could only be in the cool of the evening and night hours. We scrambled up a hillock where some sandstone rocks offered shade, and decided that the chests the sick beast had been carrying should be hidden there, and that we would eat and drink as much as possible so as to lighten the remaining load as best we could. The rest was a long one, but proved of little use to me. My heart was hammering, my temples throbbing, my tongue clove to my palate. The others relished the dried camel flesh which can be eaten uncooked; but I found it impossible to swallow the dry substance, with its strong, salty taste. I tried at least to eat some dates, but their sweetness was repugnant to me. I hoped to get some sleep, but the feverish agitation of my overtired body prevented it. I lay in despair, naked to the waist, on the water-skins we had just emptied, their damp coolness grateful to my burning skin, and tried in vain to slake the fire within me with the water—ice-cold from evaporation through the fibres of the skins. The sun rose higher and higher; noon came; the shadows began to lengthen; I felt with horror the steady approach of the moment when we must resume our journey, for which no feeling of invigoration or hopefulness prepared me.

At four in the afternoon we set out once more. The chests were left behind on the hillock; the weak camel was driven along without a load, while Bû Zeid's beast carried the two remaining water-skins, their contents considerably reduced.

Scarcely had we left our resting-place than I began to stagger forward mechanically, dimly resolved to hold on until night brought another short period of rest, but with slight hope of succeeding; and we had agreed that in such an event whichever of us could go no further must be left to his fate, each being equal in face of the ever-growing danger to our lives. My knees were trembling and my skin, usually dried by the desert air even in periods of the greatest exertion, was bathed in sweat.

At sunset we climbed up from the valley to the edge of the stony plateau through which it ran, and in the evening light Tummo suddenly appeared again before us, looking much nearer than we had expected. That same morning we had thought that it would take several days to reach, but now its familiar outline and the details of its rugged features were so clear that we felt convinced it could not be more than one day's journey away. Hope revived in me, though fatigue still threatened to gain the upper hand. Then, in this completely barren region, we came upon a little hollow where the ground was covered with Hâd (a thorny plant on which camels feed). Since Tummo now seemed so close, and Bû Zeid and the Tubu youth were anxious to spare their camels, they urged us not to deny the weary, famished beasts this refreshment. We lay down, the camels began to feed, and under the influence of renewed hope I fell asleep.

Gustav Nachtigal, *Sahara und Sudan*, Vol. I, Berlin, 1879.

*Overleaf:* TIMBUKTU 1828

The most important of the ancient caravan routes across the western Sahara led from Tangier, by way of Fez, to Timbuktu in the Sudan, a desert city whose legendary renown lasted throughout the Middle Ages. Its trade lay in Moslem hands, and only very rarely did a Portuguese or Italian merchant enter its closely-guarded precincts. A young Frenchman, René Caillié (1799–1838) set himself the formidable task of penetrating, alone and without support, the mysteries of this city, and at the same time helping to open up the western Sahara. In his poverty-stricken boyhood he had been an ardent reader of travel books, which had left him with a thirst for greatness and wide spaces, and at the age of twenty-nine he turned from great reading to great action. After spending some time in Senegal, he boldly joined a caravan which was travelling south from the coast of Sierra Leone. The pretence of being a young Egyptian Moslem, eager to return home, was his only protection against the fate that had recently befallen Laing—the first Englishman in modern times to reach the enigmatic city, following in the footsteps of Mungo Park; Laing had been assassinated by fanatical Moslems at the gates of Timbuktu. No description of the route was available. Caillié made notes as he went along, under the pretence of writing out passages from the Koran, and with the help of a pocket compass which he kept carefully hidden. On 20th April 1828 he at last entered the town which at that period had dwindled to a mere shadow of its former splendour. From the top of a sand dune he made a drawing which the engraver subsequently transformed into a work of art of classical simplicity. The city lies amid barren wastes of sand. The larger houses belonged to Arabs; the negroes and slaves lived in hemispherical huts. Almost all supplies had to be imported from the south. The caravan approaching on the right, coming from the north, recalls the town's importance as a trading post, turntable and place of refreshment for caravans travelling between the Sahara and the Sudan. The principal buildings were mosques with rectangular towers. On 4th May Caillié, still disguised, had to set out northwards again. He reached Tangier on 7th September in a state of complete exhaustion. His worn-out body survived only ten more years, but his report on his journey was published in 1830, so his life's ambition was fulfilled.

CASTEEL DEL MINA ten tyde
der PORTUGESEN.
The CASTEL DER MINA in
the PORTUGESS time

THE PORTUGUESE FORT OF S. JORGE DA MINA ON THE WEST COAST OF AFRICA

In the late Middle Ages, when the Portuguese were looking for a sea route to India, one of their chief ambitions was to investigate the entire west coast of Africa. They established a chain of settlements from one end to the other, of which this fort, built on the Gold Coast in 1482, is one. It stood on a low-lying tongue of land, protected by rocks on the seaward side from possible attack by European vessels, and easily defended against African raids from the interior. Its high walls and out-works protected the proceeds of the Portuguese trading operations—gold, ivory and slaves—and large reserves of drinking water, food and ammunition for Portuguese seafarers.

Christianity had its rights as well; the church, one of the focal points of the settlement, stood on the spot where the first commander to land there had ordered Mass to be celebrated immediately after his arrival. In similar settlements in the Congo estuary the Portuguese had already begun to establish bishops of African blood. On the water we see some of the little sailing boats used by the natives for fishing, with two merchant vessels inshore, and a man-of-war partly concealed by a decorative and heroic-looking cloud of powder-smoke. It was with ships like this that the Dutch captured the neglected fort from the Portuguese in 1637, after a siege.

GUSTAV NACHTIGAL IN COOL QUARTERS AT KUKA (1870)

Like all living-quarters in equatorial Africa, those occupied by the explorer Nachtigal (see page 309), were designed with the aim of defeating the blistering sun. The tiny windows and the entrance, with its reed curtain, opened into an inner courtyard; pitchers of water stood under the shade of a roof. On the right is the cooking-place, with a gecko on the wall above it. The majority of such courtyards were shaded by trees. This *Balanites aegyptiaca* has weaver-birds' nests hanging from its branches, and herons, storks, vultures and mischievous monkeys live in it. In the courtyard there are also ducks from Lake Chad, geese, a spotted hyena and a neat striped mongoose. An example of Nachtigal's keen interest in ethnography is provided by the enlarged reproduction *on the right* illustrating an episode that occurred during a foray by the Baghirmi in 1872 when, armed with lances, javelins and a few flintlocks, they swooped down on the peasant-farmers and hunters of Kimre. The defenders have erected a store-hut on a platform built among the second circle of branches of the cotton-tree that served them as a fortress, with a fortification higher up. Nachtigal looked on in horror as the fanatical attackers flung themselves on wounded enemies who fell from the tree and mutilated them with bestial cruelty; however, the people of Kimre were not subdued.

*Overleaf:* PLAN OF THE RUINED TEMPLE OF UMMEBÊDA IN THE SIWA OASIS. This plan was drawn during the struggle to explore the eastern side of North Africa's desert belt. In the fertile hollow of the Siwa oasis, in the Libyian desert, the Pharaohs had once built a temple to Amon—a place of spiritual life surrounded by wide, death-dealing wastes. Nearby there was a famous oracle. This plan shows the ruins of the great temple precincts; (a) may have been the atrium, (b) marks the remains of a surrounding enclosure, (c) some broken fragments of architecture, (d) is one corner of the outer wall, which enclosed a rectangle 360 feet long and 295 feet wide. All the more recent enclosures (e) were to protect the gardens of date-palms; (g) is an Arab house. This is the state in which the place was seen by the archaeologist Frédéric Caillaud (1787 to 1869) when he went there in 1819 and 1820, about a quarter of a century after its rediscovery by W. G. Browne. He could make only a brief halt in the oasis, for the superstitious inhabitants of Siwa feared that the presence of foreigners would dry up the pools of fresh water on which their lives depended. Caillaud's 'letters of introduction', signed by the highest authorities in Cairo, had no effect.

*Caption for pages 318 and 319 on page 320*

314

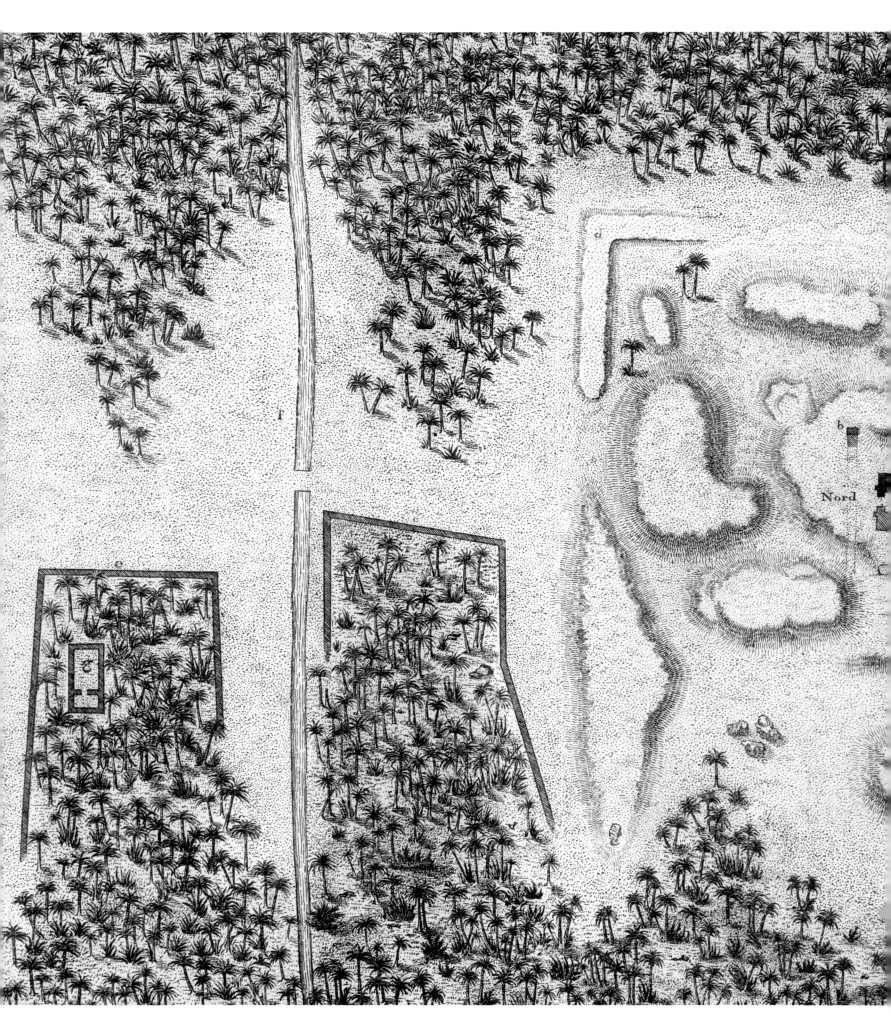

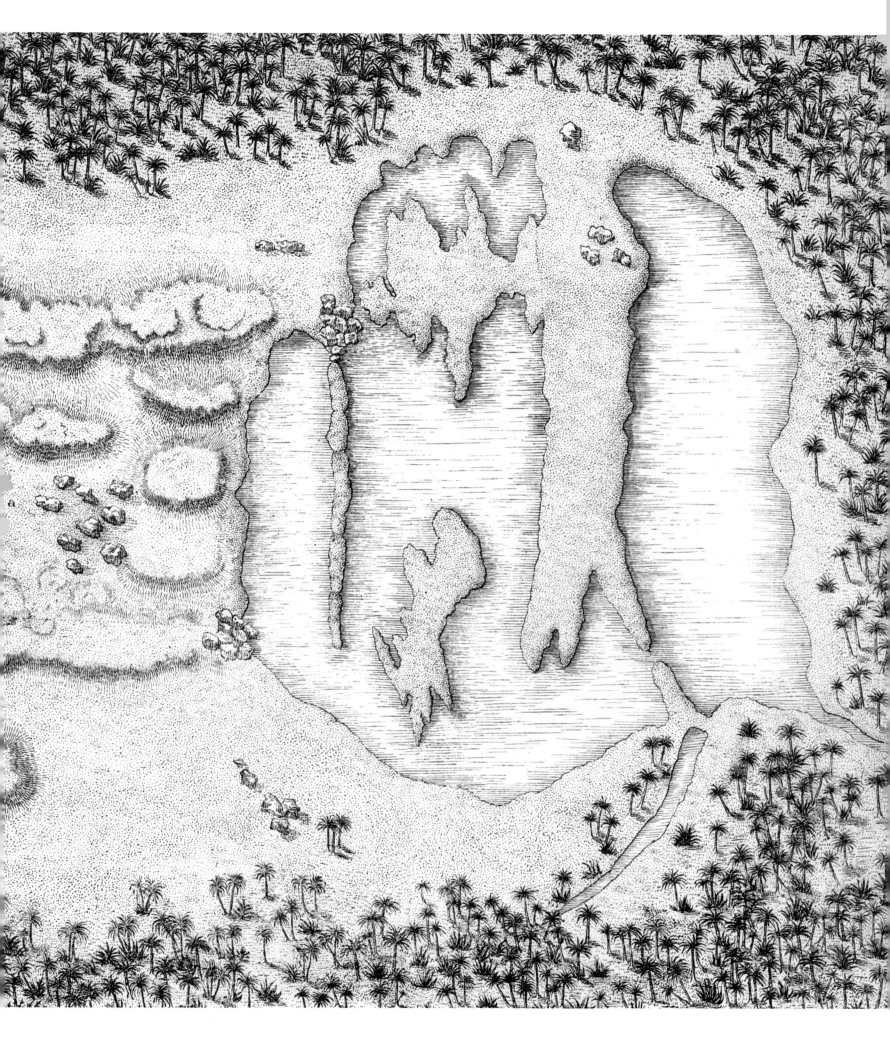

THE SANDSTORM—TRADITIONAL ENEMY OF CARAVANS

*Pages 318 and 319:* A MIRAGE IN THE DULLUL VALLEY IN THE SHOA MOUNTAINS OF SOUTHERN ABYSSINIA. The German landscape painter Johann Martin Bernatz (1802–78), who accompanied a British expedition to Shoa in 1841–43, was fortunate enough to see a remarkable mirage in a remote mountain valley that lay glittering in the desert sunlight. This apparent lake was simply an artifice of nature, an airy nothing. The bluish 'water' rose and fell, keeping time with the watcher's movements; it concealed everything that lay beneath, including parts of an approaching caravan, while faithfully reflecting all that rose above its level. The whole lake vanished when a cloud covered the sun, but reappeared as the cloud moved on. In the left foreground, marked by a circle of stones, are the lonely graves of warriors killed here at some earlier time.

Bernatz was a member of one of the many small expeditions sent out to Ethiopia in the first half of the nineteenth century, usually with instructions to investigate the sources of the Blue Nile and the lie of the mountains, and incidentally to discover markets for European goods. In the period from 1837 to 1848 the brothers Antoine and Arnaud d'Abbadie crossed Abyssinia from north to south; fourteen years later their immense, carefully-prepared map began to appear, and

was henceforth the mainstay of all explorers travelling in that part of Africa, which borders one of the mightiest deserts of the world.

*Above:* This forbidding scene was drawn by the English naval officer George Francis Lyon (1795–1832). For the time being the riders, with cloths bound round their faces, are holding their own against the rising hurricane, but soon all will be at a standstill. Even tents provided little protection. Sorest-tried were the slaves, in their blue and white striped clothes; not being allowed to ride they became far more exhausted than the rest of the party, but no-one helped them, and many of the weaker slaves would lose their lives on these desert crossings. In 1818 Lyon had joined a fellow-countryman named Joseph Ritchie, who wanted to go from Tripoli, by way of Murzuq, to the region of Fez, which was then little known. On 20th November, 1819, Ritchie died of dysentery; Lyon, sick too, and penniless, turned back to Tripoli, where he arrived more dead than alive, in March, 1820. All that remains of the episode is a report, little read nowadays, and a few drawings, recording for later generations the misery of men, women and children exposed without succour to the desert.

SOMEWHERE BETWEEN LAKE NGAMI AND THE ZAMBESI: AN OX-WAGON BATTLING ITS WAY THROUGH THE TALL GRASS AFTER THE RAINY SEASON

At about the time when Caillié reached Timbuktu, a fifteen-year-old factory worker in the Scottish village of Blantyre was studying far into the night, determined to educate himself. This was David Livingstone (1813–73), whose courageous self-sacrifice had its roots in a poverty-stricken childhood. At an early age the example of a missionary to China, and the travel books that he read with enthralled attention, had determined him to take up mission work of the most strenuous kind. With the help of the London Missionary Society he trained as a doctor. In 1840 he left England and began to practise in a village in Bechuanaland, South Africa. He taught the alphabet both to children and the studiously-minded local chiefs, he tended the sick, he tilled the soil; when he toured the district in an ox-wagon the Negroes would travel for hours to bring patients to him. Time strengthened his resolve to penetrate the completely unknown region north of the Kalahari, travelling as both missionary and explorer. His first journey, in 1849, took him to Lake Ngami; on his second, in 1852, he reached the upper waters of the Zambesi, passing through territory where the painter Thomas Baines, one of his later companions, was to make the picture seen above.

*Page 323, bottom:* In the course of his travels Livingstone encountered many columns of Negro slaves, driven like cattle by Arab slave-traders on an endless, wretched cross-country march. The men were yoked in pairs by two branches joined to form a fork, with a crosspiece to prevent them from working their heads free, and the women and children were made to walk alongside. Livingstone also witnessed the most terrible of all the cruel spectacles that the Dark Continent had to offer—the atrocious deaths of exhausted slaves, left behind by the caravans, sometimes tied to trees; and this in regions where hyenas were always on the prowl. Occasionally the people of some neighbouring village would rescue the exposed victims and nurse them back to health—but only to sell them all over again. What the traders could not purchase from the chiefs, they stole after setting fire to a village. In righteous wrath Livingstone took up the fight and became, in his writings and on his travels, one of the most vigorous opponents of slavery among Wilberforce's successors. His achievements as an explorer are inseparable from his generous determination to help the people of unknown Africa by rescuing them from their superstitious fears and from the bodily dangers that beset them.

LIVINGSTONE STRUGGLING DOWN THE KASSAI RIVER TOWARDS THE WEST COAST OF AFRICA

Livingstone was the first white man to cross Africa south of the equator, from coast to coast. With only twenty-seven trusty companions—men of the Makololo tribe—he first made his way westwards from the upper Zambesi to the port of Luanda, in Portuguese Angola. He traversed marshes, primeval forests, the territory of hostile tribes (feuds between villages and tribes were one of the ancient scourges of Africa), travelling by boat, riding or walking. The journey lasted about six months and he undertook it with scarcely more equipment than would befit a European butterfly-collector. This picture shows him two-thirds along his way. From Luanda he returned to his starting-point and then crossed the other half of the continent, travelling eastwards along the Zambesi. On 20th May, 1856, nearly two years after leaving Luanda, he and his faithful followers arrived on the shores of the Indian Ocean, at Quelimane—a Portuguese area.

*Overleaf:* THE VICTORIA FALLS FROM THE EAST. Livingstone's reports, and the lectures he delivered in England in 1856–58, shattered at one blow the widespread belief that Central Africa was one tremendous desert, and substituted the colourful picture of an immensely fertile, well-watered plateau, covered with forests and grasslands. Here nature was still waiting for men to develop her resources, and many races and tribes were in need of help towards better conditions of life. The most thrilling episode in Livingstone's career as an explorer had occurred in November 1855, when he discovered the huge waterfalls of the Zambesi. In the middle of a stretch of park-like grassland appeared a fissure, 98 feet wide and over 300 feet deep, cleaving the grey-brown basalt rock. The river, over 1,860 yards wide at this point, plunged foaming into this narrow ravine. Hurtling against the opposite wall, it flung up columns of spray to a height of 330 feet above the cliff top, where they were visible from a great distance. The spray fell back in a steady shower, watering a luxuriant mass of tropical vegetation dominated by the two- or three-branched candelabras of the aloe, tipped with their flame-red flowers. Thomas Baines (1822–75), who made this picture, was well acquainted with Africa. In 1858 he accompanied Livingstone on another expedition along the Zambesi, and in 1861, when travelling with James Chapman, he was the first artist to record this incomparable scene. To do so he had to perch on the edge of the dizzy precipice, soaked to the skin, deafened by the roaring cataract, and tormented by flies.

*Pages 326 and 327:* LIVINGSTONE'S 'MA-ROBERT' MEETS AN ELEPHANT ON THE ZAMBESI. Livingstone's vivid prophetic imagination foresaw a future in which roads would be cut through Africa, carrying the riches of the continent—ivory, cotton, rubber, skins, etc.—to market in the rest of the world. Not until the Africans could be persuaded to work systematically, by themselves or side by side with Europeans, to develop the wealth of their own territory would many of them become entirely immune to the temptations of the slave-trade.

A bold but unpractical means to this end was the two-masted paddle steamer *Ma-Robert.* On his return to Africa in 1858 Livingstone tried to use this vessel for exploring the Zambesi and some of its tributaries, intending to turn her over afterwards for use as a trading steamer. With him on board were thirty-five men, including a doctor, Kirk, and the artist Baines. The launch was flat-bottomed, with a 12 h.p. steam engine; she had large awnings to provide shade, and for good luck she was named after Livingstone's wife (following the native custom of calling a mother by her son's name). But the ship was ill-starred. Livingstone, a self-willed man, was inclined to rub his colleagues up the wrong way; the engine required mammoth supplies of wood for fuel, and the clumsy craft frequently ran aground. It was not long before Livingstone went back to land-travel to investigate the mysteries of the great African lakes and their surroundings.

STANLEY'S EXPEDITION CROSSING THE FLOODED MAKATA VALLEY

From 1866 onwards Livingstone thrust far into the unknown regions to the west of Lake Tanganyika, and after 1869 no more news of him reached the outside world. Thereupon the American newspaper magnate Gordon Bennett, hoping to make a sensational 'scoop', sent a young journalist, Henry Morton Stanley (1841–1904), to look for the vanished explorer. Stanley, who came of a poor family in England, had made adventurous progress since his arrival in America. He collected a party of about 180 natives and set out for Ujiji, on Lake Tanganyika, whither Livingstone was believed to have gone. The rainy season set in, and by the time the expedition reached the grasslands along the Makata river these were flooded. The only solution was to wade slowly and painfully across. Porters fell sick, nearly all the pack-animals died; the Negroes had to carry on their heads not only the tents, ammunition, tools, medical supplies and so forth, but large supplies of beads, rolls of wire and lengths of cotton material as well, these being the local substitutes for dollar notes. Fan-palms and thorn-bushes emerged from the muddy waters, the Usagara Mountains closed in the western horizon—and far beyond them, somewhere, was Livingstone....

*Page 329, top:* THE MEETING ON 28TH OCTOBER 1871. At the end of October 1871, after an eight months' journey, Stanley at last reached the shores of Lake Tanganyika. By this time his party had shrunk to about fifty men. Livingstone was indeed at Ujiji; he had arrived not long before—ill, exhausted and destitute, hostile natives having robbed him of all his possessions and even of his medical supplies. Stanley fired a salute from all his guns and advanced at the head of his column, flying the Stars and Stripes and the flag of the Sultan of Zanzibar, to greet the missionary who had not set eyes on a white man for six years. The meeting between the young journalist in the up-to-date white solar topee and the prematurely aged explorer with his old-fashioned oilskin cap took place outside Livingstone's hut, with a group of friendly villagers in the background. Stanley had brought news, funds and medicines, and his arrival put fresh life into Livingstone who made an unforgettable impression on Stanley, not only as the greatest of African explorers but as an exceptionally noble human being. Livingstone would not be persuaded to return home, but gave Stanley his diaries to take back to England.

*Below:* LIVINGSTONE'S LAST STEPS

Livingstone was already in his fifty-third year when he set out from Zanzibar, in 1866, on his last journey into Africa. For many years he had belonged heart and soul to the vast continent, in whose soil his wife had been laid to rest four years previously. Accompanied by a few natives, he struck westwards from Lake Tanganyika and discovered Lakes Bangweulu and Mweru and the Lualaba, a tributary of the Congo. Stanley brought news of these discoveries to the outside world, after accompanying Livingstone on a journey to explore the northern end of Lake Tanganyika.

Livingstone devoted the last years of his life to the great problem of the sources of the Nile, but without solving it. In 1873 he was advancing painfully through the region round Lake Bangweulu, so weakened by dysentery that his faithful Negroes finally had to carry him on a litter. Some of them went ahead, to set up a hut for the night in the village of Chitambo. The villagers watched with silent respect as Chuma and Susi, the most devoted of his servants, supported Livingstone's last weary steps. This was on 29th April. It was in this hut that his life ended. Far into the second night after his arrival he was found dead, kneeling beside his bed, his face in his hands, by the light of a single candle. His heart was buried near the village. The story of how his two most faithful companions carried his body and his scientific notes to Zanzibar, in the teeth of all manner of dangers, constitutes an African epic whose spiritual quality is worthy of Livingstone's own heroic life.

EXPLORER IN A TAIL-COAT: STANLEY ADDRESSING THE ROYAL GEOGRAPHICAL SOCIETY IN FEBRUARY 1878

*Left:* DAVID LIVINGSTONE. It was a mere handful of individuals who gradually unveiled for mankind the picture of the earth as it really is, and who strove in the face of every conceivable discouragement, to diminish man's inhumanity to man throughout its old and new territories. For the achievement of these two noble purposes these few were ready at all times to sacrifice health, fortune and life itself. Livingstone was one of them, and his face bears the marks of struggle and sacrifice. His written words remain, long after his death, for those who seek the truth about Africa. 'Nothing but the most pitiable puerility would lead any manly heart to make their [the natives'] inferiority a theme for self-exaltation;' and this, addressed to the Africans who are compelled to struggle for self-recognition, often bemused by the conflicting claims of illiberal ideologies which are alien to their nature: 'We hate those stupid revolutions which might sweep away time-honoured institutions, dear alike to rich and poor.'

*Above:* Stanley is seen, at the peak of his career, addressing a brilliant audience. The bearded figure in the middle of the front row is the Prince of Wales, with Prince Louis Na-

poléon on his left; on the platform, to the right of Stanley, sits Sir Rutherford Alcock, President of the Royal Geographical Society, and on the left is Dr Moffat, the old missionary who had been Livingstone's father-in-law and the first to turn his steps, when he was a young medical student, towards Africa, the land of his destiny. Stanley is describing one of the greatest feats in the history of exploration. In 1874–78 he had crossed Africa, in 999 days, from Zanzibar to the mouth of the Congo, travelling with eighteen canoes down that mighty river largely through completely unknown territory, as only the lower reaches had so far been explored. Of his original force of 359 men, which he led with relentless energy, only about a hundred Negroes completed the journey and they were as exhausted and famished as Stanley himself. England rejected his proposals for opening up the country, but Leopold II of Belgium appreciated their possibilities, and it was in his service that Stanley began in 1879 to lay the foundations of the Congo as a State, building roads, organizing shipping, and concluding treaties with local chiefs.

BABOONS CONDUCTING AN EXPERT RAID ON A COCO-NUT PLANTATION

The first attempt to draw a detailed picture of the natives, plants and animals of the Cape territory in South Africa was made by Peter Kolb, of Ansbach (1675–1726). Kolb's life began and ended in poverty, but fortune smiled on him during the fourth of its five decades. Patrons who recognized his talents had him trained in astronomy and mathematics and sent him out in 1705 to Capetown, the new Dutch settlement, to test certain novel methods of calculating latitude and longitude. Once there his field of activity widened beyond all expectation; he became secretary of the Dutch East India Company and made frequent journeys into the interior, half a century after the first Dutch expeditions had penetrated it. Parts of his comprehensive description of the manners and

customs of its original inhabitants, the Hottentots, are useful to ethnologists even nowadays. In 1715 Kolb, by then nearly blind, returned to Germany for the sake of his health; and from that time until his early death he cheerfully occupied the miserably-paid post of headmaster at Neustadt-an-der-Aisch school.

*Above:* The cunning strategy of thieving baboons, as described to Kolb. The stolen coco-nuts are tossed swiftly and neatly from hand to hand as far as the verge of the forest. There the notorious freebooters would line up again and again and repeat the operation until all the nuts were safely stowed in their cache.

## Scenes of Hottentot Life

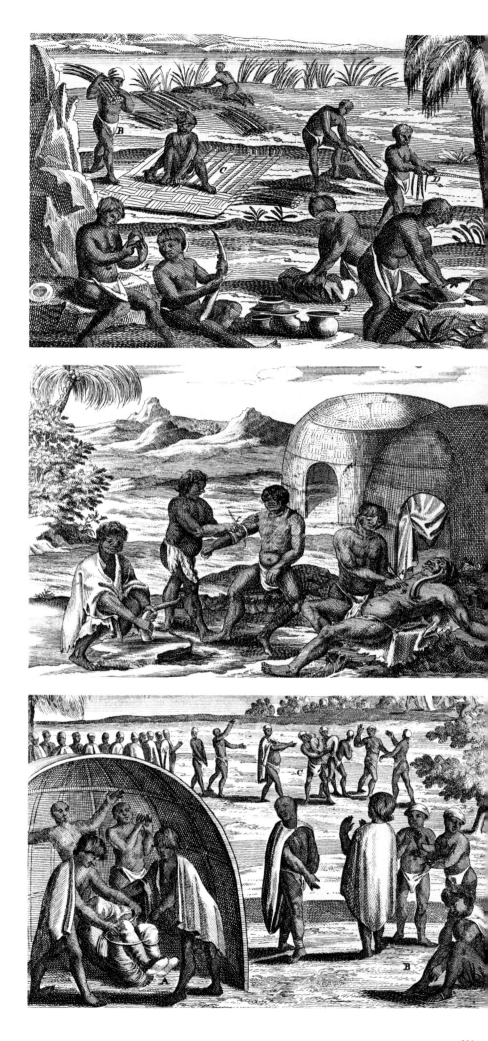

*Above:* HOTTENTOT CRAFTSMEN. A. Making bracelets from elephants' tusks by slicing them into disks. B and C. Making mats out of the tough matweed. The material is alternately soaked and dried in the sun until it becomes pliable and can be used for thatching huts. D. Twisting coarse rushes into ropes. E. Making pots, without a wheel, using only knives and deft hands.

*Centre:* HOTTENTOT DOCTORS. A and B. Scarifying flesh. In the left foreground the edges of a cow-horn are being ground smooth. The horn is pressed on the painful spot and then removed; a few incisions are made in the flesh, and the horn is again applied to the spot, which is now bleeding freely, and left there until it is filled with blood and falls off by its own weight. C. Opening a vein. After a tourniquet has been fastened above the spot, a slight incision is made in the vein. Subsequently herbs are laid on the wound or it is anointed with grease.

*Below:* HOTTENTOTS AND THEIR DEAD. A dead man—or even, not infrequently, a dying man—is wrapped in a cloth and bound up in a crouching position (A). Friends and kindred gather in a semicircle (B), break into the lament for the dead, to the accompaniment of hand-clapping. The whole village, wailing loudly, follows the bearers (C) to the cave or hole where the body is to be laid. Ant-heaps, stones and so forth are thrown into the grave —evidently for fear the dead may return as an evil spirit to haunt the living.

*Overleaf:* COOK'S FLAGSHIP LYING OFF CAPETOWN

In 1652 the Dutch had constructed, six or seven miles north of the Cape of Good Hope on the site of a settlement founded by their East India Company in 1602, a large naval base where their ships could break the toilsome voyage to or from India, which lasted several months. James Cook, too, used to put in here during his voyages round the world, and this illustration records a visit in October 1772, on his way to the Antarctic. It is a reproduction of an oil painting by William Hodges, the expedition's artist, and shows Cook's famous flagship *Resolution,* dropping anchor at the foot of Table Mountain; the Lion's Head peak is seen on the right. Close beside the sea are the fort, the church, and the little European-style town itself. Cook's logbook describes a typical visit: the inspection of the vessel by the Commander of the port and a doctor, permission to go ashore, a thundering salute from the ship's guns answered by the same number of gunshots from the fort, the ceremonial visit to the Governor, and the transportation of the sick to hospital. After this the ship was overhauled—she had been severely buffeted by storms at sea—stores were replenished and instruments checked. On 22nd November the flotilla put to sea again, after the flagship and the fort had taken formal and gallant farewell of each other with the fifteen gunshots prescribed by etiquette.

WATER-BUCKS IN A PAPYRUS THICKET BESIDE LITTLE LAKE WINDERMERE

The great explorers who pushed forward into the interior of Africa to the south of the desert belt found animal life of an incomparable richness and variety. Then followed the mass murder of the great African fauna. In the mid-twentieth century the American writer Fairfield Osborn, referring in his book *Our Plundered Planet* to the world-wide and ever-increasing desecration of nature, was to exclaim wrathfully 'Blind to the need of co-operating with nature, man is destroying the sources of his life.' The ideals and achievements of the explorers had been betrayed and abused.

*Above:* The marshes beside Little Lake Windermere, in the Karagwe territory, west of Lake Victoria. It was not far from this expanse of steppe and parkland that in 1859/60 an

Englishman, J. H. Speke, found the answer to the ancient riddle of the Nile. His conclusions were confirmed by Stanley in 1887–89. One of the principal tributaries of the White Nile flowed out of Lake Victoria, a veritable inland sea in the depths of Africa; and the largest river running into Lake Victoria from the west was the Kagera, which could therefore be regarded as the real source of the White Nile. Speke also discovered Little Lake Windermere in December 1861. His name has come down to modern times as part of the scientific nomenclature of the water-buck, classified by P. L. Sclater, the zoologist, as *Tragelaphus Spekii*. This animal, whose favourite food is the tips of papyrus shoots, has unusually long, outspread toes and thick coat, and is thus excellently equipped for life in marshy country.

FIVE O'CLOCK IN THE AFTERNOON IN A DINKA CATTLE-PEN ON THE BAHR-EL-ABIAD

The original purpose of the expedition led by the German botanist Georg Schweinfurth in 1868–70 was to investigate the hydrographical situation in the Nile Valley above Fashoda; but its most valuable results were achieved in the ethnological field. Our picture shows (top left) two wealthy Dinka Negroes sitting outside a rest-hut two or three miles from their home. Their tall, narrow-headed slaves have just rounded up for inspection all their masters' fortune. About two thousand cattle, humped above the shoulder, have been driven into the pen and tethered in their respective places. The slaves have collected sun-dried cattle-dung and are now setting fire to it. Thick smoke will soon rise and hang above the cattle-pen, protecting men and beasts throughout the night from mosquitoes, the ancient scourge of Africa.

*Overleaf:* BARON KARL KLAUS VON DER DECKEN'S EXPEDITION SETTING UP CAMP ON LAKE TEKA (enlarged reproduction). 'Towards one o'clock', writes a member of the party, 'we came to a marsh...and set up our camp under a magnificent, strangely shaped tree...I lay awake for a long time on my simple couch, listening to the chirrup of an occasional cricket, watching the fireflies darting merrily about among the reeds, and following the changing course of my own reflections.' Perhaps also reflections about death, that invisible member of every expedition? This first journey into the land of the Masai and the regions around the Kenya and the Kilimanjaro was concluded successfully, but four years later, in 1865, von der Decken and three of his companions were murdered by natives on the Juba river.

# POLAR REGIONS

The Arctic makes its appearance fairly early in history as a dim, legendary region on the furthest horizon of the European and Asian peoples. As men travelled north, a great change gradually stole over the friendly face of the earth, till a point was reached from which an expanse of deathly whiteness stretched as far as the eye could see. Any vessel unluckily caught by the ice was in the greatest danger. Yet the Arctic and Antarctic lured many explorers with a spell stronger than that of any other part of the globe; for the visitor to their fantastic prospects of ice and snow felt as though transported to another planet, floating disembodied in the chill of interstellar space. Fridtjof Nansen declared that the polar world was an alliance between death and beauty.

When the English merchant Robert Thorne wrote in 1527 to his king, Henry VIII, suggesting that he should open the much-desired trade with China by following the shortest route, across the North Pole, he added that earth had no land that could not be inhabited and no sea that could not be sailed. These words anticipated the bold, challenging spirit of the Arctic explorers. Thorne also gave the main reason why the Arctic sea voyages of the sixteenth and seventeenth centuries were undertaken. The young English, Dutch and French nations, vigorous and enterprising, were eager to find new routes to the Far East without crossing the path of the Spanish and Portuguese. And they hoped to find them by sailing the unknown seas that washed the north coasts of Asia (the 'North-East Passage') and America (the 'North-West Passage'), or by cutting straight across the equally unknown North Pole.

Not one of their principal aims was achieved in the sixteenth century, nor in the seventeenth or eighteenth centuries either. This part of the globe—the most difficult of access, except for the Antarctic—began to give up its secret only after centuries of unremitting, stubborn investigation—exemplified by the fanatically systematic approach of John Davis, who devoted three voyages (1585–87) to thrusting further and further into the Strait that now bears his name.

Once the Napoleonic wars were over John Barrow, Secretary to the Admiralty, exhorted his fellow-countrymen to renew the attempt to solve the problem of the three routes to Asia across the Arctic, though by that time they were no longer of much practical importance. Vitus Bering had long ago completed the notions of Siberia's northern coast-

◄ AFRICA'S DELIGHT IN RHYTHM

Two musicians, members of the lively, intelligent Mandara tribe, as Dixon Denham saw them when, with Oudney and Clapperton, he arrived in the vicinity of Lake Chad after a pioneering journey across the Sahara from Tripoli. One of the facts established by this expedition was that the mysterious Niger, which runs now north, now south, did not, as had often been supposed, flow into Lake Chad.

line. But the tremendous number of expeditions required to open up the channels that run among the bewildering maze of islands off the Canadian coast is evident from the fact that the map of this region is more thickly studded with the names of different explorers than that of any other. But seamen were more daring by this time; they allowed their ships to become ice-bound, used them as bases for further progress on foot, and were sometimes away for years on end. The boldest exploit was that of Nansen. In 1893–95 he allowed his *Fram*—a small ship with a curved bottom that the ice could not crush—to be carried far northward in the drift. But even Nansen, of course, never succeeded in reaching the Pole.

It was not until the nineteenth century that explorers deliberately set themselves to learn the difficult art of wintering in polar regions, by studying the customs of its most skilled exponents, the Eskimoes. This led to the triumph of Robert Peary, the American explorer of Greenland, who in 1909 was the first to reach the North Pole (see page 363).

In 1878/79 the Swedish polar explorer A. E. Nordenskiöld was the first to find a way through the North-East Passage, whilst the North-West Passage was mastered by a young Norwegian, Roald Amundsen, in a three-year voyage made with six companions, keeping fairly close to the north coast of America.

Amundsen attributed his success in great part to the little petrol engine with which his craft was equipped. And indeed the internal combustion engine, once its early unreliability had been overcome, changed the whole complexion of geographical exploration by tremendously reducing its difficulties. In 1899, when the importance of the Arctic from the economic, meteorological and military standpoints, and even from that of transport, was already gaining wide recognition, the first Russian ice-breaker, *Yermak*, made its maiden trip, under the command of Makarov; and in 1926 the American Richard E. Byrd flew over the North Pole from Spitzbergen, a few days before Amundsen, Ellsworth and Nobile crossed the Pole to Alaska by airship. Three years later Byrd looked down on the South Pole from the warm cabin of his aeroplane.

But all the really decisive feats of exploration were achieved without the help of machines. Did Byrd's conscience prick him when he remembered the great days of the past and thought of the whale-fishers and seal hunters who were probably the first to set eyes on the Antarctic coasts? When he recalled Bellingshausen, Wilkes, Dumont d'Urville, J. C. Ross, de Gerlache, Drygalski and other pioneers; or C. E. Borchgrevink, the Norwegian who was the first to winter in that continent, in 1899? Did he feel inferior to those who had penetrated the interior on sledges and on foot, until in 1911/12 they had reached the South Pole? It seemed like a magnanimous act of expiation when Byrd had himself set down in the frozen Antarctic, to spend a whole long polar night in utter solitude in the world's southernmost weather station. His book *Alone* tells the thrilling story of how, manfully defying fear and sickness, he in his turn experienced that great toughening of fibre and spiritual uplift which was the finest gift the polar regions bestowed upon their early unmechanized explorers.

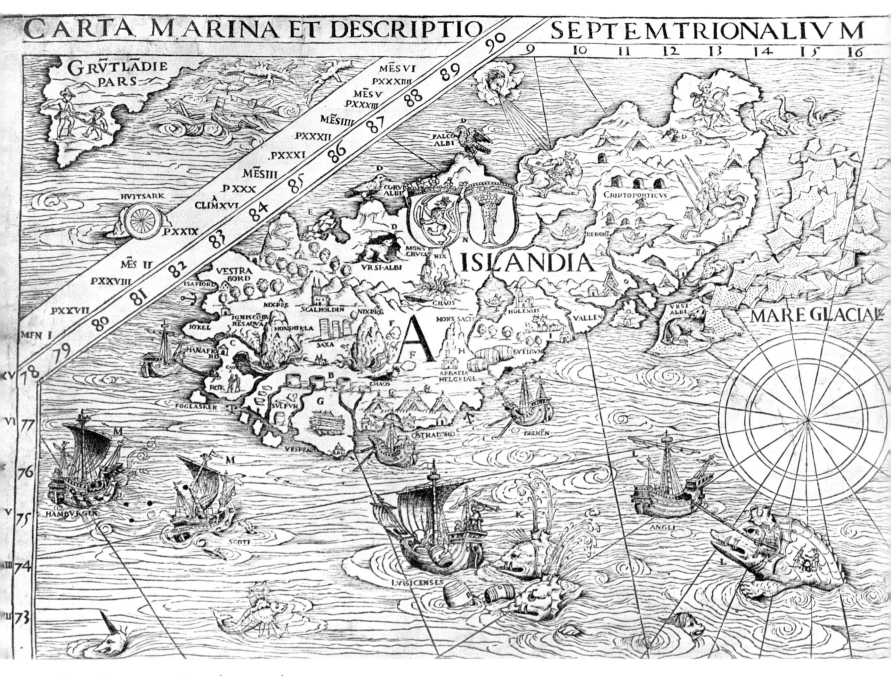

CARTA MARINA ET DESCRIPTIO SEPTEMTRIONALIVM

ON THE FRINGES OF THE ARCTIC (ABOUT 1539)

Section A of the *Carta Marina* drawn up in nine parts by the Swedish Bishop Olaus Magnus (1490–1558) makes the first contribution to an accurate picture of the far north. Olaus Magnus paid several visits to the north of Sweden in 1518–20 and travelled on missions as far afield as Warsaw, gathering material wherever he went, and supplementing it from various sources, including the maps of the Viking world drawn up by one of his contemporaries, the Dane Claudius Clavus Niger. Above, left, we see the southern tip of Greenland, and in the centre the outline of Iceland, broken up by its fjords. At the top, a horse and rider are shrinking from the northerly blast. The approach to one stretch of coast is barred by ice floes (above, right). The surrounding inscription asserts that the Arctic day may last six months ('me[nse]s VI') and that part of the population lives underground ('Criptoporticus'), in troglodyte fashion. In this region the fur of dark-coloured animals turns white, as is frequently indicated

by the word 'albi' placed beside pictures of bears (ursi), ravens, hawks, etc. (D). The presence of trees and groups of above-ground houses does, it is true, suggest the recurrence of warmer seasons, some of them stand near the 'chemical melting-pots' of the Far North: (B) marks the sources of hot and cold streams and sulphurous springs. (A) indicates two mountains—an imaginative rendering of the Icelandic volcanoes. (G) denotes one of the population's sources of wealth —they are piling fish as high as the eaves of a house. Whalefishers were already finding their way to Iceland and Spitzbergen. As is shown by the exchange of cannon balls taking place on the bottom left, the trading vessels and whalers sent out by England, Scotland and the aspiring Hanseatic League were already vying for control of the area. (K) marks the zone where giant whales were liable to appear—an emergency which sailors meet by rolling barrels off the decks and blowing trumpets, to drive them away.

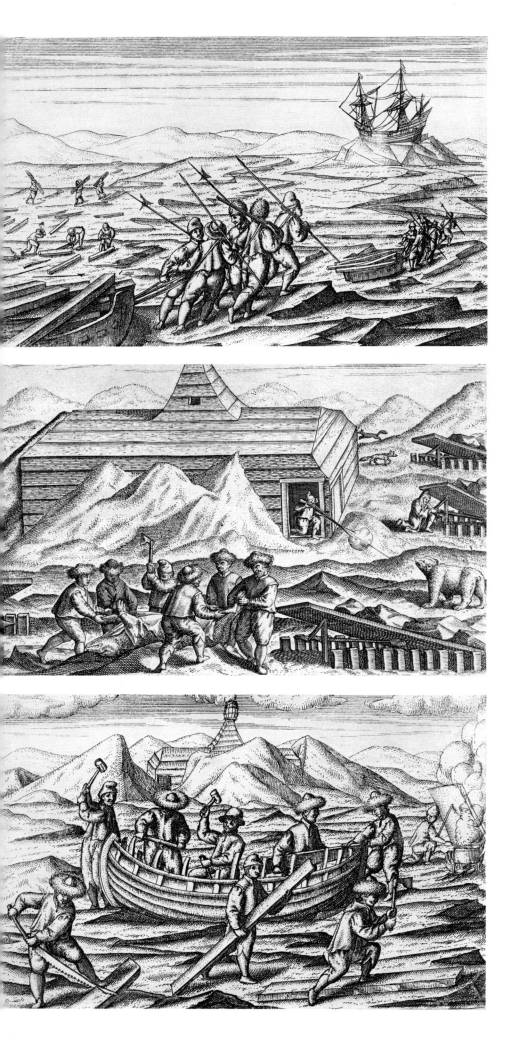

## Willem Barents and the North-East Passage

In the sixteenth century the French, English and Dutch were young nations, bending their will towards the future with all the vigour of the Renaissance. The ambition of their explorers, merchants and colonists to win overseas territories was foiled, thwarted by the world monopoly granted to Spain and Portugal by the Pope. All that could be done in the southern hemisphere was to penetrate by stealth into some of the regions these two countries controlled. In the north, however, there were certain routes along the northern borders of the recently-discovered American continent, or to the east, following the Siberian coast, which, though not yet sailed by any ship, seemed to promise unobstructed access to China and India.

The Dutch, with the English close on their heels, took the arduous course round Lapland to Archangelsk. Their attempts to sail further in a north-easterly direction were defeated, like those of their predecessors, by the old enemy—the drifting ice-floes that perpetually barred the way. The most memorable of the three expeditions sent out from Holland in 1594–97 was the third, led by Willem Barents, a seafarer with great experience of the far north—who on the second of these expeditions had rediscovered Spitzbergen, known earlier to the Vikings. But his fame rests chiefly on the feat of being, with his crew, the first to survive a winter in the Arctic. Willoughby had succumbed when his ship became ice-bound off the Kola peninsula in 1553/54. In the autumn of 1596, after sailing round the northern end of Novaya Zemlya, Barents was cruising among the ice-floes in a fruitless search for open water and a route to the more distant Siberian coastal territories. Suddenly his retreat was cut off; the ice had closed round his ship, and his crew of twenty-seven realized that they were to face the oncoming Arctic winter on the uninhabited north-eastern coast.

*Above:* Caught in the ice, their ship was thrust upwards and slowly crushed. Meanwhile, however, they had built a hut with driftwood—the trunks and branches of trees—and the forecastle timbers, and had collected firewood, though in these labours they had to be constantly on guard against prowling polar bears.

*Centre:* With the approach of the polar night the largest of the animals they hunted moved southwards. The Dutch had already caught polar foxes in traps, and killed bears with their muskets.

*Below:* 'On 27th January 1597 one of our people went outside and saw the sun. He called us all forth, and we perceived the sun lying low on the horizon. And we thanked God from our hearts for His great mercy.' So writes Gerrit de Veer in his report on this expedition, which breathes the spirit of Calvinism. But they had to hold out for another eighteen weeks before they could escape from the Arctic. Their ship was completely unseaworthy, so they made alterations to the jolly-boat and one of the lifeboats—raising the gunwales for example—while the snowdrifts round their hut were still deep. At last, on 13th June they pushed off. On 20th June Barents died; he had been ill for some time, worn out by the strain of his responsibilities. A few of the other men died of scurvy on the way home. Finally a Dutch trading vessel picked up the exhausted survivors near the Kola peninsula; there were thirteen of them.

BARENTS AND HIS COMPANIONS WINTERING IN THE ARCTIC

It was in this hut that the Dutch sailors fought their stubborn battle against the death-dealing cold of the Arctic winter. A fire was kept up day and night, and the sick lay close to it. When ice formed on the plank partition behind the bunks, they heated stones beside the fire and used them as foot-warmers. When the polar night descended on the hut and the island, they melted bear's fat to feed their faint-burning lamps. At times one of them would read aloud to the company. To keep vermin within bounds they were forced to take an occasional bath in a tub (right); and when at last the sun again shone on the group of stiff-limbed men, weary from inactivity, Barents ordered them out of doors to do gymnastics. The bales of woollen cloth entrusted to them by

Dutch merchants to be bartered for furs were carefully stored in the hut; only in the direst extremity would they help themselves to a little of this much-needed source of warmth; and when at last, in June 1597, they left their winter quarters, the unsold bales were stowed with scrupulous care in their two overloaded boats. The clock on the wall was a cherished companion; when it finally stopped they had to make do with an hour-glass. Nearly three centuries later, Elling Carlsen, a Norwegian fisherman, came accidentally upon this winter hut. Its contents were still undisturbed, including the clock whose last chimes had fallen on the ears of Barents and his few companions so long ago. In a powder-horn on the hearth was the report which Barents had left.

*Below:* EDWARD PARRY'S ATTEMPT TO REACH THE NORTH POLE (1827)

As early as 1527 an English merchant, Robert Thorne, tried to persuade King Henry VIII to open up a trade route to China by sending his ships across the North Pole—then entirely unknown territory—along a route, already thought of by Columbus, which was to be as direct as Thorne's letter. Indeed, for a long time the North Pole route was regarded as no more than the boldest alternative—investigated, among others, by Henry Hudson in 1607—to the vainly-sought North-West and North-East Passages. In the eighteenth century, traders' speculations were superseded by scientists' questions as to what the North Pole territory was really like. Just three hundred years after Robert Thorne's letter to Henry VIII, another Englishman, Edward Parry (1790–1855), broke away from the established custom of trying to reach the Pole with sailing ships. He made his attempt from Spitzbergen, first by water and then across the ice, using two heavy boats mounted on runners. His companions were J. C. Ross (see page 369) and twenty-five sailors. They hauled the boats over the ice with ropes, sleeping in them at night, beneath sails. In places the ice was divided by streams of water; at other points it was piled into hummocks. The twenty-seven men rowed and hauled their burden for sixty-one days, out and back. They reached a point only some 160 miles north of their ship; they had travelled a much greater distance, but the ice had been drifting southwards all the time. On reaching 82° 45' latitude north, they turned back. Not until fifty years later was their distance exceeded, and then only by very little.

JOHN ROSS AND LIEUTENANT PARRY MAKE CONTACT WITH UNKNOWN 'ARCTIC HIGHLANDERS' IN PRINCE REGENT'S BAY IN 1818

In 1818 the British government resumed the search for the North-West Passage and the polar route, and John Ross was one of the first explorers to be sent out, with two ships. He penetrated further than his forerunner, Baffin, into Smith Sound and Lancaster Sound, which it was thought would ultimately prove to lead to the desired goal. Among the important results of the expedition was the discovery of the Etah Eskimoes, the northernmost of the earth's human population. A white flag was hoisted to show the peaceful intentions of the ships, which the Eskimoes greeted reverently as huge, divine birds. Their timidity was overcome by dint of presents and kind words, the latter furnished by John Sacheuse, a mission-educated Eskimo who had come along as a stowaway. Mirrors, shirts, European knives and beads were received with cries of joy by these representatives of a primitive though ancient culture. Sacheuse painted this scene in his simple style.

*Overleaf:* PARRY'S SHIPS 'HECLA' AND 'GRIPER' WINTERING IN MELVILLE SOUND (1819/20). Ross had scarcely got back to England to report his partial success, before the government sent a fresh expedition northwards under the leadership of Edward Parry. Luck was with Parry, and his ships sailed 'along the Arctic boulevards' as far as Melville Sound. Impenetrable ice-fields barred their way to the Bering Strait so, in the autumn of 1819, Parry resigned himself to seeing his vessels caught in the ice off Melville Island. As the polar night dragged on, ice piled up around the ships and hungry wolves made their appearance. On the shore of the island, to the left of a great block of sandstone which became famous in the annals of Arctic exploration (see page 351), a hut was built for use as an observatory. We see a man melting ice over the fire, for drinking water. The sails were spread out to form a roof for extra warmth. This picture (enlarged here) was made by W. Westall from a sketch by Lt. Beechey.

AN EVERYDAY MIRACLE OF THE ARCTIC—THE ESKIMO'S WARM SNOW-HOUSE

Edward Parry was a brilliant innovator. In 1819/20 he had ventured upon an Arctic overland journey lasting several weeks—something hitherto only attempted by Cossacks—using his ice-locked flagship as a base. Now he adopted some original ways of coping with the difficult human problems of a long winter in the polar regions. Himself only thirty years old, he had picked a crew aged between seventeen and twenty-one years, adventurous lads to whom the word mutiny was unknown. He kept up not only their health but their spirits, by organizing a school, maintaining a continual series of scientific observations, and arranging for recreation as well. The *Hecla* was the first Arctic expedition ship to have its own newspaper and its own theatre. The sun had no sooner vanished below the horizon, to remain invisible for several months, than the first performance of a popular operetta entitled *Miss in her Teens* was given amid general hilarity.

Parry also tried a new method of approaching the North Pole (see page 346) and paid more attention than his fore-runners to Eskimo life, though he learnt far less from it than Peary, for example, was to later. Parry's report on the 1821-23 expedition is unusually detailed in its descriptions of the 'outposts of humanity' he visited.

*Above:* The Eskimoes needed only snow and a knife to build their winter igloos. They cut the snow into short blocks and laid these in a circle on the ground as a foundation. They then added further layers, narrowing the circle as they went up, so that the finished structure was hemispherical. Projections were whittled away with the knife, and cracks were stopped up with a handful of snow. A big block of ice was wedged in the top to serve as a window, through which filtered a dim light. Entrance was made on hands and knees along a kind of tunnel which led to an opening cut in the snow wall. The artist has filled out his picture of Eskimo building operations by including some of the few possessions that these hardy people required—harpoons, kayaks and sleigh-dogs.

## Eskimo Life

*Above:* An Eskimo stalking a seal. Parry was quick to make friends with the Eskimoes. They were allowed on the ship, and some of them soon learnt 'the art of opening and shutting a door'. On 16th February, 1822, a party of eight hunters passed the ship (seen in the background), and Parry joined them. One of them crept up to windward of a sleeping seal, clutching his harpoon—but this time he was unlucky.

*Centre:* Eskimoes speeding along on their sledge, with their hair flying in the wind. These were always noisy occasions, the men shouting and the dogs barking. The leading dog deals energetically with his quarrelsome team and obeys the voice of his master.

*Below:* Eskimoes would sometimes wait for hours beside small humps, like molehills, in the ice; one man would perhaps bend down, listening, while another stood with his harpoon at the ready, its rope held in his hand or coiled round his arm. Sometimes they built a low wall of snow to protect them from the wind while they stood there on the alert for any sign that a sea-lion or walrus was moving under the ice. The man in the background on the right has enlarged the opening in the hope of reaching his prey more easily.

*Overleaf:* McClure's 'Investigator' approaching the Southern Point of Banks Island on 7th September, 1850. In 1848 and the succeeding years, after Sir John Franklin with his two ships, *Erebus* and *Terror,* had vanished into the desolate ice-labyrinth in search of the North-West Passage, more than forty expeditions went out to search for him and to explore on their own account—a tremendous rescue bid. McClure was commissioned by the government in 1849 to penetrate eastwards beyond Bering Strait. He was the first to reappear at the other end four years later—though not, it is true, on his own ship. On 7th September, 1850, McClure steered his *Investigator* towards the barren southern promontory of Banks Island, landed, and hoisted the Union Jack. He and his companions stayed ashore for an hour, collecting plants and mineral specimens. The sea was comparatively free of ice, though during the previous night the ship had been buffeted against drifting floes with a violence that flung several of the crew out of their bunks.

This island is associated with two triumphs scored by McClure's expedition and with many of its sorest tribulations. On 26th October, 1850, sailing through the Strait on its eastern flank, the explorers came out into Melville Sound, which was then ice-bound—they had found the first North-West Passage. In 1851 McClure failed in his attempt to sail home round the southern point of the island and along its western and northern coasts. He did, indeed, discover this second North-West Passage, but the ship had to spend a further winter in the ice. McClure left a message under the sandstone block on Melville Island (see page 347) where Parry's report had been laid. McClintock, blocked by ice off Delay Island, discovered this—the world's most lonely letter-box—and in April 1853 McClure and his company were rescued by sledge from their dangerous quarters on *Investigator.* And so it was that two explorers, one coming from the western end of the passage and the other from its eastern end, met with a handshake in the middle.

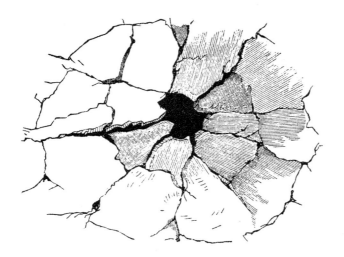

A Live Ice-Breaker in Smith Sound—the Walrus

Even before 1857, when the tragic fate of Franklin's expedition was discovered, polar explorers began once more to be fascinated by the great controversy as to whether there was a stretch of open sea between the ice pack to the north of the Canadian islands and the North Pole, or whether the Pole could be reached dryshod, so to speak, across the ice. In contrast to Parry's experiment in 1827 with his boats on runners, several explorers in the eighteen-fifties and 'sixties tried to prove the theory of a 'wet' Pole. Their field of investigation lay to either side of Greenland, the great island stretching—nobody could say as yet how far—towards the Pole. The 'American route' to the north followed the west coast of Greenland to the still unexplored Smith Sound, and Elisha Kent Kane, a Philadelphia doctor, was at work here in 1853–55, following the route of the Englishman E. A. T. Inglefield, R.N. Kane had a brig, *Advance,* and seventeen men under his orders. It was not long before he was obliged to leave his ship and take to sledges. During this journey he often came upon one of those holes in the ice, picturesquely ringed by two concentric circles of cracks which bear witness to the force with which a walrus has charged up from under the water to break itself a breathing-hole.

*Below:* During the second ice-bound winter the crew of the *Advance* had built up a store of dried meat and barrels of herrings not far from the ship. On 7th October, 1854, a white bear with her cub arrived to loot this hoard of delicacies. The Eskimo dogs flew at her, but she shrugged them off. Bullets seemed hardly to penetrate her thick fur. With disconcerting nonchalance she rummaged among the treasure until, wounded at last, she began to weaken. She was then given the *coup de grâce,* and her cub was captured. The mother's stomach was found to be completely empty—Arctic starvation had given her the courage of despair. That same hunger, and the piercing cold, were the arch-enemies of the trapped crew. They survived only because they found helpers among the Etah Eskimoes living farther south and because they began to use their ship as firewood. In the end, though scurvy-ridden and wretched, they managed to make their way south in two boats.

KANE AND SEVEN COMPANIONS RECONNOITERING NORTHWARDS

Kane wintered very far north, at latitude 78½ degrees. His meteorological observations were of great importance, and so were his maps, for on various toilsome trips northwards he charted more than 960 miles of previously unknown Greenland coast, discovering, on his way, the Humboldt glacier, which is over 60 miles wide. The lively picture reproduced above illustrates the trials of such a journey. The men, all volunteers, are hauling a sledge loaded with their tent, theodolite, cooking apparatus, furs and food supply. Beyond jagged peaks of ice lie the frozen wastes of Greeland. Crevasses must be bridged, with infinite labour. The sledge is pointing northwards, towards the polar sea of Kane's dream; the men of one sledge party believed they had seen its waves glittering in the far distance from the most northerly point of their journey. Kane never reached it.

*Overleaf:* KANE'S BRIG 'ADVANCE' IS ICE-LOCKED IN SMITH SOUND. The sketch from which this picture was made dates from the spring of 1855, when only five men, weakened by privations, were left to tend their companions, who lay sick with scurvy on board the ice-bound *Advance.* Kane, too, was ill and care-worn, fearing that the brig was destined to become a floating coffin for his expedition; but he nevertheless drew endless satisfaction from the beauty of the icebergs as they drifted away from Greenland and moved southwards in ghostly fleets. A few weeks earlier the returning sun had cast its first gleam over the wintry desolation; now its horizontal rays touched the icebergs, their young light mingling with that of the pale moon. 'It is a landscape such as Milton or Dante might imagine', wrote Kane in his journal, 'inorganic, desolate, mysterious. I have come down from deck with the feelings of a man who has looked upon a world unfinished by the hand of its Creator.' In the same year they had to abandon the ship. Dr Hayes, one of Kane's party, returned in 1861 to the spot where they had passed that dire winter, but by that time *Advance* had vanished without trace. The illustrations to Kane's report are remarkably forceful, for they were made, from Kane's own sketches, by a great American marine painter, James Hamilton. The reproduction seen here is considerably enlarged.

Stand 2. Mai

Stand 10. Mai

THE FIRST VIEWS OF FRANZ JOSEPH LAND DRAWN BY JULIUS PAYER IN 1874

August Petermann, the German geographer, was one of those who were inclined to believe that the North Pole was surrounded by a great expanse of open sea. His tireless encouragement confirmed Julius Payer (1842–1915), an Austrian cartographer, and Karl Weyprecht, a naval lieutenant, in their plan to seek a route over the Pole to the Bering Strait and investigate a warm stream they had already discovered, to the east of Spitzbergen, in 1871. But no sooner had their ship—the *Tegethoff*, provisioned for a thirty-month voyage —left the north coast of Novaya Zemlya, at the end of August 1872, than she was caught in a mass of ice from which she never again emerged. Nearly a year later, when the crew were stoically resigning themselves to a second winter in the Arctic, a miracle of polar history occurred. The ice, archenemy of explorers, carried its prisoners to the very place they had wanted to reach—a stretch of undiscovered Arctic coast. 'It was about the middle of the day, and we were leaning on the rail and staring out into the drifting fog, through which the sun broke from time to time, when a curtain of mist

drew suddenly aside, revealing a line of rugged cliffs to northwest of us; and within a few minutes these had taken on the aspect of a radiant Alpine landscape!' The actual exploitation of their discovery could not begin until the spring of 1874. The Austrians began to cover the territory in a series of hazardous sledge-trips which took them as far as 160 miles northwards. They saw Franz Joseph Land while it still lay under the snowy mantle of early spring—an unpopulated waste, almost bare of vegetation, a region of mighty glaciers, grey rocks, snow-covered plains, and fjords in which the ice was melting. It was an archipelago of islands in a frozen sea.

The panoramic view reproduced above was one of the last of the expedition's many drawings, made on 10th May, 1874. Ten days later they had to abandon ship in a hurry, for their dwindling stores and the advancing season would allow of no delay on the return journey. They had travelled a thousand miles by sledge and boat when at last, on 24th August, they were picked up by a Russian fishing vessel near the southern tip of Novaya Zemlya.

THE FUNERAL OF KRISCH, THE SHIP'S ENGINEER

In 1874 the Austrians left one of their number in a lonely grave among the rocks. Julius Payer included the spot in his panoramic view, and made a picture of the burial scene to relieve his own distress. The ship's doctor had discovered nearly a year before that Krisch, the chief engineer, was suffering from pulmonary tuberculosis. Almost until the last the dying man had begged to be taken on one of the sledge-journeys into the newly discovered territory. He died on 16th March, 1874, and on 19th March they carried his body through a heavy snowstorm, under a lowering sky, to a height overlooking the shore on Wilczek Island, where they had first set foot on Franz Joseph Land. 'Here we laid his earthly remains in a cave between two columns of basalt, and placed a simple wooden cross above it. It was a melancholy last resting-place, surrounded by all the symbols of death and separation, far from every human creature.... We repeated aloud the prayer for the dead....' On 15th May, five days before their departure southwards, Payer returned to bid a last, silent farewell to his lost comrade.

*Overleaf:* THE AURORA BOREALIS SEEN FROM BOSEKOP IN FINNMARK, ON 6TH JANUARY, 1839. In his masterly book, *Die österreichisch-ungarische Nordpolexpedition 1872–74,* Julius Payer allocated several pages to a description by Karl Weyprecht, second in command of the *Tegethoff,* of the mysterious play of light which spreads silently across the night skies in the polar region, assuming the form of hanging draperies, clustered rays, or circling candelabra, all glowing with unearthly, evanescent colours. The Austrians were tireless in their attempts to establish some connection between these northern lights and terrestrial magnetism, weather, temperature, the season of the year, and so on. Several other nineteenth-century Arctic expeditions likewise collected a wealth of data on the subject. In particular the *Commission scientifique du Nord,* sent out by the French with the corvette *La Recherche,* made a systematic classification of the rapidly-changing phenomena while they were in the European waters of the polar region. Its records included this bow of light, which spanned the horizon from east to west.

THE NORTHERN POLAR CIRCLE *(circulus arcticus)* AS GERHARD MERCATOR (1512–94) IMAGINED IT

# Robert Peary reaches the North Pole

The North Pole was reached on 6th April, 1909—by the American Robert Peary, who carried tenacity and organisation to the point of genius. Since 1898 he had gone nearly every year to Greenland, making bold sledge expeditions to explore the coastal regions, and travelling right across the northern end of this largest island in the world. He failed in several attempts to reach the Pole. Success came at last when he set out from Cape Columbia, on the northern tip of Ellesmere Land, where the *Roosevelt* lay at anchor to serve as a base for his operations. Peary knew that Eskimo methods of travel offered the best chance of overcoming the tremendous difficulties involved. He had built up a highly-organized system by which the journey was divided into five stages, with a camp at the end of each, so that the last team of five men, headed by their fifty-two-year-old leader, could keep enough strength in reserve for the final effort.

During the daily march my mind and body were too busy with the problem of covering as many miles of distance as possible, to permit me to enjoy the beauty of the frozen wilderness through which we tramped. But at the end of the day's march, while the igloos were being built, I usually had a few minutes in which to look about me and to realize the picturesqueness of our situation—we [Peary, four Eskimoes, and the Negro Henson] the only living things in a trackless, colourless, inhospitable desert of ice. Nothing but the hostile ice, and far more hostile icy water, lay between our remote place on the world's map and the utmost tips of the lands of Mother Earth.

I knew of course that there was always a *possibility* that we might still end our lives up there, and that our conquest of the unknown spaces and silences of the polar void might remain for ever unknown to the world which we had left behind. But it was hard to realize this. That hope which is said to spring eternal in the human breast always buoyed me up with the belief that, as a matter of course, we should be able to return along the white road by which we had come.

Sometimes I would climb to the top of a pinnacle of ice to the north of our camp and strain my eyes into the whiteness which lay beyond, trying to imagine myself already at the Pole. We had come so far, and the capricious ice had placed so few obstructions in our path, that now I dared to loose my fancy, to entertain the image which my will had heretofore forbidden to my imagination—the image of ourselves at the goal...

As there were indications that it would clear before long, two of the Eskimoes and myself made ready a light sledge carrying only the instruments, a tin of pemmican, and one or two skins; and drawn by a double team of dogs, we pushed on an estimated distance of ten miles. While we travelled, the sky cleared, and at the end of the journey, I was able to get a satisfactory series of observations at Columbia meridian midnight. These observations indicated that our position was then *beyond* the Pole.

Nearly everything in the circumstances which then surrounded us seemed too strange to be thoroughly realized, but one of the strangest of those circumstances seemed to me to be the fact that, in a march of only a few hours, I had passed from the western to the eastern hemisphere and had verified my position at the summit of the world. It was hard to realize that, on the first miles of this brief march, we had been travelling due north, while, on the last few miles of the same march, we had been travelling south, although we had all the time been travelling precisely in the same direction... Again, please consider the uncommon circum-

◀ THE NORTHERN POLAR CIRCLE *(circulus arcticus)* AS GERHARD MERCATOR (1512–94) IMAGINED IT

Mercator, the Flemish-German geographer, drew up the most advanced of the sixteenth-century maps, and his new-style projection placed him among the most important reformers in the history of cartography. His *Atlas* began to appear in 1585. The sheet dealing with the Arctic, in which some slight alterations were made by his son Rumold, was included in the complete edition, published posthumously, in 1595.

The fascination the map has for students of the history of exploration is due to the clarity and simplicity with which it illustrates the views held in 1600 about the polar regions and the northern magnetic pole. In regard to both we find a mixture of fact and fancy. The earliest attempts to discover North-West and North-East Passages had already added certain definite features to the map, but in the west only Greenland and Davis Strait are accurately shown. Surprisingly enough, there is already an inlet of sea dividing Asia from America—the mythical Anian Strait, first mentioned by the Venetian J. Gastaldi in 1562.

Late medieval traditions still linger around the northern polar region; Mercator found them in a book —now lost—called *Inventio Fortunatae* (1360), believed to have been written by Nicholas of Lynne, which declared that the North Pole was surrounded by four great islands, lying in the 'Amber Sea' and separated by four broad, rapid currents flowing towards the Pole. The Pole itself was a very tall black rock.

One of the most mysterious of natural phenomena —the magnetic force pervading the whole terrestrial globe—is presented by Mercator in the naive form provided by popular legend. Mercator assigns a location to one of the poles of this force by putting a magnetic mountain—rumoured to draw the nails out of ships' timbers—in the sea to the north of Anian Strait. He sets it well away from the North Pole, for seamen had long ago realized that the compass needle did not point due north. On the strength of a later series of calculations he moved it nearer to the North Pole, to the spot indicated by the little circle on the map. The true magnetic pole was not discovered until 1831, when James Clark Ross, the navigator, found it on the Canadian peninsula of Boothia Felix. In the corners Mercator gives maps of Friesland, the Faroes and the Shetlands.

stance that, in order to return to our camp, it now became necessary to turn and go north again for a few miles and then to go directly south, all the time travelling in the same direction.

As we passed back along that trail which none had ever seen before or would ever see again, certain reflections intruded themselves which, I think, may fairly be called unique. East, west, and north had disappeared for us. Only one direction remained and that was south. Every breeze which could possibly blow upon us, no matter from what point of the horizon, must be a south wind. Where we were, one day and one night constituted a year, a hundred such days and nights constituted a century. Had we stood in that spot during the six months of the Arctic winter night, we should have seen every star of the northern hemisphere circling the sky at the same distance from the horizon with Polaris (the North Star) practically in the zenith.

DUMONT D'URVILLE'S SHIPS CAUGHT IN THE ANTARCTIC ICE

The next five illustrations relate to the heroic age of Antarctic exploration (1838–43), during which an American expedition led by Charles Wilkes, a French expedition under Dumont d'Urville and an English expedition under James Clark Ross were vying with one another in the attempt to obtain, at long last, some factual information about this unknown polar region. This was at a time when sections of the coast had long been familiar, from a distance, to Norwegian and English whalers, and in 1820 Bellingshausen, the German-Russian explorer, had discovered the shores of Alexander I Land.

In the Antarctic summer of 1838/39, Dumont d'Urville sailed from Tierra del Fuego intending to follow Weddell's route through the ice-floes and into the open polar sea. But this time there were treacherous drifting floes and advance was impossible. For four days and nights his two vessels sought a way back to the safety of the open sea. Finally, as the wind strengthened, the commander gave the desperate order to crowd on all sail and ram the ice-pack at this last moment before it froze into one solid mass. Seven hours later the ships were safe. This picture shows them during the preparations immediately preceding the break-through. The fog has thinned out and for a short time the *Zélée* is visible from the *Astrolabe*. Two officers are trying to determine the position of the ships. Sailors are chipping ice from the *Astrolabe's* sides and bringing some of it on board in baskets, to be kept to provide drinking water. Arctic petrels are flying above. The thunder of the waves where safety lay could be heard a few miles ahead....

*Overleaf:* 'ASTROLABE' AND 'ZÉLÉE' IN THE DREADED ANTARCTIC STORM-BELT. At the end of June 1838 the two French vessels, sailing north-west of the South Orkneys, were caught in one of the fierce storms to which the zone of frequent low pressure lying between latitudes 50 degrees and 60 degrees south owes its particularly bad reputation among seamen. In the background we see little islands, covered with snow and ice. The presence of scattered ice-floes in the sea made it essential that the ships should be able to change course rapidly. So they could not reef all sail. Finally they reefed the top-sails and relied solely on the stormsails. Whenever it was possible, explorers kept to the tradition of having two ships. In foggy weather or snowstorms, *Astrolabe* and *Zélée* maintained contact by firing a gun every half-hour and by signalling with bells; at night they sent up rockets; and from time to time in clear weather the captain of the second vessel was summoned by a flag-signal to a conference aboard the flagship.

*Right:* THE FRENCH PLANTING THEIR FLAG ON ADÉLIE LAND (21ST JANUARY 1840). In the late autumn of 1839, *Astrolabe* and *Zélée* again sailed southwards, this time into a region diametrically opposite the Weddell Sea. They had already passed through a belt of loosely drifting ice into a sea 'never ploughed by any ship before us', when the approach of land was indicated by great blocks of ice showing no trace of weathering, and by the presence of arctic petrels, penguins and seals in great numbers. On the following day they came in sight of a long coastline shrouded in snow and ice from which a few grey rocks projected. They could find no landing-place, for the ice-cliffs fell straight into the sea. Late in the afternoon of 21st January 1840, both ships sent their jolly-boats to investigate, under the command of an officer. The penguins stared in blank amazement at these visitors—there were no humans on the sixth continent. The explorers landed on a little rocky island just off the mainland, and one of the sailors from the *Zélée* hoisted the French flag. The party could not cross to the mainland be-cause of the difficult ice conditions. As we see above, the expedition's artist—Louis Le Breton, who was also *Astrolabe's* surgeon—was already at work. Some of the others chipped specimens of stone out of the granite-hard rocks. A few days later the ships were driven westwards by a storm, through dangerous ice-fields, always in sight of the coast of what Dumont d'Urville had named 'Adélie Land' after his wife. On 29th January one of Wilkes's ships was sighted unex-pectedly, but soon vanished from view again. With the possible exception of an occasional whaler blown off her course, no ship had arrived in these waters since history began; but now, suddenly, two were too many. An ugly rivalry between France and America, in which a certain whaling captain called Balleny took a hand, prevailed for some time after this—overshadowing the one important fact, that Adélie Land and Wilkes Land had been discovered independently.

*Below:* 'ASTROLABE'S CREW CELEBRATING THE DISCOVERY OF ADÉLIE LAND. 'Although we had not yet reached the polar circle', writes Dumont d'Urville, 'our crew waited no longer, but summoned "Father Antarctic" on deck. They presented all kinds of quaint scenes; there was a masked procession, a sermon and a banquet. It all ended with dancing and song.' During this mummery, serious work continued uninterrupted on board the ship which—with a few others—had established the existence of a polar continent.

*Overleaf:* J. C. Ross discovers an Active Volcano in the Antarctic. We have already met J. C. Ross (1800–62), the British polar explorer, as one of Parry's companions and as the discoverer of the north magnetic pole (see pages 346 and 363). In 1841 he was only 160 miles from the position of the south magnetic pole (accurately determined by Gauss's calculations) when pack-ice obliged him to turn back. All the same, his incursions into the Antarctic (1839–43) were more productive than those of his rivals in the pioneering days. His ships *Erebus* and *Terror* brought back a mass of observations about terrestrial magnetism and the northern lights, and great collections of plants, animals and geological specimens; and still more important, Ross discovered the towering ice barrier, hundreds of miles in length, that bears his name—the outer edge of a shelf of ice extending southward to a depth of 516 miles. This was to be the starting-point of the explorers who set out half a century later to try to open up a route through the interior as far as the Pole. Ross also discovered Victoria Land; but his most extraordinary find was, perhaps, an active volcano 13,122 feet high. At the foot of this mountain lay the white ribbon of an ice barrier against which the waves dashed high. To the left was the white, rounded top of Beaufort Island. The volcano still bears the name of Ross's flagship, *Erebus* (foreground), while a smaller, extinct crater is named after his second vessel, *Terror.* Both ships were lost in Franklin's search for the North-West Passage.